SOCIAL STRUCTURE AND CHANGE

SOCIAL STRUCTURE AND CHANGE

Volume I:
Theory and Method—Evaluation
of the Work of M. N. Srinivas

EDITORS

A. M. Shah
B. S. Baviskar
E. A. Ramaswamy

SAGE PUBLICATIONS
NEW DELHI/THOUSAND OAKS/LONDON

Copyright © A. M. Shah, B. S. Baviskar and E. A. Ramaswamy, 1996

First published in 1996 by

Sage Publications India Pvt Ltd
M–32, Greater Kailash Market–I
New Delhi 110 048

Sage Publications Inc
2455 Teller Road
Thousand Oaks, California 91320

Sage Publications Ltd
6 Bonhill Street
London EC2A 4PU

Published by Tejeshwar Singh for Sage Publications India Pvt Ltd, phototypeset by Line Arts Phototypesetters, Pondicherry and printed at Chaman Enterprises, Delhi.

Library of Congress Cataloging-in-Publication Data available.

ISBN: 0–8039–9261–0 (US–HB)   81–7036–494–9 (India–HB)
      0–8039–9262–9 (US–PB)   81–7036–495–7 (India–PB)

Sage Production Editor: PAYAL MEHTA

In Honour of M. N. Srinivas

CONTENTS

PREFACE

In 1982 several old students and friends of Professor M. N. Srinivas suggested that we organise a festschrift for him. The circle of his students, colleagues and friends is so large and diverse in academic interests that we thought they could not be requested to write papers on any one particular theme. We therefore decided that we would request them to write on topics of their own choice, and then group the papers according to the major themes emerging from them. The response was overwhelming. As many as 46 scholars promised to contribute papers. Some of them took more time than others in sending their papers. The process of commenting on the papers, returning them to the authors for revisions, and editing the revised papers was far more time consuming than we had anticipated. While some papers required little editing, others had to be edited in two or three stages. Only two authors did not respond to our comments and therefore their papers could not be included. Since the time lag between the finalization of the papers and approaching the publisher was long, we had to give an opportunity to the authors to update their papers if they so desired. A few of them took this opportunity to send entirely new papers; one paper was withdrawn at the last stage.

Considering the large number of papers, it was obvious that they could not be included in one volume. It was therefore decided to publish them in several volumes. However, the grouping of papers proved to be a difficult task. We tried several combinations and finally decided to publish the papers in five volumes. We then requested one of the contributors to each volume to write an introduction to it.

The papers included in the present volume focus on theory and method in the study of social structure and change, mainly through a critical examination of Professor Srinivas' work on India but also in other ways. The papers included in Volume 2 will focus on various aspects of life of women in Indian society; the theme of Volume 3 will be complex organizations and urban communities; Volume 4 will discuss various aspects of development and ethnicity; and the focus in Volume 5 will be on kinship and religion. The contributions in the five volumes cover a wide variety of structures and institutions and theoretical and methodological issues in the context of India as well as other societies. The papers presented here focus on a broad spectrum of themes in sociology and social anthropology which Professor Srinivas has either himself worked on or encouraged others to work on. We are honoured to dedicate these volumes to him.

The secretarial expenses involved in our editorial work have been met from a small fund created by a few friends and from grants made year after year by the Centre of Advanced Study, Department of Sociology, University of Delhi. We are grateful to these friends and the Department.

We thank V. S. Parthasarathy for his help in preparing the bibliography of Professor Srinivas, and Shalini Suryanarayana for preparing the index.

We are grieved to inform the demise of two of the contributors to the present volume, I. P. Desai and Milton Singer, before the festschrift could be published. They were among the very close friends of Professor Srinivas and gave us a lot of encouragement in our work. We pay our respects to their memory.

A. M. Shah
B. S. Baviskar
E. A. Ramaswamy

INTRODUCTION

A. M. SHAH

We have brought together in this volume papers connected directly or indirectly with the writings of Professor M. N. Srinivas and with the theoretical, methodological and professional issues arising out of them. Included here are contributions by Milton Singer on Srinivas' *Religion and Society among the Coorgs of South India*, R. S. Khare on *Social Change in Modern India* and *The Remembered Village*, I. P. Desai on *Social Change in Modern India*, J. V. Ferreira and P. C. Joshi on *The Remembered Village*, and T. N. Madan on *Social Change in Modern India*. In addition, there are essays by M. S. Gore on professionalization of social sciences, and John Barnes on ethical issues in social science, themes on which Srinivas has also written. The papers discussing Srinivas' writings go far beyond them. Thus, we have rich discussions on the semiotics of ritual, the processes of social change in complex societies and the methods of studying them, the legacy of social thought in Germany and Japan, the aims and methods of sociology and social anthropology, and the role of the sociologist in his profession as well as in his society's transformation.

Milton Singer in his paper 'On the Semiotics of Ritual: Radcliffe-Brown's Legacy' traces the development of Radcliffe-Brown's ideas on the interpretation of rituals, beginning with the first edition of *The*

Andaman Islanders (1922). He offers an incisive reading not only of all of Radcliffe-Brown's well-known publications but also of his lesser known lectures on primitive religion delivered at the University of Chicago in 1932 and published in the University's student journal, *Anthropology Today*, in 1956. Singer also draws our attention to a number of important events in the intellectual life of Radcliffe-Brown as well as of many of his predecessors, contemporaries and successors. Most important, he shows how the 1932 'Lectures on Primitive Religion' were the first appearance of Radcliffe-Brown's 'genuine structuralism' antedating his second lecture on totemism (1958 [1952]) in which Lévi-Strauss first noticed it. 'Beginning with Radcliffe-Brown's first lecture on totemism in 1929, one can trace an explicit and continuous development of a generalized theory of ritual symbolism in the formulations of 1931, 1932, 1939, 1945 and 1947.' This, as well as Singer's another paper, 'A Neglected Source of Structuralism: Radcliffe-Brown, Russell and Whitehead' (1984a), should be an eye-opener to many of Lévi-Strauss' admirers.

Singer weaves Srinivas' study of Coorg rituals deftly into the account of Radcliffe-Brown's legacy of the semiotics of ritual. He locates Srinivas' use of the concept of ritual idiom in the context of the universe of Radcliffe-Brown's general ideas. He draws our attention to Radcliffe-Brown's statement on the analogy between rituals and language in his little read and discussed 'Foreword' to Srinivas' Coorg book.

Radcliffe-Brown not only enunciated the concept of ritual idiom but also devised the rules of method to discover the meaning of rituals. Srinivas used three rules, two taken from the second edition of *The Andaman Islanders* and the third from Radcliffe-Brown's lecture on taboo. Radcliffe-Brown believed that the interpretations and explanations of rituals, myths and legends are concrete, vague and inconsistent, and while they need to be taken as data (the first rule of method), they should be supplemented by the anthropologist's more systematic, abstract and explicit interpretations. Srinivas did precisely this in his book on the Coorgs. In Section II of Chapter 3 of the book he states 13 parts of the ritual complex of *mŭrta* (part of the ritual complex of *mangala*) and in the subsequent sections—generally one section on each of them—unravels their meaning. In the process he provides an interpretation of the symbolism of Coorg ritual.

Singer shows how Radcliffe-Brown's

functionalism was combined with structuralism by the early 1930s, both in the sense that society was conceived as organized in a structure of social groups and social relations, and in the larger sense that the objects towards which ritual attitudes are directed, in rites or myths, are coordinated with the social structure.... In other words, there is a similarity between the structure of social relations (the 'social structure') and a wider structure that includes the ritual relations between a society and natural phenomena. These 'analogies of structure', as Lévi-Strauss called them, include both Lévi-Strauss' 'postulate of homology between nature and culture' and Radcliffe-Brown's principle of 'dual opposition'.

It is this legacy of functionalism combined with structuralism which is reflected in Srinivas' Coorg book. And it is remarkable, Singer points out, that Srinivas has achieved this combination in the context of a civilization and not just a primitive isolate.

R. S. Khare in his paper 'Social Description and Social Change: From Function to Critical Cultural Significance' provides a wide ranging critique of Srinivas' contribution to Indian sociology against the backdrop of Khare's assessment of the work of Dumont and Marriott. In doing so, he focuses his attention mainly on Srinivas' three major books: *Religion and Society among the Coorgs of South India*, *Social Change in Modern India*, and *The Remembered Village*.

According to Khare, 'Srinivas might be most evidently functionalist in his book on the Coorgs.... Over time, he increasingly concerned himself with meanings.' Khare suspects that this shift was probably due to Evans-Pritchard's shift from 'function to meaning'. As a matter of fact, however, as Singer has forcefully pointed out, the concern for meaning was a part of Radcliffe-Brown's legacy.

Srinivas is viewed by many, including Khare, as an empiricist. We shall see how I. P. Desai views him as an empiricist. Khare writes,

Overall Srinivas... uses ethnographic writing as a multipurpose template for reporting data, capturing Indian socio-cultural conditions, and a sociological analysis. His analysis remained rooted more in 'empirical data' than rested on a critical evaluation of other scholars' ethnographies and theories. Srinivas favoured a certain 'reasonableness' in analyses and conclusions, which should find support in the data put to 'rigorous testing before they can become valid generalizations.'

It is, again, due to this empiricism that, as Khare puts, 'one of Srinivas' common concerns is to explain India by a range of (historically changing) ideas, representations, contexts, experiences and actions. According to him, single, simple essentialist theories, however well crafted, do not adequately explain the lived, diverse and contentious India.' Not only that, Srinivas also portrays the 'reasonableness' of Indians. Khare concludes, 'In my reading of Srinivas... this general cultural sense repeatedly comes through.'

According to Khare, Srinivas' work intuitively weaved 'facts', 'meanings' and 'interpretations' together. 'Srinivas was at his best when he grappled with social issues and changes intuitively.' In other words, he does not apply formal rules of method, the kind which he used to interpret the meaning of rituals in his book on the Coorgs. However, this intuition was born out of long experience of fieldwork in diverse settings and his being a native anthropologist. As it were, he went straight to the meaning without always applying the rules of method. As Khare states, 'His methodological and analytic constraints remained unstated and implied.'

Khare sees Srinivas moving from functionalism (as in the Coorg book) to the study of diverse and changing India. Khare devotes a major part of his review of Srinivas' work to this aspect. In the end he also suggests and elaborates that 'India needs a self-aware critical ethnography (which links with but is not limited to Srinivas' initiatives) to address the increasingly unmanageable subject of Indian cultural diversity.'

I. P. Desai in his paper, 'The Western Educated Elites and Social Change in India', provides a critical re-reading of Srinivas' *Social Change in Modern India* with a focus on the Western educated elites. He examines the validity of Srinivas' views of 1966 in the present context. By and large he is appreciative of the 1966 analysis but doubts its relevance today.

Desai's basic position, elaborated not only here but in his other writings as well, is that sociologists should be concerned not only with the analysis of empirical situations but also with the concept of what he calls 'the desirable type of society'. From this point of view, he finds that in Srinivas

there is the tendency to be empirical, so much so that it might lead to the trend of his becoming an empiricist—someone might add if he is not already one. His tendency to emphasize the 'what' and 'why' of an enquiry need not be deplored. I would only like it to be seen with reference to the future type of society to be envisaged.

Desai believes that 'the society envisaged by the directive principles given in the Constitution of 1950 should be the society desired by us'. However, he bemoans that 'The Western educated elite which is believed to have framed the Constitution, does not want to defend it—the same elite the formation of which Srinivas delineates in *Social Change in Modern India*.' Srinivas said that the discovery of India's past 'produced a certain amount of palaeocentrism in all educated Indians and, as is well known, a great past can be either energiser or opiate. In the main, however, it acted as energiser, and has provided modern India with a mystique for national identity as well as development.' In his comment on the draft of Desai's paper Srinivas has elaborated,

Energising palaeocentrism is again two fold. It may make possible the introduction of changes in the society to accommodate new forces while maintaining the fiction that the changes only mean a movement into a purer past, or it may become mere revivalism. Revivalism, it must be stressed, involves action while opiate does not. It rests content with glorification of the past.

Desai believes that at the present time the Western educated elite is the 'energizer' of fundamentalism in all the religious communities. 'These elite are closer to political and economic power today than they were about 20 years ago, and the threat to Indian society from their ideology is not less, if not greater, today'. 'If Srinivas was writing today he would have had to deal with the conflict between liberalism and illiberalism in the political as well as social fields brought about by these post-independence developments'. Nevertheless, 'The rise of fundamentalism of the Indian variety, though unanticipated, comes as no surprise if we agree with Srinivas' (about palaeocentrism in the educated Indian acting as an energizer).

Desai believes in the unity of thought and action. He dismisses thought unrelated to action as 'contemplative thought', and says, 'My perception of Indian intellectuals and academicians is that they are indulging in contemplative type of thinking'.

Desai discusses Srinivas' classic statements on conflict at some length. (Khare also briefly discusses them.) Srinivas said, 'Developing countries are today arenas for conflict between the old and the new.... A theoretical approach that regards conflict as abnormal, or that invests equilibrium with the special value in the name of science, can be a handicap in developing societies'. Srinivas then distinguishes between forms of conflict that can be resolved by the existing institutional mechanisms, and the more fundamental conflicts that threaten the entire social order. Desai comments, 'Srinivas wrote this in 1966 when the prospects appeared bright for achieving the new order by resolving conflicts with the help of the existing institutional mechanisms.' Desai then raises his favourite question of the desired type of society. For him,

> the correct question would have been: What is 'new' in the direction in which India is moving?... If development is taken as something new, ... are we or are we not entitled to question the nature of that development and the direction in which it is moving.... But that question implies characterization of the whole. Srinivas probably doubts if societies exist as wholes. In keeping with that doubt, he goes by parts and is concerned largely with the question as to how that development is taking place.

J. V. Ferreira in his paper, 'The Therapy of Methodological Reversal', makes a strong counter-affirmation against the encroachments of positivism of the natural sciences into social sciences and cultural disciplines. He takes us on a journey through German social thought to show how 'the most seminal ideas in countering the encroachments of positivism and in strengthening the humanistic approach in social sciences have arisen in the German-speaking countries.' He then discusses how these ideas have diffused in England and America.

Ferreira pleads for such a methodological reversal in India. He argues that 'forgetting or ignoring our roots, we followed blindly in the footsteps of a rigorous British empiricism, and, therefore, adopted the positive methods as primary and science as understood in the West till recently as our guiding star.' A reversal of this trend would be in harmony with 'our philosophic-social heritage and a cultural conditioning', in brief, with our 'spirit', and 'it can be engineered by force of self-assertion' and 'through the assimilation of personalist philosophy'. 'The net result... is very likely the eventuation of a heightened creativity in social sciences... in India'.

Ferreira views Srinivas' *The Remembered Village* as 'a foreshadowing' of such a methodological reversal. 'Its ethnographic material... has been transmuted by the memory and aesthetic intelligence of the ethnographer into a work of art.' It also signifies how 'the trajectory

of Srinivas' scholarly life has moved upwards from the descriptive–
diffusionist ethnography of his first phase with Ghurye as his guide,
to the analytical ethnography of his second phase under the influence
of Radcliffe-Brown, and finally to social anthropology as art, if not
as historiography, of his third phase in the light perhaps of Evans-
Pritchard's affirmations of this effect.'

P. C. Joshi has devoted his entire paper to an evaluation of Srinivas'
The Remembered Village. Like many others, he considers this work
as 'an intensely human document... [having] as much the rigour of a
sociological study as the charm of a novel which is appreciated both
by specialists and non-specialists alike. [It] is marked by maturity
born of prolonged reflection over facts observed 35 years ago.' In this
context, Joshi dwells at some length on the value of the fieldwork
method of social anthropologists who view society from the bottom
as contrasted with urban planners, economists, politicians, administrators and the elite who view society from the top. He hopes that
'works such as *TRV* will exercise a humanizing influence on urban
politicians, planners and administrators who are often ignorant about
rural communities but play such an important role in the decisions
affecting them'. Srinivas, according to him, is not opposed to the
concept of sponsored rural change or rural planning but questions 'the
concept of planning and intervention from above without a grasp of
the problems and processes at the village level.'

For Joshi, *TRV* also reveals the growth of Srinivas as a social
scientist. 'He began by applying his moral and intellectual resources
derived from his brahmanical culture and Western education to the
field study of a village. But contact with rural people helped him to
shake off many, though not all, pre-conceived ideas and prejudices
about them that he had acquired as a brahmin and as a Westernized,
urban intellectual.'

Joshi highlights how Srinivas indicates the shift in his orientation
between the time he did his fieldwork and when he wrote *TRV*.
'...when Srinivas did his fieldwork he was oriented primarily towards
exploring and emphasizing the stability of the traditional social system.... But in *TRV* he has tried to identify elements of change... and
has shown much greater awareness of the conflicts growing within
the social system.' Joshi therefore labels *TRV* as 'Rampura Rediscovered'. He suggests that this change in Srinivas' orientation came
about not through the theoretical but through the intuitive route.
(Khare also makes a similar remark on intuition.) Joshi repeats his

observation of absence of theoretical interpretations in Srinivas when he discusses the themes of 'continuity *vs* change' and 'caste and class' in *TRV*.

Joshi identifies five themes in Srinivas' account of the contrast between the old and the new in *TRV*: (*a*) rural-urban integration, (*b*) the changing economy, (*c*) dominant caste *vs* new class, (*d*) harmony *vs* conflict, and (*e*) continuity *vs* change. Joshi believes that in developing these themes Srinivas has not accorded sufficient weight to the economic factor, which reduces the explanatory power of the concept of dominant caste.

T. N. Madan in his paper, 'Westernization: An Essay on Indian and Japanese Responses', takes off from Srinivas' ideas on Westernization expressed mainly in *Social Change in Modern India*. In particular, he contrasts Srinivas' assessment of optimism about the future of modernizing India on the one hand and the attitudes of ambivalence, self-criticism—even self-debasement—palaeocentrism, crude caricaturing of Western life, and Xenophilia on the other hand. Madan provides an interesting and rather provocative account of Indian and Japanese responses to Westernization. His main concern is to demonstrate the complexity and ambivalence of attitudes towards Westernization in the two cultures. He expresses many doubts, questions and misgivings about current theories. In the process he develops his own view that

> all paths of development need not lead to the same kind of culture and society, or that Western society or, for that matter Westernized Japanese society, provides the rest of the world its best or only paradigm of development.... [because] at the core of the notion of Westernization lies the notion of cultural arrogance and politico-economic power and, therefore, the so-called 'burden' of modernizing the world.

M. S. Gore in his article 'Challenges to the Professionalization of Social Sciences in Asia' discusses the problems of research policy formulation faced by major funding organizations like social science research councils. In the process he raises several pertinent questions regarding the nature of social sciences, their role in social development, ethics of social scientists, indigenization of social sciences in non-Western countries, prioritization of goals of research, and so on.

John Barnes in his paper 'Unavoidable Compromises in Social Research' pleads for recognition of the fact that there is an ethical dimension of social inquiry. This dimension arises out of the fact that social researchers have moral relations with the subject of their research—human beings. In other words, social researchers and human beings are part of a moral community. Barnes then proceeds to show how in most instances of social research ethical compromises are unavoidable. These are due to the fact that the moral community comprises individuals and groups with diverse ideas and interests. Every actual social configuration that might conceivably become the object of empirical inquiry is characterized by a certain amount of social conflict and a certain amount of social consensus. In the choice of the configuration for inquiry the researcher has to make a compromise which falls along a continuum between the two. The second kind of compromise is between commitment and impartiality, i.e., between the enthusiasm necessary for practical action and the scepticism that is rightly demanded by science. The third compromise is between the researcher's role as a scientist and as a citizen. There is also a compromise between frankness and concealment vis-à-vis the people being studied. Barnes' advice is: 'Social scientists should aim at securing public recognition for combining the journalist's sceptical curiosity and the novelist's empathic perspicacity with the physician's professional reticence and fidelity to the data.' This is similar to Srinivas' ideas expressed in many of his writings on methodology. Finally, Barnes states that one can only give 'guidance... and not prescription, for it acknowledges that in social research there are no perfect ethical solutions but only uneasy compromises.'

This volume concludes with a biographical essay on Srinivas by me and a bibliography of his publications.

1

ON THE SEMIOTICS OF RITUAL: RADCLIFFE-BROWN'S LEGACY

MILTON SINGER

INTRODUCTION

The perennial debates among anthropologists about the relative historical and causal priorities of ritual and myth reached a temporary equilibrium by the end of the First World War with the emergence of a synchronic functionalism. The Durkheimian formula that ritual is a dramatization of myth, and that myth is oral ritual, seemed to concede

Acknowledgements: I am grateful to Fred Eggan, Helen Singer, and M. N. Srinivas for a careful reading of the paper and for helpful comments on it. I have consulted Sol Tax's original notes on Radcliffe-Brown's 1932 Chicago 'Lectures on Primitive Religion' as well as the slightly edited version of these lectures that was published in the University of Chicago student journal *Anthropology Today* in 1956.

Professor Srinivas recalls that Radcliffe-Brown's use of the term 'ritual idiom' at Oxford in 1945–46 emphasized the recurrent characteristic expressions of ritual in a culture rather than the total meaning of a ritual system as in 1932 (Srinivas, personal communication 2 June 1983). Such a difference in emphasis is probably explained by something to both the ritualists and the intellectualists. Malinowski's additional argument that myths are the charters legitimizing social institutions and practices did not upset the functionalist equilibrium. So far as the anthropological theory of myth and ritual is concerned, that equilibrium lasted a full generation. It was transformed when Claude Lévi-Strauss applied a structural analysis to some Pawnee myths in order to show that they represented 'a permutation of certain rituals, not only of the same tribe, but also of other people' (Lévi-Strauss 1963a: 240 [1956], 1976 [1971]).

Calling his method 'structural dialectics', Lévi-Strauss applied it to the problems of totemism (1963 [1962]), to the structure of primitive thought (1966 [1962]), and to a large corpus of North and South American myths (1964 [1970] seq.). His acknowledged source of inspiration for the method was Saussure's structural linguistics, especially as interpreted by Jakobson ([1940] 1978: Preface). Saussure's vision of a science of signs lying at the heart of social life, which he called *semiology*, became for Lévi-Strauss a programme for anthropology, at least those portions of it not already preempted by linguistics—'to which it adds many others, such as mythical language, the oral and gestural signs of which ritual is composed, marriage rules, kinship systems, customary laws, and certain forms of economic exchange' (1976: 9 [1960]).

In adopting Saussure's semiological programme for anthropology, Lévi-Strauss recognized that his 'structural dialectics', which aimed to show that myth and ritual were structural transformations of identical elements, by no means assures an automatic procedure for discovering the meaning of the elements of ritual and myth.

The value of ritual as meaning seems to reside in instruments and gestures: it is a *paralanguage*. The myth, on the other hand, manifests itself as *metalanguage*; it makes full use of discourse, but does so by situating its own significant oppositions at a higher level of complexity than that required by language operating for profane ends.

---

the fact that Radcliffe-Brown's interest in the 1932 lectures was to compare religious systems in all societies, while in 1945–46 there was an additional focus on the ritual of a particular religious system, such as that presented in Srinivas' Coorg data. In the 1922 edition of *The Andaman Islanders*, Radcliffe-Brown's rules of method are distributive rather than holistic because he focused on a particular culture, and he had not yet formulated a concept of a ritual system or a social system.

Our method comes down, then, to postulating an analogy of structure among various orders of social facts and language, an analogy which constitutes the social fact *par excellence* (1976: 66).

The structural analogies between language and various orders of social facts, as seen by Lévi-Strauss, reflect 'a vast system of communication' among individuals and groups with several perceptible levels. In the case of myths, the communication is from gods to men, and, in rites, from men to gods. But 'the divine interlocutors are not partners, like others, within the same system of communication. Men conceive them as images or projections of the system' (1976: 66).

The historical significance of Lévi-Strauss' suggestion that ritual ought to be analysed as a language was discussed in Edmund Leach's article on 'Ritual' (1968). In this article Leach also seems to accept Lévi-Strauss' interpretation of ritual as a means of communication, and proposes that the term *'ritual'* be used to denote the communicative aspect of behaviour. This proposal raises a question which Leach's article formulates incisively but does not answer (Leach 1968: 524): 'If ritual be that aspect of customary behaviour that "says things" rather than "does things"...how is it that, in view of the actors (and even some analysts), ritual may "do things" as well as "say things?"' (cf. Tambiah 1973).

Not all the symbolic theories of ritual that appeared in the 1950s and 1960s followed the model of structural linguistics and structuralism. In Max Gluckman edited *Essays on the Ritual of Social Relations* (1962), dedicated to the memory of Van Gennep and also paying tribute to Radcliffe-Brown, Victor Turner introduced an analysis of 'Three Symbols of Passage in Ndembu Circumcision Ritual' which was structural–functional and broadly semiotic. Turner focused on symbols as a process that was at once psychological, social and cultural. The analysis postulated the multivocality of symbols in relation to 'a spectrum of referents', and distinguished three levels of meaning for interpreting symbols: native *exegesis*, the symbols' *position* in a total configuration of symbols that express native beliefs and values, and the *operational* level of symbol use in the context of social action and social structure. Putting the three levels of meaning together, Turner interpreted the Ndembu circumcision ritual as a 'primitive sacrament' that symbolizes the novice's passage from an amorphous state of 'filthy' childhood to 'clean' and mature masculinity (Turner in Gluckman 1962: 173).

In later formulations, Turner generalized his analysis of ritual to apply to both modern and primitive societies and showed how the phases of transition rites observed by Van Gennep can be applied to the 'social drama' of conflict ('breach', 'crisis') and to conflict resolution ('redress'). Freudian and Jungian interpretations of the biological role of symbolism were also incorporated into his theory of the ritual process (Turner 1969; 1974; 1979; 1982a; 1982b). Most significant in the present context is Turner's recognition that his three levels of meaning are 'roughly similar' to Peirce-Morris' division of semiotics into *syntactics* ('positional meaning'), *semantics* ('exegetical meaning') and *pragmatics* ('operational meaning') and align Turner's theory of ritual with a Peircean semiotics rather than with a Saussurean semiology (Singer 1978), Turner's theory of ritual, moreover, grew out of Radcliffe-Brown's earlier synthesis of Van Gennep, Durkheim and Shand. Turner's teacher at Manchester, Gluckman, had heard Radcliffe-Brown's lectures at Oxford in 1938–39. Gluckman invited Radcliffe-Brown to repeat the theme of those lectures at Manchester in 1949–50. Recollecting in 1974 the Oxford and Manchester lectures, Gluckman wrote, 'What I think has been sadly neglected is the crucial work which R–B did on symbolism...' (Gluckman, personal communication, 5 January 1974).

When Turner heard his lectures at Manchester, Radcliffe-Brown had already formulated a structural–functional analysis of ritual and myth in the Andamans and in Australian totemism and was well on the way towards a general semiotic theory of social and cultural symbolism. Significantly, both Turner and Srinivas added an analysis of the ritual process to Radcliffe-Brown's synchronic functionalism.

Commenting on a draft chapter of my book I had sent him that included a description of Radcliffe-Brown's theory of cultural symbolism, Professor M. N. Srinivas wrote me in the Fall of 1982 that underlying Radcliffe-Brown's 'analysis of ritual and dance was the assumption that ritual is a language, and that the anthropologist must decipher the language' (Srinivas personal communication, 14 September 1982). Srinivas also reminded me that two chapters of his own book on the Coorgs of South India applied the idea of ritual idiom to Coorg material and that when Srinivas was analysing his Coorg field materials at Oxford in 1945 under Radcliffe-Brown's supervision, Radcliffe-Brown was talking about 'ritual idiom' (Srinivas 1982).

Although I had read Srinivas' *Religion and Society among the Coorgs of South India* in 1953, one year after it was published and a year before my first trip to India, and had found its concepts of 'Sanskritic Hinduism' and 'Sanskritization' useful in applying to India some of Robert Redfield's ideas about the structure and organization of a civilization, I did not appreciate at that time the theoretical and historical importance of Radcliffe-Brown's idea of 'ritual idiom' or of Srinivas' application and development of that idea in his Coorg monograph. I was not alone in neglecting these early sources for the idea of a ritual idiom. Discussions of linguistic or symbolic theories of ritual rarely mentioned 'ritual idiom' (Firth 1973: 138 is a notable exception), and the authors of ethnographic studies who continue to make effective and creative use of the idea, including some of Radcliffe-Brown's students and colleagues, do not always refer to Radcliffe-Brown's early formulations or to Srinivas' classic monograph (cf. Barth 1975: chs. 1, 17, 23).

INTERPRETING RITUAL AND MYTH IN THE ANDAMAN ISLANDS

The essential features of Radcliffe-Brown's theory of ritual idiom are summarized in his 'Foreword' to Srinivas' book on the Coorgs. His is a behaviouristic, structural–functional, and semiotic theory based on an analogy with language:

> Just as different societies have different languages so also they have their different systems of ritual idiom, and it is the task of the social anthropologist to investigate a system of ritual idiom in the same way that he studies a language. In any system of ritual, each ritual has its meaning, and the totality of such meanings constitutes the idiom of that system (Radcliffe-Brown in Srinivas 1952: vi).

How a social anthropologist who does not yet know the idiom comes to learn it is of course a problem of anthropological as well as linguistic method. Radcliffe-Brown recommended that the social anthropologist should 'seek to observe how people act as a necessary preliminary to trying to understand how they think and feel', since 'the religion of a people presents itself in the first instance not as a body of doctrine, but as what we may call "religious behavior" as a part of social life'. In the following sentence, Radcliffe-Brown praises Srinivas as 'a trained anthropologist who is himself an Indian, and who has therefore an understanding of Indian ways of thought which it is difficult for a European to attain even after many years' and one who has produced 'a scientifically valuable and objective account of the religious behaviour of a particular religious community' (Radcliffe-Brown in Srinivas 1952: v).

One feature of Radcliffe-Brown's theory of ritual idiom that is omitted from his 'Foreword' to Srinivas' book on the Coorgs is a description of the rules of method that a social anthropologist should use to discover the meanings of ritual actions. The omission is puzzling, since the rules are an essential and distinctive feature of Radcliffe-Brown's theory of ritual idiom and are explicitly stated in all his earlier references to the theory, beginning with the formulation of the rules in the first edition of *The Andaman Islanders* (Radcliffe-Brown 1922: 234–35).

It is possible that Radcliffe-Brown may have omitted to state the rules in his 'Foreword' to Srinivas' book because he did not think they were needed by an Indian social anthropologist who was already acquainted with some of the languages and much of the ritual idiom. Besides, Srinivas had already completed his field observations before he went to Oxford and began his analysis of the data under Radcliffe-Brown's direction. This plausible explanation for his omission of the rules fails to explain why Srinivas himself states the rules of method in the only reference to Radcliffe-Brown in his book (Srinivas 1952: 72).

In Chapter III of the Coorg study, which is entitled 'The Ritual Idiom of the Coorgs (1) The Ritual Complex of Mangala', Srinivas points out that in every society certain 'ritual acts' and 'ritual complexes' comprising several individual ritual acts, frequently repeat themselves, and that several such ritual complexes and some individual ritual acts 'might be together knit into a still wider ritual whole which repeats itself occasionally' (Srinivas 1952: 70). Referring specifically to the typical ritual complex of *mūrta*, which includes salutation, Srinivas writes:

> The ritual complex of *mūrta* consists of several ritual acts, and it is proposed to discover the meaning of each of them by the application of the three rules formulated by Professor Radcliffe-Brown. (1) 'When the same or similar custom is practiced on different occasions it has the same or similar meaning in all of them.' (2) 'When different customs are practiced on one and the same occasion there is a common element in the customs.' (3) 'If two rites are

found associated with one another on different occasions then there is something in common between the different occasions.'

The first two rules are identified by Srinivas as emerging from the second edition of Radcliffe-Brown's *The Andaman Islanders* (1933: 2, 235) and the third from his lecture on taboo ([1939] 1952: 36).

The semiotic character of these rules of method would not be immediately apparent if they were not directly associated with the language analogy. This is not a hypothetical speculation, for in the first edition of *The Andaman Islanders* there is no explicit statement of the language analogy to accompany the rules of method (Radcliffe-Brown 1922: 234–35). In fact, as formulated in the first edition, the rules do not refer to 'ritual' or to 'ritual idiom' but to 'customs' and 'ceremonies'.

From the retrospective standpoint of Radcliffe-Brown's 1932 Preface to the second edition and other later formulations of the language analogy, one can infer that the rules of method were intended to be semiotic (Radcliffe-Brown 1952 [1939]: 144–46). *Within* the text of the first edition there is also some support for symbolic interpretations of specific rituals and ceremonial customs (for example, painting the body with white clay on the occasion of a birth or death, and the mutual embracing of bride and bridegroom in the wedding ceremony). Radcliffe-Brown's interpretations of these and other 'ceremonial customs' leave little doubt that he perceives them as ritual actions whose meanings depend, not on the spontaneous feelings of the individual actors, but on the customary and obligatory social character of the actions. The actions are 'symbolic'—express sentiments and 'symbolize' certain social values.

'The social union is symbolized or expressed by the physical union of the embrace' (Radcliffe-Brown 1922: 236). The marriage ceremony, wrote Radcliffe-Brown, 'brings vividly to the minds of the couple and also to those of the spectators the consciousness that the two are entering upon a new social relation of which the essential feature is the affection in which they most hold one another' (1922: 236). From the point of view of the witnesses, the ceremony marks a recognition of 'the change of status of the marrying pair', who must henceforth be treated as responsible adults rather than as children (Radcliffe-Brown 1922: 237).

Radcliffe-Brown describes how he arrived at his interpretation of the embrace in the Andaman marriage ceremony. Assuming a universal psychological law that 'everywhere in human life the embrace is employed as an expression of such feelings as love, affection, friendship, i.e., the feeling of attachment between persons', he inferred that the meaning of the marriage ceremony is readily seen as bringing 'the man and woman into a special and intimate relation to one another' (Radcliffe-Brown 1922: 236).

A more explicit application of the rules of method is illustrated by the Andamanese custom of relatives weeping over the bride and groom on the occasion of marriage. To interpret this custom, Radcliffe-Brown collates it with the principal occasions of ceremonial weeping: (*a*) when friends or relatives meet after a separation; (*b*) at the peace-making ceremony of former enemies; (*c*) by friends of mourners at the end of a period of mourning ; (*d*) by friends and relatives over a corpse; (*e*) over the bones of a dead man or woman recovered from the grave; (*f*) on the occasion of a marriage; and (*g*) by the female relatives of a boy or girl at his or her initiation ceremony (1922: 239).

Applying one of his postulates of method, Radcliffe-Brown assumes that 'one and the same rite has the same meaning in whatever circumstances it may take place' (Radcliffe-Brown 1922: 240). Analysing the several occasions for ceremonial weeping, he concludes that the common element in all of the occasions is

> the affirmation of a bond of social solidarity between those taking part in it, and...producing in them a realisation of that bond by arousing the sentiment of attachment.... In all instances...the purpose of the rite is to bring about a new state of the affective dispositions that regulate that conduct of persons to one another, either by reviving sentiments that have lain dormant, or producing a recognition of a change in the condition of personal relations (Radcliffe-Brown 1922: 245).

Although Radcliffe-Brown's interpretations of weeping and embracing appeal to 'fundamental laws regulating the affective life of human beings' (for example, that weeping is an outlet for emotional excitement, that an embrace is an expression of feelings of attachment between persons), he nevertheless insists that the sentiments expressed in the ceremonial customs are not spontaneous expressions of individual feelings (which may also be expressed on occasion) but are obligatory social duties to be performed on specified occasions. 'It is the duty of everyone in a community to give presents at a wedding;

it is the duty of relatives to weep together when they meet' (Rad-cliffe-Brown 1922: 246).

There is a reciprocal interaction between the ceremonial custom and its psychological basis; on the one hand, 'on every occasion of the rite [weeping] there is a condition of emotional tension due to the sudden calling into activity of the sentiment of personal attach-ment'; on the other hand, the obligatory rite 'compels the two partici-pants to act as though they felt certain emotions, and thereby does, to some extent, produce these emotions in them' (Radcliffe-Brown 1922: 241).

This interpretation of embracing and weeping at the time of mar-riage and on other occasions when the Andamanese display such behaviour illustrates how Radcliffe-Brown applies one of his rules of method for discovering the meaning of particular ceremonial customs. The method obviously includes assumptions that the ceremonial cus-toms constitute a closely connected system of obligatory behaviour on specified social occasions, that such behaviour is more or less standardized in form but has a psychological foundation, that the observance of the ceremonial customs marks changes in the social status of at least some of the participants in the ceremonies, and is thereby a means of keeping alive in them those collective sentiments relating to such changes and to the solidarity and continuity of society. These assumptions, taken together, constitute a novel synthesis of Durkheim's theory of collective representations, Van Gennep's theory of the 'rites of passage', and Shand's theory of 'sentiments'. The synthesis is explicitly formulated in Radcliffe-Brown's definition of 'ceremonial' in *The Andaman Islanders* (1922: 328–29) as collective actions, required by custom, performed on the occasion of changes in social life, and expressing the collective sentiments relating to such changes. (The use of Durkheim's, Van Gennep's, and Shand's concepts was acknowledged only in later years.)

Another later addition to the definition of 'ceremonial', as defined above, is the assumption that ceremonial customs can be interpreted as a kind of language, a 'ritual idiom', in terms of a general theory of cultural symbolism. It is possible that Radcliffe-Brown already had the language analogy in mind as early as the first edition of *The Andaman Islanders*. However, there are no explicit references to it in the 1922 edition; the earliest reference to it I have been able to find is his 1931 Presidential address 'On the Present Position of Anthro-pological Studies' (Radcliffe-Brown 1958: 67–69).

In spite of the fact that Radcliffe-Brown had not yet arrived at an explicit formulation of the language analogy for interpreting ritual in the first edition of *The Andaman Islanders*, he had begun to pay some attention to symbolism and the processes of 'symbolic thought' in Andamanese ritual. This is particularly striking in his interpretation of the Andamanese custom of painting the body with white clay and red paint during initiations, marriage and mourning ceremonies, and dances. Not only does he apply his rules of method to discover the meaning of this custom, he also discusses the variety of symbolic patterns involved and why they are an appropriate means for expressing the particular meanings on different occasions. To paint one's body with patterns of white clay to resemble turtles and pork after consuming such foods is a means of expressing solidarity with these species and thereby avoiding the dangers associated with the consumption of such foods. Painting circular patterns on the bodies of boys and girls during initiation symbolizes the camp, the communal hut, and the village, that is, society and social life in general. The body paintings in this case are interpreted as protecting the initiates from danger by a power that is inherent in society (1922: 314).

The most detailed illustration of 'symbolic thought' in Andamanese ritual is Radcliffe-Brown's interpretation of the custom of hunters to paint their bodies with zig-zag patterns of white clay and red paint after a successful hunt. The 'symbols' in this case are interpreted by the anthropologist as expressing a sense of euphoria, well-being and esthetic pleasure in one's appearance and success. Any light or bright colour is associated with well-being and fine weather; honey and snakes symbolize fine weather and well-being; and the zig-zag patterns represent a particular species of snakes (1922: 316). Some of these associations are culturally and perhaps geographically distinctive of the Andamans. Others, for example, colour symbolism, may have a universal psychological basis. In any case, Radcliffe-Brown's hypothesis is that the Andamanese 'customary regulation of personal ornament is a means by which the society acts upon, modifies and regulates the sense of self in the individual'. This hypothesis is derived from 'a commonplace of psychology that the development of the sense of self is closely connected with the perception of one's own body' and the general recognition that 'the development of the moral and social sentiments in man is dependent upon the development of self-consciousness, of the sense of self' (1922: 315).

As a kind of negative test of his hypothesis, Radcliffe-Brown cites the prohibition of painting with white clay to a mourner, a homicide, or a sick person, each of whom is excluded from social life and whose social value is thus diminished (1922: 316).

The discussion in the first edition of *The Andaman Islanders* of painting the body with white clay and red paint and of the ceremonials of embracing and weeping, makes little reference to how the Andamanese interpreted them or to the linguistic accompaniments to the rites. That is perhaps as much to be explained by the way the monograph is organized and Radcliffe-Brown's sceptical attitude towards native exegesis as it is by the Andamanese ritual. Following the precedent set by his teacher Rivers (1906 [1967]), Radcliffe-Brown sharply separated description from interpretation, and 'customs' from 'beliefs'. 'Ceremonial customs' are restricted to non-verbal behaviour and 'beliefs' to verbally articulated expressions in myths and legends. In addition, Radcliffe-Brown believed that the Andamanese interpretations and explanations of their rituals, myths and legends are concrete, vague and inconsistent and while they need to be taken as data (the first rule of method), they should be supplemented by the anthropologist's more systematic, abstract and explicit interpretations (1922: 324, 396–97).

In the chapter dealing with the Andamanese beliefs, myths and legends, Radcliffe-Brown found the same processes of 'symbolic thought' he had already observed in their ceremonial customs. He compared the often inconsistent, concrete and metaphorical symbolic processes to those observed in dreams and in art (1922: 397). Since the purpose of the legends is to express sentiments and desires of various kinds, 'the *either-or* relation is inadmissable owing to the very nature of the thought process itself' (1922: 396). Although in their everyday practical life, the Andamanese are 'excellent observers of natural phenomena and are capable of putting their observations to practical use', their myths do not follow the laws of logical reasoning. The explanation, Radcliffe-Brown offers, is rooted in a kind of psychological law governing the use of symbols to express emotions:

> ...A mind intent on expressing certain feelings, faced with two alternative and equally satisfactory but inconsistent symbols, will hesitate to choose between them even at the command of the desire for logical consistency. It will cling as long as possible to both of them (1922: 397).

Andaman mythology follows such a psychological principle:

> The view of lightning as a person who shakes his leg seems to express in some way certain notions of the natives about lightning.

The alternative explanation of lightning as a fire-brand thrown by *Biliku* [a female deity] also satisfies in some way his [the 'native's'] need of expressing the impression that the phenomena make upon him. In spite of the inconsistency he clings to both symbols as best he can (1922: 397).

The 'symbols' in this case are personifications of a natural phenomenon which appeal 'through the imagination, to the mind's affective dispositions' (1922: 397). By using such symbols and metaphors, the Andamanese legends and myths express the social values of proper conduct, of the past and tradition, of familiar places and landmarks, of the weather and seasonal changes, and of interesting jungle birds and other creatures. Taken together, the legends express a system of social values or sentiments upon which Andamanese society depends for its survival. The legends represent for the Andamanese a moral and material order of the universe, that is, a cosmology, fragmentary and inconsistent but capable of systematization by the anthropologist.

Radcliffe-Brown's conclusion from his symbolic interpretation of the Andamanese legends and myths is that their function is 'exactly parallel to that of ritual and ceremonial':

They serve to express certain ways of thinking and feeling about the society and its relation to the world of nature, and thereby to maintain these ways of thought and feeling and pass them on to succeeding generations. In the case of both ritual and myth the sentiments expressed are those that are essential to the existence of the society (1922: 405).

Beliefs and customs of the Andamanese are religious, for 'they believe in a moral power regulating the universe, and they have organized their relations to that power by means of some of their simple ceremonies.' Radcliffe-Brown, however, did not find it possible, in the Andamans, to separate a definite entity which we call religion 'from things that may more appropriately be regarded as art, morality, play, or social ceremonial' (1922: 405).

The religious or, in Durkheim's terms, the 'sacred' character of the ceremonial customs is experienced by the Andamanese as the collective force of society through a sense of moral obligation in ritual and in the collective emotions of dances. This 'moral force' of society is projected onto the world of nature and all objects of social value. The

beliefs about the moral powers of society are implied by the Andamanese's ritual actions but are not formulated explicitly by them.
'They are not capable of thinking about their own sentiments except
in vague notions.'

RITUAL IDIOM, THE LANGUAGE ANALOGY AND SUBSTITUTION SYMBOLS

The exact parallels that Radcliffe-Brown noted between the Andamanese legends and ritual ceremonies, a parallelism in the processes
of 'symbolic thought' as well as in social function, indicate a pervasive
and implicit preoccupation with the problem of symbols and their
interpretation in the first edition of *The Andaman Islanders*. Yet there
is no explicit language analogy in the first edition and no general
theory of symbolism to explain how the meanings and functions of
verbal signs in legends can be 'exactly parallel' to the meanings and
functions of weeping, embracing, painting the body with white clay
and red paint in life cycle rites and in other ceremonial customs. The
answers to this will be found by taking into account the explicit
formulation of the language analogy and the theory of 'ritual idiom',
and of a general theory of cultural and social symbols, all of which
appear in the 'Preface' to the second edition (1933) of *The Andaman
Islanders* and in the 1932 'Lectures on Primitive Religion'.

The 'Preface' to the second edition of *The Andaman Islanders*
(1933) is quite explicit in its reference to the language analogy.
Radcliffe-Brown points out that although the fifth and sixth chapters
deal with the 'meaning' and 'function' of rites and myths, he gave
no definitions of these terms, and now supplies them:

> Just in the sense that words have meanings, so do some other things
> in culture—customary gestures, ritual actions and abstentions, sym-
> bolic objects, myths—they are expressive signs. The meaning of a
> word, a gesture, a rite, lies in what it expresses, and this is deter-
> mined by its associations within a system of ideas, sentiments and
> mental attitudes.

The application of this analogy to ethnology will provide

> a method of determining meanings as effective and free from
> 'personal equation' as the methods by which a linguist determines

the meanings of words or morphems in a newly studied language. Ethnology is faced with the dilemma that it must either give up forever all hope of understanding such things as myth or ritual, or it must develop proper methods for determining as accurately as can be what meanings they have for the people to whose culture they belong (Radcliffe-Brown 1933: viii–ix).

This formulation of the language analogy is obviously a slightly more complete variant of the formulation in the 'Foreword' to Srinivas' book on the Coorgs. Other variants of the analogy appear in several of Radcliffe-Brown's lectures and articles between 1931 and 1952. One of the most interesting of these appears in his 'Lectures on Primitive Religion' delivered at the University of Chicago in the winter of 1932. The notes of these lectures taken by Sol Tax were published by the Student Anthropology Club of the University in April 1956.

The concept of 'ritual idiom' was probably first introduced in these lectures and explicitly linked to the language analogy:

Every given culture has its ritual idiom and just as you cannot understand language idiom without the whole language, you must get the entire ritual system and culture.

For method, you must use the lexicographer's—you collect all examples of uses of a word and find what is in common—and that is the meaning, either precise or vague (and needing a description).

The word may have separate meanings, and you must find the link between the meanings. *Mana* means (1) authority or power, and (2) a process of thought, and you must get examples of each. Same with ritual: in the Andamans there is the rite of obligatory weeping; collecting all instances, there are both one-sided and mutual weeping. We see here that it is a rite of *separation* from others or of *reunion*. It expresses social attraction. Any change of human relations in this way brings on the rite. We get this by the comparative method. How do we check these results? The rite is combined with others—and considering its combination with other rites and analyzing its part in each of the others, we get a check. A third check is to ask the people what the rite means: this may be the same as yours; at least it *must fit in*. When you have made a study of a ritual system you get general principles that run through—and you can check each interpretation by the general principle. This is the method as laid down in *The Andaman Island-ers* (Radcliffe-Brown 1932: 8).

By 1932, Radcliffe-Brown obviously regarded his 1922 rules of method for the interpretation of ceremonial customs as following the lexicographer's method, although this was not explicitly stated in the first edition of *The Andaman Islanders*. It is of greater interest that the 1932 lectures contain the rudiments of a general theory of cultural symbolism that is intended to apply to both ritual and myth and is illustrated with material from Australian totemism as well as from *The Andaman Islanders*. The theory is well grounded in an interpretation of ritual and religious belief that explicitly draws on Durkheim's *Elementary Forms of the Religious Life*, Van Gennep's *Rites of Passage* and the works of the members of the French sociological school. The following summary statement about transition rites reveals how Radcliffe-Brown constructed a distinctive synthesis from such sources:

> *Summary*: Transition rites can be generalized into a tendency to treat with the ritual attitude any change which takes place in the relation of the individual to the society. The most important occur at birth, initiation, and death. Ritual and adoption of the ritual attitude are an expression of the social value of the object or the occasion. *The social importance of the occasion is indicated and expressed by the rites*. The things which affect the society are death, birth, etc.; these are important things in the life of a small group and ritual expresses this (Radcliffe-Brown 1932: 15. Italics in original).

This passage stresses the social function of ritual in expressing attitudes and sentiments towards objects and towards the changing social status, and 'social personality' of individuals that have significance and social value for the solidarity and continuity of a society. This function of ritual was already recognized in the first edition of *The Andaman Islanders*. The novel features introduced in the 'Lectures on Primitive Religion' is a discussion of the nature and kinds of symbols, and of the ritual idiom through which these functions of ritual are performed.

In both ritual and mythology, there is a process of substitution whereby something comes to represent something else. Symbolism is an example of such a process, and it is of two kinds: (1) a purely conventional sign stands for something else, and there is no good reason for the symbol—like language symbols; no correlation of form of word and meaning; (2) the symbol is by its form appropriate to represent the thing to which it refers. Where we have (1) we can never, by taking the *sign*, find what it stands for.

Shaking hands and smiling are examples of collective representations in class (2). Another example is from language: when you want words to describe enthusiasm, you use such words as 'ardent' and 'zeal'; if you know the language, you see that they are metaphors referring to 'heat'. We use it to represent mental eagerness. This is a process of substitution, and is an appropriate metaphor; ardour seems like heat to us, though we can not define why. This occurs in diverse cultures, too, such as China and Australia (Radcliffe-Brown 1932: 5–6).

Some of the colour symbolism, according to Radcliffe-Brown, is universally distributed and probably has a physiological basis in human nature. The colour red, for example, is important ritually in most parts of the world and is used to symbolize energy, vitality or violence. 'Red produces energy physiologically…You put maniacs in a blue room, and depressives in a red room' (1932: 6).

Denying that he derived social symbols from physiological reactions, Radcliffe-Brown emphasizes that he is interested in social symbols and that 'the production of social symbols is a social matter', although 'many of them are based on psychic reactions on which a system of communication is built' (1932: 6).

Black and white, up and down, right and left, clockwise and counterclockwise are some of the oppositions which have a physiological foundation.

Communication is the essence of human life; we communicate ideas by language (animals have none) and we *also* have means of communicating emotions (and animals do this—such as the sight of white under a rabbit's tail which sets off rabbits; there is no convention, but a communication of emotion). This is the basis on which human society starts and builds up a system of which ritual is a part (and art another). Where there is a common ritual idiom in different cultures, it is wrong to assume it must have been diffused; the very fact that it is accepted by different cultures shows that it is grounded in human nature. Why did they all accept a symbol? Because it had an appropriateness: it is rooted in psychophysical processes (Radcliffe-Brown 1932: 6–7).

Although many of the examples of 'ritual symbols' cited in the lecture notes on 'Primitive Religion' suggest that the symbols in ritual and myths and legends are 'natural', physiologically grounded rather than 'conventional', such a generalization needs to be qualified in several respects. The lectures indicate that words, too, are used in rites and myths as proper names, spells and prayers, commands, and the like. These words usually do not express their meanings because of their form; are they, then, conventional signs or natural symbols grounded in physiology? On the other hand, a handshake or an embrace may express friendly feelings and have a psychological basis. Yet, it is not customary in all societies and may be circumscribed by all sorts of conventions in those societies where it *is* customary.

To consider such possibilities it is necessary to elaborate upon Radcliffe-Brown's classification of 'natural' and 'conventional' symbols in the direction of a Peircean semiotics. Within that analytic framework, 'natural' signs may designate their objects because of some resemblance in form. The Andamanese circular patterns of clay body paintings which resemble their circular huts would be an example. Using Peirce's terminology, we may say that the circular patterns are 'iconic' signs, as are most diagrams, pictorial images and metaphors. The use of white clay and red paint in the body paintings is *said* to express euphoric feelings because white and red are believed to stimulate such feelings psychologically. In Peirce's terminology, these white and red paintings would be called 'symptoms', or 'indexical' signs, of euphoria. While the circular patterns and the colours of the clay body paintings are both 'natural' symbols, we cannot be equally certain that the circles have a physiological basis or that the colours resemble euphoric feelings in form (cf. Needham 1982: 32–52). In *The Andaman Islanders* Radcliffe-Brown constructs several long chains of symbolic associations to link the circles and colours with other objects in the Andamanese experience.

Radcliffe-Brown's distinctions between 'conventional symbols' and 'natural symbols', and between symbols that have a psychophysical foundation and those that are socially imposed, raise the question as to which kinds of symbols are used in ritual and myths. The 1932 'Lectures on Primitive Religion' do not contain an explicit general answer to this question. Judging, however, from the specific illustrations discussed, it seems that the distinctions were not intended to be mutually exclusive. Weeping and embracing may have a universal psychological basis, but as obligatory, formal and customary behaviour at marriages and funerals, they are socially imposed and include a conventional dimension. In the case of such mixed symbols it becomes necessary to analyse their components and organization, as well as their relations to social and individual contexts, in order to determine their meanings and functions. Radcliffe-Brown reformulated Durkheim's emblem theory of totemism in order to deal with mixed social and cultural symbols in rites and myths.

THE TOTEMIC CONNECTION

Radcliffe-Brown's symbolic analysis of ritual and myth grew out of his studies of Australian totemism as well as his field studies in the non-totemic Andamans. What is most distinctive of his analysis is his formulation of a general theory to fit both cases. The 1932 'Lectures on Primitive Religion' already document some of the major advances toward such a general theory, for example, the replacement of Durkheim's definition of totems as 'sacred' plants, animals, and natural phenomena represented by emblems ('the totem is the flag of the clan') by a new theory of 'ritual attitudes' towards any objects that are 'important' and thus have 'social value' for the life of a social group. This reformulation includes the Andamanese ritual attitude towards turtle and pork, two chief foods, as well as towards the cicada, which represents the seasons. The cicada in the Andamans and the eaglehawk in Australia are objects of a ritual attitude not because they are 'good to eat' but because they are 'substitution symbols' for something else that is of direct importance to social life. In this sense they are like Durkheim's 'emblems', even if they are not carved or painted.

A flag, a king, a phrase like 'my country' can become 'substitution symbols', concrete objects which represent more remote and less tangible objects towards which sentiments are expressed:

> A group's solidarity depends on a sentiment of solidarity (patriotism, *espirit de corps*). The sentiment must be given frequent expression—and it preferably should be collective. But your social group is not an immediate object of perception: it is hard to see it, so you substitute an immediately perceptible object which becomes

representative of the society...kings are sacred in Africa, etc. because they are tangible representatives of 'national unity', etc. Kings
can then be objects of ritual. The king is made king partly by
religious ceremony—he is a *sacred* being. Other symbols can be
used, such as the *flag*, which is only a designed cloth—but an object
of strong emotions. Emotion is directed to the flag, but that is only
a representation of something not immediately perceptible, though
it becomes the *chief object* of sentiments.

In order to express the sentiment collectively you have to have
a substitute object, and the sentiment becomes attached to it; it may
even be difficult to see what the real object is. An apparently
insignificant thing can become the object of ritual. The grasshopper
in East Africa represents grass, cattle, etc. In Andamans, the cicada
(an insect) is important ritually, cannot be killed, etc.; it represents
the procession of day and night and the seasons [its routine: it sings
certain hours in certain seasons]. The same thing can stand for a
number of nonperceptible objects; and the same object can be
represented by a variety of things (Radcliffe-Brown 1932: 8).

A second step in Radcliffe-Brown's progress towards a general
semiotic interpretation of ritual and myth was to show that Australian
totemism was not restricted to clans, but extended to moieties,
'hordes', totem centres, males and females, and individuals, each kind
of social subdivision being represented by its own totem and totemic
cult. The fact that these social subdivisions were often characterized
by binary oppositions (of clans, moieties, sexes, etc.) led Radcliffe-
Brown to identify a principle of 'dual opposition'—a *structural opposition* at the level of antagonism and friendship in social relations,
and a *logical opposition* at the level of symbolic representation:

In a totemic people...they start by regarding all these things [as]
sacred. But the society is subdivided into groups (moieties and
clans)...they often divide up nature in the same way and establish
special ritual relations between homologous parts of society and
nature.

The moieties have reciprocal functions. There is a conception of
dual oppositions, this is the basis of animals, etc. to represent the
moieties.... In the simplest form, you get just animals and plants
paired off, some in one moiety and opposing ones in the other
(1932: 24).

Societies with moieties frequently seek a general principle of dichotomy on the basis of which they classify everything in nature. The dichotomy varies in different places: 'land' vs. 'water', 'upstream' vs. 'downstream', 'heaven' vs. 'earth'...The way the oppositions in nature are represented is based on the social relations that exist (1932: 25).

...By means of mythology and ritual 'a philosophy of nature' is established, particularly a classification of nature, usually by analogy with the social structure. Totemism is a process by which the whole universe is built up into a single structure, and you establish between parts of the structure relations of the same kind as social relations (1932: 24).

We cannot regard this as a natural order alone but also a social and moral order. There is a social bond between all people and aspects of nature (1932: 28).

The classification of nature into dichotomous classes is based on dual social divisions and at the same time is a construction of a cosmology which includes both nature and society.

The chief semiotic means for incorporating the natural world into the social structure is through metaphors that personify natural phenomena in myth and ritual. To 'personify' is to treat a natural phenomenon as if it were a person, an act of a person, or the result of the act of a person. For Radcliffe-Brown, the basis of personification is psychological; it is a means of expressing and organizing emotional experiences, especially as found in relation to people in early life. 'Personification establishes personal relations with objects not primarily personal. This is part of the process of establishing between man and nature a set of relations similar to social relations of man to man' (1932: 30).

The objects and phenomena that are personified in myth and ritual, whether in totemic or non-totemic societies, are selected because of their social value for the community. They either have a direct social value, for example, rain in Africa and the north-south monsoons in the Andamans, or the objects selected symbolize something of social value, for example, the cicada in the Andamans whose life cycle represents the seasons, and the deity Baiume in New South Wales who represents the moral and social order of the tribe (1932: 30–33).

Some of the stages in Radcliffe-Brown's generalization of Durkheim's theory of Australian totemism to a special case of ritual relations between human societies and nature are explicitly described in the 'Lectures on Primitive Religion' (1932): the redefinition of the 'sacred' in terms of a ritual attitude, the parallels between social segmentation and ritual differentiation, the generalization of totems and totemic emblems into 'substitution symbols' that represent different kinds of social groups, and the building up of cosmologies through personification of the natural world in symbolic dual divisions. The generalization is intended to include non-totemic societies such as the Andamans as well as totemic societies. The method used is abstractive generalization from the comparison of similarities and differences.

The 1932 'Lectures on Primitive Religion' are neither the first nor the last discussion of Radcliffe-Brown's 'genuine structuralism' antedating his second lecture on totemism (1958 [1952]), in which it was first observed by Lévi-Strauss. Beginning with Radcliffe-Brown's first lecture on totemism in 1929, one can trace an explicit and continuous development of a generalized theory of ritual symbolism in the formulations of 1931, 1932, 1939, 1945 and 1947. Just as the Australian ethnographic sources of the generalization are evident in the 1931 monograph on *The Social Organization of Australian Tribes*, so are the Andamanese ethnographic sources evident in the 1922 edition of *The Andaman Islanders*.

Warner's further generalization and application of Durkheim's emblem theory to ancestral flags, cemeteries, historic houses, costumes and ships of a New England community reversed Durkheim's original analogy from 'the totem is the flag of the clan' to 'the flag is the totem of Yankee City' (Warner 1937 [1958]); 1959; Singer 1982a). Although more receptive to Durkheim's emblem theory of totemism than Radcliffe-Brown's, Warner's application of the theory to the symbolic life of an American urban community was entirely consistent with Radcliffe-Brown's theory of social and cultural symbolism.

DOUBLE OPPOSITION AND CREATIVE SOCIAL SYMBOLS

Lévi-Strauss' criticism of Radcliffe-Brown's explanation for the selection of ritual objects or symbols in mythology and ritual is based on the charge that it is too functionalist, utilitarian and naturalistic. The objects are selected because they are 'good to eat', not because they are 'good to think'. Radcliffe-Brown denied the utilitarian charge but did not deny his functionalism and naturalism.

That his theory of ritual or 'sacred' objects is functionalist is well-known from his often repeated statements that the function of rituals and myths is to express and perpetuate those sentiments towards the objects on which the existence and continuity of a society depends. It has not, however, been well recognized that this functionalism was combined with structuralism by the early 1930s, both in the sense that society was conceived as organized in a structure of social groups and social relations, and in the larger sense that the objects towards which ritual attitudes are directed, in rites or myths, are coordinated with the social structure.

> For primitive man the universe as a whole is a moral or social order governed not by what we call natural law but rather by what we must call moral or ritual law...
> In Australia, for example, there are innumerable ways in which the natives have built up between themselves and the phenomena of nature a system of relations which are essentially similar to the relations that they have built up in their social structure between one human being and another (Radcliffe-Brown 1952 [1929]: 130).

In other words, there is a similarity between the structure of social relations (the 'social structure') and a wider structure that includes the ritual relations between a society and natural phenomena. These 'analogies of structure', as Lévi-Strauss called them, include both Lévi-Strauss' 'postulate of homology between nature and culture' and Radcliffe-Brown's principle of 'dual opposition', (Radcliffe-Brown 1958: 118), as may be seen in the following illustration from Radcliffe-Brown's 1929 lecture on 'The Sociological Theory of Totemism':

> By the fact that each clan has its own totem there is expressed the differentiation and opposition between clan and clan: the kangaroo men not only recognize the bond that unites them as kangaroo men but also recognize their difference from the emu men and the bandicoot men and so on.... The wider unity and solidarity of the whole totemic society is expressed by the fact that the society as a whole, through its segments, stands in a ritual relation to nature as a whole (Radcliffe-Brown 1952 [1929]: 130–31).

The structure of ritual relations towards natural phenomena are homologous to some social relations. Whether all social relations are ritualized is an open question in Radcliffe-Brown's theory of ritual. His definition of a ritual relation as a socially imposed attitude towards an object that involves 'some measure of respect expressed in a traditional mode of behavior with reference to that object' does not imply that all social relations are respect relations (Radcliffe-Brown 1952: 123; compare Eggan 1955 [1937]: 27–29, 75–81, 516–17; Fortes 1969: 45–50).

An essential feature of Radcliffe-Brown's analysis of ritual relations as involving two homologous structures of relations, social and natural, is that the system of natural relations is used to mediate and symbolize the system of social relations. The structure of differences and similarities between kangaroos and emus is used to symbolize the structure of differences and similarities between kangaroo men and emu men. Whether the mediation is based on perceived similarities and differences in natural species or on their fanciful personifications, whether the natural species themselves are the emblems of social groups or the emblems are carved and painted designs, the important fact is that the expression of respect (or disrespect) towards the emblem in a traditional mode of behaviour triggers a significant social interaction among the members of the social groups whose emblems are the objects of a ritual attitude. Radcliffe-Brown's description of sex totemism in New South Wales graphically illustrates how a relation of ritual disrespect towards the emblems mediates a relation of structural opposition between the social groups represented by the emblems:

> An Australian camp includes men of a certain local clan and their wives who, by the rule of exogamy, have come from other clans. In New South Wales there is a system of sex totemism, by which one animal species is the 'brother' of the men, and another species is the 'sister' of the women. Occasionally there arises within a native camp a condition of tension between the sexes. What is then likely to happen, according to the accounts of the aborigines, is that the women will go out and kill a bat, the 'brother' or sex totem of the men, and leave it lying in the camp for the men to see. The men then retaliate by killing the bird which in that tribe is the sex totem of the women. The women then utter abuse against the men and this leads to a fight with sticks (digging sticks for the women, throwing sticks for the men) between the two sex groups in which a good many bruises are inflicted. After the fight peace is restored

and the tension is eliminated. The Australian aborigines have the idea that where there is a quarrel between two persons or two groups which is likely to smoulder, the thing to do is for them to fight it out and then make friends. The symbolic use of the totem is very significant. This custom shows us that the idea of the opposition of groups, and the union of opposites, is not confined to exogamous societies (Radcliffe-Brown 1958: 25–26).

This example probably served Radcliffe-Brown as a concrete prototype of how a cognitive relation of 'opposition' between the symbols of two cultural categories ('men' and 'women'), and a social relation of 'structural opposition' between two kinds of persons, men and women, are mediated in a context of social interaction by the symbolic representations, or totems, of each group.

Radcliffe-Brown's theory of ritual implies that totems (and other ritual objects) are not only symbolic representations of particular social groups and categories of persons and their relations; but they also symbolize more abstract and intangible entities such as the power of society, the natural order and the moral order. In a society with some complex social differentiations, as in aboriginal Australia, there will be some kind of ritual hierarchy among the ritual objects that symbolically represent different social groups and subgroups. The hierarchy will depend on three major factors: the social value and importance of the groups and objects symbolized, their existing and past positions in the social structure, and the nature and extent of the ritual and mythological symbolization. The roles of the first two factors are fairly obvious in Radcliffe-Brown's functional theory of ritual. If the function of ritual is to express and keep alive those social sentiments and values on which a society depends for its existence and continuity, then the socially important objects, persons and events will be ritualized, and the more important they are, the more intensified the ritual will be.

The activities of symbolization in ritual and myth are not entirely passive and dependent. While many ritual objects are good to eat, many are not, and derive their importance and social value from their aesthetic qualities (the colourful plumage of birds and the rainbow serpent), the unusual and regular sounds of insects (the cicada), or other striking and memorable features that serve to mark some important occasion. The medium may not be the entire message, but symbolization, as Whitehead and advertisers have observed, enhances the importance of what is symbolized (Whitehead 1927 [1959]: 63). Whitehead's *Symbolism: Its Meaning and Effect*, especially the third chapter, is cited as 'an admirable brief introduction to the sociological theory of symbolism' in Radcliffe-Brown's note appended to his lecture on 'Taboo' (1952: 152). Whether a particular object chosen as an object of ritual attitude is good to eat or not, it soon gets embellished by the arts of carving, painting, drawing, dance and drama, song and story in ritual and cultural performances which render it difficult to distinguish religion from art, morality, play, or social ceremonial (Radcliffe-Brown 1922: 405; see also Singer 1982a: 90–91).

CONCLUSION: TOWARDS A SEMIOTIC THEORY OF RITUAL

The significance of Radcliffe-Brown's contribution to a semiotics of ritual consists not so much in his early recognition of ritual as a language, or as a 'ritual idiom' whose meaning can be investigated by a method analogous to the lexicographer's method of learning the meaning of words of an unknown language. The language analogy as Radcliffe-Brown applied it to ritual was suggestive rather than literal or exact. The important suggestion was his recognition that ritual acts differ from technical acts 'in having in all instances some expressive or symbolic element in them' (1939: 49). This led him to the insight that ritual actions are often 'symbolic actions', and make use of 'symbolic representations' in myths and rites. A general definition of 'symbol' and 'meaning' as reciprocal ('whatever has meaning is a symbol and the meaning is whatever is expressed by the symbol') and a classification of symbols into 'conventional' and 'natural' quickly followed. His use of this definition and classification of symbols in the analysis of ritual and myths did not fall into the trap of creating mutually exclusive categories of symbols. Guided in part by the precedents of Durkheim on totemism and Van Gennep on the rites of passage, Radcliffe-Brown developed a concept of 'social and cultural symbol' as a kind of complex sign which represented a natural phenomenon at the same time that it emblematized a social group (Singer 1982a). To study rites as symbolic expressions of sentiments and social values, and of the cosmological ideas and beliefs associated with the rites, in a particular society, became a programme for field research and theoretical construction which has stimulated anthropologists for several generations since.

In spite of considerable progress and controversy, at least two of Radcliffe-Brown's formulations still survive: one of these is the definition of a ritual attitude as 'the attribution of ritual value to objects and occasions which are either themselves objects of important common interests linking together the persons of a community or symbolically representative of such objects' (Radcliffe-Brown 1952 [1939]: 151). A second contribution is his formulation of a principle of 'dual opposition' comprising a 'structural opposition' between social groups or individuals, and a homologous 'logical opposition' between 'symbolic representations' of these groups or individuals in rites and myths. These two contributions may not be precisely linguistic, but they are semiotic, semiological and even structural; as Lévi-Strauss recognized, semiotic because a triadic relation between two subjects linked to one another by a common interest in an object or in a substitute symbol for such object, semiological because ritual is to be analysed as a sign system, and structural because Radcliffe-Brown's principle of 'dual opposition' is practically identical with Lévi-Strauss' postulate of homology between nature and culture.

In his 1971 article on 'Kimil: A Category of Andamanese Thought', Leach argues that Radcliffe-Brown 'did not in fact make a structuralist analysis of Andamanese myth, but he came close to doing so' (Leach 1971: 25). Although Leach finds *The Andaman Islanders* 'biological-functional' in its attitude towards structure rather than 'mathematical-logical', he credits it with 'embryonic structuralist insights' (Leach 1971).

Another explanation for Radcliffe-Brown's early deficiencies as a structuralist is that the first edition of *The Andaman Islanders* uses a Tylorian global concept of culture ('the whole mass of institutions, customs and beliefs of a given people', 1922: 400) that includes social organization. An explicit concept of 'social structure', including the kinship system, and a complementary concept of 'culture' as social usages and symbol systems in which the social structure is expressed were not explicitly formulated until the 1930s. The 'embryonic structuralist insight' of *The Andaman Islanders* included structural homologies between nature and culture based in part on observation and in part on metaphors that personified nature or naturalized persons (as in the naming of girls according to the 'calendar of scents', Radcliffe-Brown 1922: 311–12). It was not, however, until Radcliffe-Brown tried to systematize the description of Australian classificatory kinship systems and analyse the relation of social differentiation to ritual differentiation in totemism did he see the need for a narrower concept of social structure and a wider concept that included ritual structure (Radcliffe-Brown 1931: 32). This was the situation, I believe, that led him to develop a mathematical-logical conception of social structure in the 1930s, deriving in part from Russell and Whitehead's philosophy of events and relational structures (Singer 1973; 1984a).

Radcliffe-Brown's generalization of Durkheim's theory of totems as 'sacred' emblems or 'collective representations' into a theory of social objects that have social values for a society, or are substitute symbols for such objects, marked the transformation of his functionalist theory of ritual into a *structural*–functionalist and semiotic theory. While the transformation was cumulative and can be discerned with hindsight, in embryo, in the 1922 edition of *The Andaman Islanders*, it was not explicitly formulated until the late 1920s and the early 1930s. Only then does it appear that Radcliffe-Brown's theory of rituals as collective and obligatory 'ceremonial customs' which express the social sentiments of solidarity, attachment and similar emotions, on important occasions in social life, is a functionalist synthesis of Durkheim's theory of 'collective representations', Van Gennep's theory of 'rites of passage' and Shand's theory of 'sentiments'; only then do Radcliffe-Brown's distinctive contributions to the synthesis emerge. These further contributions are not a repudiation of the 1922 synthesis but a refinement and further development of it. Ritual as 'ceremonial custom' is redefined as a mode of obligatory ritual behaviour, standardized by culture and society. The 'sacred' objects of ritual become objects of a 'ritual attitude' that involves some measure of respect. They are selected as objects of a ritual attitude not solely because they are ecologically 'important' sources of food and other 'social values'; their social value is redefined to add the *internally adaptive* criteria of common personal 'interests' and shared consciousness of social relations.

While some measure of agreement about values, some similarity of interests, is a prerequisite of a social system, social relations involve more than this. They require the existence of common interests and social values. When two or more persons have a common interest in the same object and are aware of their community of interest, a social relation is established. They form, whether for a moment or for a long period, an association, and the object may be said to have a social value (Radcliffe-Brown 1952 [1929]: 140).

This definition implies that an object can 'only have a social value for an association of persons':

In the simplest possible instance we have a triadic relation: subject 1 and subject 2 are both interested in the same way in the object and each of the subjects has an interest in the other, or at any rate in certain items of the behaviour of the other, namely those directed towards the object (Radcliffe-Brown 1952 [1939]: 141).

The application of this definition of 'social value' leads to the conclusion that most ritual values are social values and that 'the primary basis of all ritual and therefore of religion and magic...is the attribution of ritual values to objects and occasions which are either themselves objects of important common interests linking together the persons of a community or are symbolically representative of such objects' (Radcliffe-Brown 1952 [1939]: 151).

The Andamanese taboos on plants and animals used as food and on other ritual objects express a social *recognition* in a standardized symbolic form, or ritual idiom, of the importance and interest of such objects:

In the Andamans ritual value is attributed to the cicada, not because it has any social importance itself but because it symbolically represents the seasons of the year which do have importance.... The reverence that the Australian shows to the image of Baiume or towards his name is the symbolic method of fixing the social or the moral law, particularly the laws relating to marriage (Radcliffe-Brown 1952 [1939]: 151).

Radcliffe-Brown has deftly combined his early definition of 'social value' in terms of the social importance of ecological conditions and processes with an individualistic interest theory of values ('an interest is always the interest of an individual', 1952 [1939]: 140). While Radcliffe-Brown's definition of 'social value' in terms of common interests did not completely transform Durkheim's 'collective representations' into individual representations, it makes possible the analysis of ritual relations in terms of interpersonal social relations, and the analysis of totems and other ritual objects in terms of a theory of substitution symbols.

The interest theory of social values was probably derived from R. B. Perry's book, *General Theory of Value* (1926), which Radcliffe-

Brown described as 'the best treatment of the subject of value with which I am acquainted' (1952 [1939]: 152; Singer 1968: 532). In this book Perry also discusses the social functions of symbols such as words and flags in creating a community of interests, and analyses Durkheim's concept of 'collective representations' (Perry 1926: 457–59, 480–87).

An interest theory of ritual attitudes, of ritual objects and of social relations enabled Radcliffe-Brown to formulate a comprehensive concept of 'social structure' as a network of social relations and to complement that concept with a concept of 'culture' as a set of social usages and rules of behaviour, and a set of social and cultural symbols (Radcliffe-Brown 1957 [1937]: 92–109). Taken together with his Australian ethnographical writings on social and ritual differentiation, the complementarity of social structure and culture was then analysed in terms of analogies of structure between social relations and the relations of their symbolic representations in myth and rite, a structural analogy which Radcliffe-Brown called 'dual opposition'.

Analogies of structure between nature and culture are seen in *The Andaman Islanders* in the 'calendar of scents', the interpretation of the category of *kimil*, and other examples. Radcliffe-Brown's structuralism, however, is not formulated explicitly and self-consciously until he begins to apply, in the 1930s, Russell and Whitehead's philosophy of reality as relational structures of events, an application that Perry's *General Theory of Value* also suggested (Perry 1926: 460–61; Singer 1973; 1984a).

Radcliffe-Brown's structuralism and Lévi-Strauss' as well do not suffice to account for the meaning of social and cultural symbols. In both cases a structuralist method of analysis is applied to the symbolism of myths and rituals, but in both cases the structuralist analysis is supplemented—by a Saussurean semantics and semiology in Lévi-Strauss' case and by a triadic semiotics and pragmatics in Radcliffe-Brown's.

Radcliffe-Brown's interpretation of 'symbolic thought' and 'symbolic action' in *The Andaman Islanders* is chiefly based on the late nineteenth century and the early twentieth century associationist psychology and psychophysiology. Only in the 1930s, when his interpretations of 'ritual idiom' are guided by the language analogy, and he distinguishes between 'conventional symbols' and 'natural symbols', do his interpretations show how cultural symbols and cosmologies mediate social and ritual relations, and thus achieves a genuine semiotics of ritual.

EPILOGUE

Srinivas at Oxford in the 1940s must have welcomed Radcliffe-Brown's suggestion that he do a structural–functional analysis of Coorg religion and society rather than a cultural–historical analysis. The functionalist style of social anthropological monograph was a novelty at that time and some of the pioneering monographs had already become classics of social anthropology, for example, Rivers' *The Todas* (1906), Malinowski's *The Argonauts of the Western Pacific* (1922), Radcliffe-Brown's *The Andaman Islanders* (1922). To a young man just embarking upon a professional career in social anthropology the new style was appealing. The suggestion was moreover appealing for deeper reasons that may not have been evident at the time to Radcliffe-Brown: a science of ritual had already been developed in Hinduism for over 2,000 years (Staal 1980; 1982). The path of ritual observance (*karma marga*) is a well-known Hindu mode of life and is recognized in modern India by the widespread use of printed ritual calendars (*panchanga*). In Sanskritic Hinduism, *karma* is usually translated both as ritual observance and as a theological doctrine of right action or *dharma*. In later Hinduism and in Buddhism the path of ritual observance was differentiated from the path of devotion to a deity (*bhakti marga*) and the path of philosophical knowledge (*jñana marga*), a differentiation somewhat analogous to the Western religious distinction of works, faith and knowledge (Raghavan 1955; Singer [1972] 1980; Das 1977; Freed and Freed 1980; Saraswati 1977).

In his Coorg study Srinivas notes the differences between the three major Hindu paths (1952: 25–26, 189, 212–13, 227, 240). His chief interest, however, was in the application of Radcliffe-Brown's theory of ritual to Coorg religious practices and beliefs and their relation to all-India Hindu practices and beliefs. The application goes considerably beyond Radcliffe-Brown's redefinition of the 'sacred' in terms of 'ritual value' and an analysis of rituals and myths in terms of 'symbolic action' and 'symbolic thought'. It also includes a detailed ethnographic description of the 'ritual idiom' and cults of different social units in Coorg—joint family, village, caste; and of the diacritical symbols of age, sex, marital status, caste, sect and other social divisions. His most original contribution to a theory of ritual is his analysis of the hierarchies of ritual purity and ritual pollution among different castes, occupations, and age and sex groups. Srinivas' linking of this analysis to social strategies that different groups adopted for changing their social and 'normal ritual status' by changing their ritual practices and beliefs generated the famous theory of 'sanskritization' and 'desanskritization', and his later theory of secularization and Westernization (Srinivas 1952: 106–7; 1962; 1966; 1976; Singer 1973; 1980: 488–507; Singer and Cohn 1968).

One explanation for Srinivas' achievement, as Radcliffe-Brown suggested in his 'Foreword' to the Coorg monograph, is that it was done by a trained anthropologist who is himself an Indian and 'who has therefore an understanding of Indian ways of thought which it is difficult for a European to attain even over many years.' To this suggestion I would like to add the supplementary explanation that by the 1940s the early synchronic functionalism of the 'primitive isolate' had begun to relax sufficiently to incorporate a study of the social organization, structure and differential spread of Hinduism in the subcontinent. Srinivas' teacher, Radcliffe-Brown, was not unaware of the Indian context of the Andamans, as his occasional reference to Hindustani or Indian beliefs testify. Nor was *his* teacher Rivers unaware of the Hindu influences on the Todas (Rivers 1906 [1967]: 457–59, 696–98). A belief that social anthropology could be applied to the 'higher religions' of ancient China, Greece, Rome, the Middle East and India was expressed by Radcliffe-Brown himself in 1945 with supporting references from Durkheim, Loisy, Fustel de Coulange, Hubert, Mauss, and Robertson Smith (Radcliffe-Brown [1945] 1952).

Perhaps it was this favourable opinion at Oxford and Manchester, his earlier training and fieldwork at Bombay under Professor G. S. Ghurye who had been a student of Rivers, and the *Toda* and *Andaman* monographs that inspired Srinivas to write a pioneer monograph on the social anthropology of Indian civilization (Srinivas 1952; Singer [1972] 1976; 1980). His contribution and Radcliffe-Brown's legacy will continue to be relevant for a semiotics of ritual even if modernization and political changes convert sacred rituals into political theatre and religion into a cultural system (Fried and Fried 1980; Geertz 1960; 1968; 1973; 1980; Meyerhoff and Moore 1977; Peacock 1968; Seneviratne 1978; Turner 1982a; 1982b).

REFERENCES

BARTH, F. 1975. *Ritual and Knowledge among the Bhaktaman of New Guinea.* New Haven: Yale University Press, pp. 207–14.

BOON, J. A. 1982. *Other Tribes, Other Scribes. Symbolic Anthropology in the Comparative Study of Cultures, Histories, Religions, and Texts*. Cambridge: Cambridge University Press.

DOUGLAS, M. 1966. *Purity and Danger. An Analysis of Concepts of Pollution and Taboo*. New York: Praeger.

DURKHEIM, E. [1915] 1947. *The Elementary Forms of the Religious Life*. Glencoe: The Free Press.

EGGAN, F. (Ed.). 1955 [1937]. *Social Anthropology of North American Tribes*. Chicago: The University of Chicago Press.

FIRTH, R. 1973. *Symbols: Public and Private*. Ithaca: Cornell University Press.

FORTES, M. 1969. *Kinship and the Social Order. The Legacy of Lewis Henry Morgan*. Chicago: Aldine.

FREED, R. S. and FREED, S. A. 1980. *Rites of Passage in Shanti Nagar*. New York: American Museum of Natural History.

FRIED, M. N. and FRIED, M. H. 1980. *Transitions. Four Rituals in Eight Cultures*. New York: W. W. Norton.

GEERTZ, C. 1960. *The Religion of Java*. Glencoe: The Free Press.

———. 1968. *Islam Observed: Religious Development in Morocco and Indonesia*. New Haven: Yale University Press.

———. 1973. *The Interpretation of Cultures*. New York: Basic Books.

———. 1980. *Negara. The Theatre State in Nineteenth-Century Bali*. Princeton: Princeton University Press.

GENNEP, A. van [1909] 1960. *The Rites of Passage*. Chicago: The University of Chicago Press.

GLUCKMAN, M. (Ed.). 1962. *Essays on the Ritual of Social Relations*. Manchester: Manchester University Press.

GRANET, M. [1933] 1973. 'Right and Left in China'. In R. Needham (Ed.), *Right and Left. Essays on Dual Symbolic Classification*. Chicago: The University of Chicago Press.

HUBERT, H. and MAUSS, M. [1898] 1964. *Sacrifice: Its Nature and Function*. Chicago: The University of Chicago Press.

JAKOBSON, R. [1940] 1978. *Six Lectures on Sound and Meaning* (Preface by Claude Lévi-Strauss). Cambridge, Mass.: The MIT Press.

LEACH, E. 1968. 'Ritual'. In *International Encyclopedia of the Social Sciences*. New York: Macmillan.

LEACH, E. R. 1971. 'Kimil: A Category of Andamanese Thought'. In P. Maranda and E. K. Maranda (Eds.), *Structural Analysis of Oral Tradition*. Philadelphia: University of Pennsylvania Press.

LÉVI-STRAUSS, C. 1963a. *Structural Anthropology*, Vol. I, 1963. New York: Basic Books.

———. 1963b. *Totemism*. Boston: Beacon Press. First published in France in 1962.

———. 1963c. 'The Bear and the Barber', *The Journal of the Royal Anthropological Institute*, XCIII: 1–11.

———. [1964] 1970. *The Raw and the Cooked. Introduction to a Science of Mythology*, Vol. I. New York: Harper & Row.

———. [1966] 1962. *The Savage Mind*. London: Weidenfeld and Nicholson. First published in France in 1962.

———. 1971. *Mythologique IV: L'Homme Nu*. Paris: Plon.

LÉVI-STRAUSS, C. [1971] 1976. 'Relations of Symmetry between Rituals and Myths of Neighboring Peoples'. In C. Lévi-Strauss, *Structural Anthropology*, Vol. II. New York: Basic Books.

MALINOWSKI. 1922. *The Argonauts of the Western Pacific*. London: Routledge and Kegan Paul.

MEYERHOFF, B. and MOORE, S. (Eds.). 1977. *Secular Ritual*. Amsterdam: Royal van Gorcum.

NEEDHAM, R. (1982). *Circumstantial Deliveries*. Berkeley: University of California Press.

PEACOCK, J. L. 1968. *Rites of Modernization: Symbolic and Social Aspects of Indonesian Proletarian Drama*. Chicago: The University of Chicago Press.

PEIRCE, C. S. 1931–58. *Collected Papers*, Vols. 1–6 (eds. C. Hartshorne and P. Weiss); Vols. 7–8 (ed. A.W. Burks). Cambridge, Mass.: Harvard University Press.

——. [1940] 1955. *Philosophical Writings of Peirce* (ed. J. Buchler). New York: Dover Publication.

——. *Writings of Charles S. Peirce* (general ed. M. H. Fisch), Vol. 1, 1857–66. Bloomington: Indiana University Press.

PERRY, R. B. 1926. *General Theory of Value. Its Meaning and Basic Principles Construed in Terms of Interest*. New York: Longmans, Green.

RADCLIFFE-BROWN, A. R. 1922. *The Andaman Islanders. A Study in Social Anthropology*. Cambridge: Cambridge University Press.

——. 1931. *The Social Organization of Australian Tribes*. Oceania Monographs. Melbourne: Macmillan.

——. [1932] 1956. 'Lectures on Primitive Religion'. Notes taken by Sol Tax. Chicago: Anthropology Club.

——. 1947. Cosmology of the Australian Aborigines. Handwritten Notes. Manchester. Compare 1932 notes.

——. [1922, 1933] 1948. *The Andaman Islanders*. Glencoe: The Free Press.

——. 1952 [1939]. *Structure and Function in Primitive Society*. London: Cohen and West.

——. [1957] 1937. *A Natural Science of Society*. Glencoe: Free Press.

——. 1958. M. N. Srinivas (Ed.), *Method in Social Anthropology*. Chicago: University of Chicago Press.

RAGHAVAN, V. (1955). 'Some Leading Ideas of Hindu Thought', *The Vedanta Kesari*.

REDFIELD, R. with M. SINGER, 1954. 'The Cultural Role of Cities', *Economic Development and Cultural Change*. II: 53–73. Reprinted in Redfield 1962.

——. 1956. *Peasant Society and Culture*. Chicago: The University of Chicago Press.

——. 1962. 'The Universally Human and the Culturally Variable; Anthropological Universtanding of Man; Societies and Cultures as Natural Systems', *Human Nature and Society*. Chicago: The University of Chicago Press.

RIVERS, W. H. R. [1906] 1967. *The Todas*. Oosterhout N. B. The Netherlands: Anthropological Publications.

SARASWATI, B. 1977. *Brahmanic Ritual Traditions in the Crucible of Time*. Simla: Indian Institute of Advanced Study.

SENEVIRATNE, H. L. 1978. *Rituals of the Kandyan State*. Cambridge: Cambridge University Press.

SHAND, F. A. 1920. *The Foundations of Character: Being a Study of the Tendencies of the Emotions and Sentiments*. London: Macmillan.

SINGER, M. (Ed.). 1959. *Traditional India: Structure and Change*. Philadelphia: The American Folklore Society.

———. (Ed.). [1966] 1968. *Krishna, Myths, Rites and Attitudes*. Chicago: The University of Chicago Press.

———. 1968. 'Culture'. In *International Encyclopedia of the Social Sciences*, Vol. 3. New York: Macmillan, pp. 527–43.

———. 1972. *When a Great Tradition Modernizes*. Chicago: The University of Chicago Press. Midway Reprints, 1980.

———. 1973. *Entrepreneurship and Modernization of Occupational Cultures in South Asia*. Durham: Duke University.

———. 1976. 'Robert Redfield's Development of a Social Anthropology of Civilizations'. In J. Murra (Ed.), *American Anthropology: The Early Years*. St. Paul, Minn.: West Publishing Co. and American Ethnological Society.

———. 1978. 'For a Semiotic Anthropology'. In T. A. Sebeok (Ed.), *Sight, Sound and Sense*. Bloomington: Indiana University Press.

———. 1980. 'Signs of the Self: An Exploration in Semiotic Anthropology', *American Anthropologist*, 82: 488–507.

———. 1981. 'On the Semiotics of Indian Identity', *American Journal of Semiotics*, 7: 85–126.

———. 1982a. 'Emblems of Identity: A Semiotic Exploration'. In J. Maquet (Ed.), *Symbols in Anthropology*. Malibu: Udena Publishers.

———. 1982b. 'Personal and Social Identity in Dialogue'. In B. Lee (Ed.), *Psychosocial Theories of the Self*. New York: Plenum.

———. 1984a. 'A Neglected Source of Structuralism: Radcliffe-Brown, Russell and Whitehead', *Semiotica*, 48: 11–98.

———. 1984b. *Man's Glassy Essence. Explorations in Semiotic Anthropology*. Bloomington: Indiana University Press. Delhi: Hindustan, 1986.

SINGER, M. and COHN, B. S. (Eds.). 1968. *Structure and Change in Indian Society*. Chicago: Aldine.

SRINIVAS, M. N. 1952. *Religion and Society among the Coorgs of South India*. London and New York: Oxford University Press.

———. 1962. *Caste in Modern India and Other Essays*. Bombay: Asia Publishing House.

———. 1966. *Social Change in Modern India*. Berkeley: University of California Press.

———. 1973. 'Itineraries of an Indian Social Anthropologist', *International Social Science Journal*, 25: 129–48.

———. 1976. *The Remembered Village*. Berkeley: University of California Press.

STAAL, J. F. 1980. 'The Meaninglessness of Ritual', *Numen. International Review for the History of Religions*, 26: 2–22.

———. 1982. *The Science of Ritual*. Poona: Bhandarkar Oriental Research Institute.

STANNER, W. E. H. 1965. 'Religion, Totemism and Symbolism'. In R. M. Berndt and C. G. Berndt (Eds.), *Aboriginal Man in Australia*. Sydney: Angus and Robertson.

TAMBIAH, S. J. 1973. 'Form and Meaning of Magical Acts: A Point of View'. In R. Horton and R. Finnegan (Eds.), *Modes of Thought: Essays on Thinking in Western and Non-Western Societies*. London: Faber and Faber.

TURNER, V. 1962. 'Three Symbols of Passage in Ndembu Circumcision Ritual: An Interpretation'. In M. Gluckman (Ed.), *Essays on the Ritual of Social Relations*. Manchester: Manchester University Press.

———. 1967. *The Forest of Symbols*. Ithaca: Cornell University Press.

TURNER, V. 1969. *The Ritual Process.* Chicago: Aldine.

——. 1974. *Dramas, Fields and Metaphors.* Ithaca: Cornell University Press.

——. 1979. *Process, Performance and Pilgrimage. A Study in Comparative Symbology.* New Delhi: Concept.

——. 1982a. *From Ritual to Theatre. The Human Seriousness of Play.* New York: Performing Arts Journal Publications.

——. (Ed.). 1982b. *Celebration. Studies in Festivity and Ritual.* Washington, D.C.: Smithsonian Institution Press.

WARNER, W. L. [1937] 1958. *A Black Civilization.* New York, Evanston: Harper and Row.

——. 1959. *The Living and the Dead: A Study of the Symbolic Life of Americans.* New Haven: Yale University Press.

WHITEHEAD, A. N. [1927] 1959. *Symbolism: Its Meaning and Effect.* New York: Putnam.

2

SOCIAL DESCRIPTION AND SOCIAL CHANGE: FROM FUNCTION TO CRITICAL CULTURAL SIGNIFICANCE[1]

R. S. KHARE

I

This paper argues the need to re-examine the wider significance of the studies of social description and social change in India, the topics to which Professor M. N. Srinivas has made a series of pioneering

[1] Written in the early 1980s for the Srinivas Festschrift, this paper now incorporates only a *limited* revision of the content and style, undertaken in the late summer of 1992. I have resisted the temptation to rewrite the whole paper, for it would have meant an entirely different one. As it now is, the paper retains most of its original content, though its introduction and conclusion have been rewritten, with a suitable addition and discussion of some recent studies.

Those interested in following up the relevant recent literature on critical debates and anthropology are provided with references which include good bibliographies.

contributions (e.g., Srinivas 1966; 1976). Such a step is necessary because some recent influential analyses, especially those of Professors Louis Dumont and McKim Marriott,[2] point out new issues and problems which previous studies either overlooked or were unprepared to recognize. Meanwhile, we have questioned several sociological and anthropological assumptions about our method, descriptive representation and theorization, most notably scientific objectivity (see Agger 1991; Manganaro 1990). In such a context of changing disciplinary assumptions, the works of M. N. Srinivas, which never clearly followed a predominant theoretical 'school', might be reviewed for their strengths and weaknesses. Though theoretically naive (hence unencumbered), these works still remain influential for describing verities of Indian social life, often in striking styles of description, narration and analysis.

An evaluation of Srinivas' work, in my view, automatically implicates the works of two other major contemporary scholars—Louis Dumont and McKim Marriott. A brief, stage setting, comparative review is in order. For example, while Srinivas' view of Indian society rested on historical and cultural diversity, Dumont's 'Indian sociology', one of the most influential scholarly efforts after the Second World War, chose to deal with Indian reality in 'ideological' terms, with the focus on the 'structural logic' of ritual status and power (Dumont 1980, also his other essential writings included therein).[3]

---

[2] As I have already argued elsewhere (Khare 1992), Dumont and Marriott extend each other's essentially *emic* studies of India. When viewed in the larger context of development of Indian sociology after the Second World War, the picture remains incomplete until Professor Srinivas' work is simultaneously taken into account. Methodologically, Srinivas' studies complement—and criticize—the 'internal' view of India which Dumont and Marriott, two outsiders, separately and together, try to provide. When the three contributions are seen together, Dumont and Marriott must cluster together for relying heavily (and explicitly) on Indology and Western sociological theories, while Srinivas stands apart for his intuitive sociological formulations and home-grown cultural aesthetics and descriptive sensibilities.

[3] Analytically, it may mean at times to distinguish between Dumont's own formulations on Indian sociology (see his writings and debates up to 1966 in the original numbers of *Contributions to Indian Sociology*, and up to 1980 in his revised and enlarged edition of *Homo Hierarchicus* and Dumont-inspired pursuit of Indian sociology by others. My concern is only with the former. I thus refer to only Dumont's use of the label 'Indian sociology'. Such distinctions are important to control the influx of other approaches and perspectives under the banner of 'Indian sociology'. A second round of critical evaluation of Dumont's Indian sociology may now be quite in order, provided we are prepared to make India *and* sociology its proper and primary subjects.

Dumont thus proposed a new methodological point of departure: That Indian society must be studied 'from within', by its own cultural configuration of values, yielding what he called 'Indian sociology'. When juxtaposed to the wide ranging concerns of Srinivas' studies on India, Dumont's approach, in some important ways, remains incomplete, ironic and paradoxical.

Incomplete because Dumont's accounts limit themselves to only traditional Hindu India. Ironic because Dumont's 'Indian sociology', while aiming to view India from 'within', actually establishes and highlights the primacy of modern Western thought for its logic of binary structures and 'total' oppositions. Dumont thus bypassed a rich and rigorous field of reasoning, relations, distinctions *and non-distinctions* which Indic (i.e., Hindu, Buddhist and Jain) epistemologies had long developed and illustrated in their own societies. And paradoxical because Dumont firmly positions the West in the background as he describes India 'from within'. Actually, the result was to alienate India from its own conceptions of moral agent, political power and cultural history.[4] From Srinivas' standpoint, to bring such a perspective to India is to see its culture only in certain favoured aspects and essences. Little wonder therefore that Indian counter-examples, anomalies and exceptions should constantly dog Dumont's 'structural explanations'.

Similarly, despite Dumont's emphasis on studying a society in 'totality' (a lesson that Marcel Mauss, Dumont's teacher, underscored), his sociology continued to exclude (or only selectively include) the fundamental *essences* of Hindu India. Here, as elsewhere, the root problem in Dumont's work might be one of sometimes inappropriate and sometimes inadequate and misfitting selections, translations and uses of 'central' Hindu principles and constructs. Rough analogies and the 'pure logic' of structural relations remained a poor, alien substitute for a closer inspection and translation of Hindu concepts and practices on their own. For example, Dumont's 'set theory of hierarchy' could hardly approach the rich fare which the

---

[4] Other recent social scientists have rarely done much better. For example, Marriott's ethnosociological approach also tries to correct this inconsistency and explores Hindu classical formulations around only certain selected (academically popularized) forms of Hindu 'cultural logic'. However, he does not give any indication of a systematic comprehension of the subject from within. Nor does he explain the grounds for his selection of some forms of Hindu reasoning and exclusion of others. And once he sociologically 'theorizes', the sociological theory *naturally* assumes its superordinate epistemological position. He lapses here much like Dumont.

classical Hindu models and popular uses had long developed on the crucial issue of 'identity and difference' or 'the one and the many' (Khare 1983). Nor does his notion of 'ritual power' adequately connect with the Hindu conceptions of *sakti*—temporal and spiritual. Similarly, Dumont's 'sociology of caste' starkly dismissed the Hindu panoply of formulations on the 'doer–experiencer' (*karta–bhokta*). To a critic, such examples convey that Dumont's ideas of the 'ahistorical', the 'social collective' and the 'holistic' (i.e., Dumont's encompassing and encompassed) unwittingly imposed on India some of the West's nineteenth century Orientalist formulations.

Further, Dumont, not unlike many other Indologists and anthropologists of his times, simply ignored the impositional role of Western knowledge, power and discourse control while working on India. His 'scientific' scholarly approach, assumed the predominance of Western ideas, methods and explanations even as he explicated India 'from within'. Locating himself squarely in the West, he found Indian reality historically remote, sociologically pre-individual, culturally pre-modern, and philosophically naive. Western sociology, in contrast, reflected for him a conscious control of its discourse by being external, exoteric, scientific, advanced and universal.

However, a proper 'decoding' of sociological and Indological ideas requires multiple unpacking of subtexts from *both*—Indian and Western—directions. And yet, it is Dumont's pioneering works that lead us toward such an exercise. Placed within the larger sociological context, Dumont's work has been an influential 'alternative' to the conventional structural–functional descriptions and analyses. Whether it is India or Europe, Dumontian sociology programme (see Dumont 1977; 1980), despite its flaws, shows us how one may compare dissimilar configurations of ideologies and values across complex cultures. Without such a comparison, we learn from Dumont, anthropology remains rootless and scotomatous.

In response to Dumont, on the other hand, Marriott's (1976; 1989) 'ethnosociological' explanations take a different approach to study (but again largely Hindu) India.[5] Based on his recent essay, his theoretical inspiration comes from the Parsonian 'system of social

[5] Such a claim should be carefully examined, especially when it methodologically shares Dumont's central premise to view Hindu India in terms of its own ideological (for Marriott, read 'cultural') formulations and concepts and their interrelationships. Not unlike Dumont, Marriott also reads selected Sanskritic philosophies and texts and

action' and its pursuit of 'interactional' (relational) properties. Transposing certain classical Hindu formulations and ethnographic relations onto his three-dimensional 'cubic' representations, Marriott provides a sociological language to describe 'accurately' the essentially transactional 'Hindu world'. Doing so, he also claims to provide a paradigm for comparative regional ethnosociolog*ies* and a universal social science (see Khare 1990). Though his cultural reading and translation of Indian texts are rigorous and his explanations insightful, his 'sociological theory' imposes new and different burdens on the Hindu system. Committed to studying Hindu India by the 'realities known to its own people', he cannot let the thought arise why his 'sociological theory' would not be alien to 'the Hindu world'. Nor would he allow the question of Orientalist vestiges and representations even in his 'explanatory science'. Nevertheless, he needs to address them.

Such limitations notwithstanding, Marriott's 'reading' of Hindu culture, by itself, provides deeper and subtler formulations than does Dumont's. Marriott is best when he, with care, formulates and organizes the basic constituents and transactions of the Hindu world. His accomplishments, however, diminish or scatter when he tries to provide a sociological explanation which would *refute and replace* contributions of Dumont's dualistic sociology. Though Marriott's sociology may have different strengths, its weaknesses are similar to Dumont's. His abstract work (see MacIntyre 1981) also quickly attracts counter-examples, anomalies and criticisms for what it includes—and excludes—of the Hindu world. He reduces Hindu India and its lived complex reality to a few paradigmatic transactional strategies.

Though the latest round of discussions (Marriott 1989) explains more, ethnosociology must still adequately address (rather than dismiss or sideline) increasing empirical and conceptual criticisms (see McGilvary 1982, for some empirical questions, and the continuing discussions in the *Contributions*). A crucial question for our discussion is whether ethnosociology, as currently formulated, explains Hindu society more and better than Dumont's Indian sociology or Srinivas' social descriptions. After a point, unfortunately, not unlike Dumont's 'pure–impure', ethnosociology also settles on its own self-justifying

---

selectively 'employs' their formulations to device a distinct sociological language for seeking 'transactional' explanations (see Marriott 1976; 1989; for the creation and extension of such a jargon around transactional—fluid and joining—strategies).

(and self-limiting) navel—the 'Hindu physics' of 'substance'. An outsider may wonder if such a locus does not somehow take impetus from American pragmatism and its notions of a 'flowing' practical reality.

The preceding review of the two scholars' works mainly highlights the differences when juxtaposed to M. N. Srinivas' descriptions and analyses of Indian society. Contrary to Dumont's early protestations, Srinivas does *not* just 'describe' India. Actually, over time, Srinivas' sociological writings have stood the test of time rather well. He preferred to view India through its lived cultural diversity, with an open mind toward both endogenous and exogenous forces and processes of social change. To obtain a fuller (but neither an exhaustive nor total) picture, one must evaluate the West-based as well as India-centred social ideas and experiences, and their directions of social change. In such understanding and writing must also be found the seeds of a 'universal sociology', and a view of India which would be neither mysterious, unique nor simply traditional.[6]

One of Srinivas' common concerns is to explain India by a range of (historically changing) ideas, representations, contexts, experiences and actions. According to him, single, simple essentialist theories, however well crafted, do not adequately explain the lived, diverse and contentious India. (I found the same to be true in my studies of the Hindu traditional and modern spheres; see Khare 1983; 1985; see also note 11.) If Dumont and Marriott rest their schemes on India's selected age-old idealized essentialist principles, then Srinivas' descriptive sociology builds on the modern secular, the rational and the 'reasonable' (including its complicity with dominant Western academic ways). If most of Srinivas' work (like Dumont's) stands prior to recent critical debates on knowledge and power, his discussions of social change (e.g., Sanskritization and modernization) also rest on the inevitable and superior forces of Western knowledge and its authority.

---

[6] However, it is easy to retrogress also. For example, if the strategy is to return somehow to a pristine or an earlier sociological theory to disentangle oneself from the conceptual puzzle the recent efforts raise, the central problem will be sidestepped rather than resolved. The central issue is to open up the dominant sociological assumptions to alternative cultural translations and formulations, whether the exercise concerns Western or Indian social orders. Only such a procedure will help explore the case for a genuinely universalized sociological formulation. Meanwhile, issues of inter- or cross-cultural translation can neither be wished away nor rendered any less real.

So far, sociology and anthropology in India have largely steered clear of such critical issues, while recently historiography, under the focus of 'subaltern studies', has initiated its critical discussions (Guha 1989; for critical anthropological commentaries, see Manganaro 1990; Khare 1992). In comparison, Dumont's 'structural sociology' and Marriott's 'ethnosociology' debilitate themselves by being aloof, technical, ponderous and self-important—all in the name of a theoretical explanation of India. Srinivas, on the other hand, shows that the sociologically complex and significant can be simply written and made sense, without numerous alien methodological assumptions and a technical vocabulary.

Writing style and interpretation have been important to Srinivas over time, though one could not attribute to him any such critical literary aspiration as we have come to expect from, for instance, Clifford Geertz (1973; 1983). Similarly, meanings are crucial to Srinivas, though he could hardly be credited with utilizing Indian symbolic logic and hermeneutics. Most importantly, his sociological writings, not given to defend any particular theoretical position, remain open to cultural richness and subtlety. But, on the other hand, this also keeps his discussions unreconciled in some important ways. For example, we do not know if he ever tried to reconcile his subtle West-inspired humanism and equalitarianism to the robust and resilient caste ordered customary India. For him, both are just there to take into account.

II

Let us now appraise Srinivas' selected works. Conventionally, we say that he 'used' the structure–function approach, directly or indirectly, in his ethnography, seeking meanings via functions, and providing a social commentary on the changing Indian society.[7]

Instead of reviewing all his writings, I will concern myself with only four writings (Srinivas 1952; 1966; 1975; 1976).[8] These writings,

---

[7] Though obviously this is not all that his bibliography reflects, these are his sustained concerns directly useful to our exercise. The 1978 review symposium of the *Contributions* has greatly helped me in the selection and analysis of Srinivas' work. I draw particular attention to Madan's overview and Srinivas' 'Reply to criticisms' (see Madan 1978).

[8] These four studies represent a range of attempts to study Indian society. When an earlier work of Srinivas (1952) is compared with a later one (1966), a movement in

in my estimation, are largely concerned with empirical specifications, functional explanations and processual changes. Placed by some within Radcliffe-Brown's school of 'structure and function', Srinivas might be most evidently functionalist in his book on the Coorgs (1952; see also Srinivas 1966: ch. 5). However, it is not the complete story for our purposes. Over time, he increasingly concerned himself with meanings. I find Srinivas' writings still significant because they variously weave subtexts and inform us (beyond rules and ideologies) about different locations, shades and purposes of social meanings.

Most often, as the Coorgs study showed, Srinivas described those aspects of social and ritual practice that helped him explicate 'meaning' within and across contexts. Though textually it may be hard to link such a concern directly to Evans-Pritchard's shift from 'function to meaning' (e.g., see Pocock 1971; Dumont 1975: 333–34), it is not improbable. Srinivas often remarked on meanings as he identified and analysed major social conditions and processes (e.g., vertical and horizontal solidarity; dominant caste; Sanskritization and Westernization). His work weaved, intuitively as far as we know, 'facts',

---

focus, explanation and perspective becomes clearly evident. Overall, the issues of empirical description and change receive constant attention. I shall argue that Srinivas' *Social Change in Modern India* (1966; lectures of 1964) is a sort of climax of logico-empirical and logico-meaningful inquiries in Indian social anthropology and sociology. It provided a larger historical, social and cultural view of India, prior to *Homo Hierarchicus*. Most investigators were then tied up with their village, caste and kinship descriptions, piecing together a regional picture. Dumont, however, had put forward his agenda for Indian sociology (and he had criticized Srinivas on his Coorg study). Similarly, Marriott's (1959) 'interactive' explanation of caste precedence and caste order had all the 'seeds' of his later 'interactional approach', though he, then, had focused on Dumont. Srinivas never directly evaluated any aspect of Dumont's work until the mid-1970s.

Srinivas' 1975 essay on the Indian village was significant in this context. It was written in response to Dumont's critique (for the discursive style, compare Srinivas 1966: ch. 5). It offered a logico-empirical rebuttal, based on historical data, but it did not reach the standards of the 1966 book. It was as if his usual analytical acuity had eluded him in this essay.

Making an incident (i.e., the burning of his field notes in Palo Alto) his ally, he was engaged, it would seem, in a new genre of description. He evolved a social description based largely on his memory of the fieldwork done long ago in a Mysore village. *The Remembered Village* (1976) represents more than an empirical description. It is a narrative in which an ethnographer discovers via memory a 'high art' to rediscover self and society. (For the place of memory in Evans-Pritchard's social anthropology, see Douglas 1980).

'meanings' and 'interpretations' together, but with what I would call balance and insight. It is these properties which open Srinivas' work to a discussion of the role of writer, writing, narrative, and literary interpretation in 'critical anthropology' of the 1990s (see Manganaro 1990). His distance from 'fashionable theories' served him rather well; it kept his 'descriptions' open to different readings.

Similarly, his methodological and analytic constraints remained unstated and implied. For example, while studying Indian social change, he (Srinivas 1966) seldom adequately described either the method underlying the selection of a major subject or of one example over others, or the justification of his conceptual scheme over those of others (see also Srinivas 1975). Yet his 1966 account of social coping mechanisms of diverse and contentious 'India' (especially after independence) allowed him to reach certain all-India sociological 'characterizations'. However, his conceptual assertions had a tentativeness, mostly because of his being an Indian social anthropologist or a sociologist, who had studied his own region and culture. He thus concerned himself with a 'double goal'—of modern scholarly objectivity and of that of a cultural insider. How? For example, 'we summon up all the willingness to think the thoughts and feel the feelings of the people whose life is involved in these facts' (Stark quoted in Srinivas 1966: 157).

Yet, if Srinivas at that time was for 'empirically rigorous testing' (see Srinivas 1966: 147–63), he seldom described in detail how such 'testing' was done. Though this 'mixed' methodological 'tool bag' conformed to the dominant major India study centres of Anglo-American anthropology (giving him required Western backing and authority in India), Srinivas was at his best when he grappled with social issues and changes intuitively. He employed his dual cultural (Indian and Western) sensibilities with success, including in *The Remembered Village*.

In his 1966 volume also, I find him welding large chunks of empirical social data rather intuitively, essentially by extending an ethnographer's nose for contextual particulars toward India's diverse regional, macro-level social configurations. He (1966: 147–55) was made especially aware of this issue by his reviewers, and he responded by amplifying the advantages and disadvantages of his being a 'sociologist' who was also a brahmin from South India. He admitted the influence of such a factor on his work (1966: 152), and, according to the call of times, discussed ways of 'reducing' such subjectivity for 'achieving greater objectivity' (1966: 154). There was, then, no need to question the goal of objectivity or of characterizing his reflections as a contribution toward 'reflexive anthropology'.

In contrast, a self-aware ethnographer's dilemmas now get wide attention. For an ethnographer must view the familiar from afar and the unfamiliar from up close (cf. Geertz 1983; Clifford 1981: 542; Manganaro 1990). Similarly, an ethnographer must realize that a socio-cultural condition involves a study of both rules as well as their modifications and transgressions. A social process yields conditional, incomplete and open-ended results; it is neither about a simple notion of progress toward modernity, nor about a simple description of 'empirical facts' under West-inspired and West-looking 'scientific conclusions'. Srinivas, in comparison, generally viewed empirical data as yielding socially contingent (logically ambiguous) directions and culturally resilient changes. (Such a change may now be characterized as 'prestructural' by some scholars, and 'poststructural' by others.) He seldom talked of 'total structural oppositions and transformations'.

Thus, it follows that Srinivas' accounts (1952; 1966) remain strikingly open to conditional and qualified interpretations of Indian society. Such formulations, though cast in an empiricist's language, provide multifaceted clues which we now value under critical sociological approaches. Yet, Srinivas synthesizes this way his all-India picture case by case and region by region, rather than favour a single 'mega-theory', straining to explain all India by a single essence. (Compare Dumont and Marriott on this issue.) But to be conditional is neither to be muddled nor to exclude from one's study disorder and conflict in favour of order and structure. Thus, Srinivas' (1966: 160) remarks:

Conflict ought to be seen as inhering in social life everywhere. The institutional devices which every society has provided for the solution of conflict may work with greater or less efficiency. Or the devices may work efficiently in some areas and not in others. There may be more conflict in some societies than in others, and in the same society there may be more conflict in some periods than in the others... But conflict as such is an inescapable part of social existence, and should be of serious concern to the sociologist.

Srinivas (1966: 161) similarly argues for 'a positive attitude [especially of sociologists from developing countries] towards social change', while distinguishing between the apparent and real dimensions of change in a developing country. But the ability to make such distinctions sharpens when a scholar applies 'his mind steadfastly on the existential reality as contrasted with the book-view of society' (preferably by 'the study of a village or a small town'), when the unity as well as the diversity of India is 'borne in mind continuously', and when the intensive studies are 'supplemented' by a macro-study (1966: 158).

Srinivas' (1966: chs. 2 and 4) discussion of Westernization and Sanskritization not only exemplifies the above intellectual location but it also concludes that the locational dilemmas are unavoidable for social scientists involved in a comparative cultural study. For example, Westernization, for Srinivas, is in various ways complex, multi-layered, uneven, conditional, and competitive force of modern history, but he assumes ethical neutrality (e.g., see 1966: 48–56 on Westernization). Similarly, if it is polysemic (he uses the phrase 'living in a pluralist cultural universe'; see 1966: 75), it also has multiple results. As he remarked at one place, 'different aspects of Westernization sometimes combine to strengthen a particular process, sometimes work at cross-purposes, and are occasionally mutually discrete' (see 1966: 53–56, for illustrations).

A process of social change in India is invariably complex and he tends to consider it under specific social conditions, whether historical or contemporary (1966: 53). Questions of interpretation, implicit political attitudes and reinterpretation only occasionally enter his discussion, especially when British and Indian cultural histories view the 'facts' differently. For example, consider his discussion of tolerance in Hinduism, and the remark, 'caste system made heresy-hunting unnecessary' (1966: 75–76). Indian thought, tradition and popular history tend to overlap in such a subject as 'cultural tolerance', making him (as some scholars would say, from an upper caste Hindu's standpoint) partial to internal devices of 'cultural adaptation' for social status quo.

For Srinivas, the conceptual significance of such cultural characteristics is relative, not ideological. Though he underscores the role and range of the cultural past and its resilience in India, he also remarks: 'The discovery of the past was not, however, without its pitfalls and dangers. It produced a certain amount of palaeocentrism in all educated Indians and, as is well known, a great past can be either an energizer or an opiate' (1966: 78–79). Srinivas must warn against 'xenophilia, palaeocentrism and communism, and the extreme idealization of Indian life and culture coupled with crude caricaturing of Western life and culture' (1966: 79–80). This 'balanced view' of Indian reality often attracts the educated Indian, 'the modern elite'. It, however, also fosters dilemmas of the 'logical middle', a condition Dumont's sociology must immediately dismiss for such a 'fundamental' opposition as the 'ahistorical' India versus the historical West.

In contrast, Srinivas finds contemporary India in the thick of historical conflicts. Yet his stance is conceptually cautious and 'politically neutral', reflecting the 'liberal' scholarly ethos of his times. If we juxtapose Srinivas' assumptions about Indian history to the concerns and criticisms now evident in, say, 'subaltern' historiography (Guha 1989),[9] we would get an idea of another recent 'shift' (apropos Dumont's and Marriott's) in scholarly concerns. But Srinivas favoured his 'balanced view', defending contextually what would otherwise appear to be 'double think' (1966: 82):

> The very people who wanted radical changes in their society, and who were most articulate in denouncing its evils, spoke, when they were addressing the West, of the past glories of India, of the versatility and continuance of its civilization, of the many saints and thinkers India had produced through the ages, and the great and noble ideas they expressed. This was not 'double think', but only that different aspects of the same complex phenomenon were emphasized in different contexts to achieve certain definite ends.

Such a remark also shows how Srinivas would juxtapose and interrelate tradition and modernity to each other. For example, describing Indian society under change, he continues to rely on the bases of traditional authority and authenticity (even as they disperse under modern contexts). Thus he discusses, though briefly, the authority of the *shastras* in castes and customs in comparative terms on the one hand, and of the application of reason to tradition in modern India, on the other (see 1966: 81–82). As a modernist, he notes how Westernization subsumes 'what may be broadly characterized as

---

[9] This whole volume represents as well as culminates in several recent critical discussions on India's history, culture and historiography. In particular, the reader may see papers by Gayatri Chakravorty Spivak, Ranajit Guha and Veena Das.

humanitarianism, by which is meant an active concern for the welfare of all human beings irrespective of caste, economic position, religion, age, and sex. Equalitarianism and secularization are both included in humanitarianism' (1966: 48). An important (and analytically revealing) qualifier, however, follows immediately in parentheses, recognizing the presence of an even wider notion of cosmic welfare in Indian thought.

In contrast to Dumont's India–West (traditional and modern) ideological opposition, Srinivas finds interstitial room for the goals of equalitarianism and humanitarianism within the complex Indian social hierarchy. In his zeal for achieving a clear and 'total' ideological contrast between hierarchical India and equalitarian West, Dumont simplifies and caricatures the thought and historical experience of an entire world civilization. On the other hand, Srinivas' allusion to the role of Western humanitarianism in modern India invites open inquiries (1966: 48–50). In particular, for example, we may compare the indigenous conception of social welfare to the Western one and examine the roles modernization, secularization and Westernization can (or cannot) play in India under different cultural, historical and sociological contexts (1966: 48–88; on Westernization 118–46).

In Srinivas' view, however, a large part of institutionalized Indian reality is not only about inequality and hierarchy. It is much more, and paradoxical. Similarly, his discussion of secularism makes him see 'rationalism' in those traditional Hindu terms and concepts (including purity and pollution) which have 'a certain amount of semantic stretch', to allow them 'to move from one meaning to another as the context requires' (1966: 119–20). Secularization is found to be a 'mixed' development, where 'Hinduism has assumed a political form in the Rashtriya Swayamsevak Sangh (RSS) and the [then] Jan Sangh' (1966: 141, my interpolation). A secular government, thus, can also become 'an unwitting but powerful agent of Sanskritization' in India by prohibiting alcoholic drinks (1966: 142).[10]

---

[10] Obviously, so much has happened in India since these lines were written. The Bharatiya Janata Party (the successor to Jan Sangh) 'swept' (especially northern) India during 1991. The so-called '3M'—Mandir–Masjid–Mandal—controversy continues to test the resilience of mixed Indian secularism and democracy. The 'Sikh problem' in Punjab tests the limits of both political and religious tolerance (and intolerance) within modern Indian culture. However, I have resisted to rewrite or expand the discussion here.

III

The above characterization of Srinivas' work, while incomplete, draws our attention to an overriding point: the value of a careful context-guided description and analysis cannot be overestimated for understanding the diverse Indian social past and present. Whether one studies a caste, a village or a process of social change in urban India, this general commonsensical approach upholds. Yet Srinivas leads us to a tantalizing ambiguity as a text maker. As Srinivas' last book (1976) attests, even the memory of an early fieldwork experience could be a resourceful 'trigger' in such a pursuit. The ethnographer, with his 'inside' and 'outside' perspective, in such an exercise frames the account of field memories as (and for) field experiences. The author 'touches' and describes people through his memories, making a sociologist's scholarly objectivity largely a habit of the mind. But, on the other hand, his memories, however vivid, can seldom be empirically certain and complete, especially when decades old (see Srinivas 1976). Many details would have to be recovered/uncovered/invented for a literary-cum-'sociological' narrative. A fieldworker's memories of (and from) 'notebooks' cannot be a substitute for the actual ones. Srinivas leaves this ambiguous text before the reader.

His previous work, in places, I believe, also informed of a literary sensibility in sociological work (e.g., 1966: ch. 5 for the roles of empathy, objectivity, micro and macro studies, and sociological analysis to uncover the social reality). A cultural empathy (an omnibus term) enabled the sociologist 'to understand what it is to be a member of the community that is being studied. In this respect, the sociologist is like a novelist who must of necessity get under the skin of different characters he is writing about' (1966: 156). This novelist-like role of the sociologist was mentioned again (1966: 157–58), but it had to await his burned notebooks and the writing of *The Remembered Village*. Yet the book could not be only a novel, for 'the sociologist is primarily interested... [in] generalizations rather than the development of concrete particularizations' (1976: 158). By such a comment if Srinivas stated his general preference, he also restricted the range of his narrative on Indian society. This would be especially true if his textual accounts were examined for how (well) they represented the cultural Other within his *own* society (on anthropology as text, see Manganaro 1990).

However, empirical and interpretative tendencies clearly overlapped in the 1976 monograph on Rampura. Since Srinivas' memories and images of the village and its people 'reworked' what he calls 'social facts', his ethnography acquired a distinct tone and texture of narration. Thus, between the two books on the Coorgs and on Rampura, Srinivas' ethnography shifted from the scientific objective goal to humanistic concerns. But he hesitated to fully recognize and explore this shift. In both, instead, he wanted the 'empirical data' to be at the centre of depicting and analysing Indian society. On the other hand, though he only occasionally concerned himself with the content of what we now call popular culture, he always wrote on it elegantly and non-technically. His earlier substantive concerns (e.g., village, caste organization, rituals, social dominance, and processes of social change) rested on a clear description of common culture, on the one hand, and on a self-aware interpretation of value issues, on the other. He approached his 'major concepts' the same way. For example, Srinivas (1976) found 'hierarchy' to be polysemous and interactional (mainly in terms of intercaste relations; see 1976: ch. 6) under widely different contexts—land (ch. 7), reciprocity (ch. 9), and Muslims (ch. 6). Adding a new direction in Indian ethnography, he discussed, though only briefly, 'face', 'friendship and enmity', 'gossip', 'envy', and 'sense of humour'. He termed these qualities of social relations (ch. 9). Such topics helped reflect not only a sociologist's own aesthetic and social sensibilities, but they also identified his qualities as a narrator.

But those studied participated only indirectly in such a narrative, often with a face, but without a voice of their own.[11] We sometimes find Srinivas (1976) struggling to overthrow the prized scholarly distance (e.g., his depiction of departure from the field). On such occasions, I find him donning his old hat (empirical social science) as well as a new cap (a self-aware Indian aestheticism and its writing). Hence, where one influence ends and the other begins in such an ethnography is almost impossible to distinguish (and counterproductive), especially when the 1976 book is read as a narrative.

Overall, Srinivas (1952; 1966; 1976) uses ethnographic writing as a multipurpose template for reporting data, capturing Indian socio-cultural conditions, and a sociological analysis. His analysis remained

---

[11] To my critical Untouchable informants, this would reflect the bias of an upper caste Hindu scholar more than the fact of burned notes. If not voices, they would ask, 'Where are the remembered echoes, especially of those low castes who in the forties dared seldom speak, unless spoken to?'

rooted more in 'empirical data' than rested on a critical evaluation of other scholars' ethnographies and theories. His writing, only rarely (see 1975), provided a sustained commentary or critique of another anthropologist's criticism. Only general (and mostly approving) comments are found on highly selected scholarly works of others. This style also agreed with occasionally providing disciplinary 'overviews' (see 1966: 155, for a remark on the internal struggle between sociology and social anthropology in India; also 158–63, for a general commentary on 'sociologists' in developing countries).

Put differently, Srinivas' attempts favoured a certain 'reasonableness' in analyses and conclusions. But such reasonableness, in his words, should find support in the data put to

rigorous testing before they can become valid generalizations. The moral, then, is that an idea is not necessarily wrong because its originator occupies a particular position in the society. Its validity or invalidity has to be independently established. In the words of Bernard Shaw: 'The test of sanity is not the normality of method but the reasonableness of the discovery' (Srinivas 1966: 154).

Thus, resting on a morally relativized approach to society, he took a multifactorial view of social reality. The modern educated Indian, I should remark, would also often share such a 'reasonableness' in perspective. In contrast, Dumont's 'structural approach', based on fundamentally opposed cultural principles (e.g., hierarchy and equality, ritual purity and impurity), would strike the same Indian as oversimplified, partial and unjustifiably reductionist. If Dumont's approach to Indian society were akin to that of the law maker Manu, then to Srinivas 'Manu would be a bad guide for field workers; urban and uppercaste sociologists in India need to keep this constantly in mind' (1966: 152).

The Indian's 'reasonableness' actually points toward a larger Indian cultural and historical commentary on tolerance of diversity and inconsistency, especially after independence. For instance, his 'reasonableness' may not rest as clearly on what the West calls 'reason and rationality' as on what the educated Indian finds contextually 'appropriate', 'tolerable' and 'moderate' for an aspiring democratic, secular and modernizing India. Such a cultural ethos of the modern, urban Indian renders the Indian cultural reality a mixed bag—diverse and internally conflicted, but still neither unmanageable nor ultimately incommensurable compared to the Indian's sense of 'reasonableness'. In my reading of Srinivas (e.g., 1966; 1976), this general cultural sense repeatedly comes through.

IV

Finally, one could argue that in some of his social descriptions and analyses, Srinivas anticipates certain aspects of the recent critical discussions going on between ethnography and modernity (or its pre-eminent social process—Westernization). I shall conclude the essay with a comparative commentary on both, suggesting that India needs a self-aware critical ethnography (which links with but is not limited to Srinivas' initiatives) to address the increasingly unmanageable subject of Indian cultural diversity. For example, while discussing Westernization and secularization in modern India, Srinivas (1966: 46–88, 118–46) offered a social commentary on the dynamics of contemporary Indian history. Yet his concerns remained very different from, for example, those of the recent 'subaltern' historiography on India (Guha 1989). He was essentially concerned with the social coping mechanisms of Indians as they faced the rather inevitable and desirable Westernization (1966: 50–56). As a concept, he found Westernization

> inclusive, complex, and many-layered. It covers a wide range—from Western technology at one end to the experimental method of modern science and modern historiography at the other. Its incredible complexity is seen in the fact that different aspects of Westernization sometimes combine to strengthen a particular process, sometimes work at cross-purposes, and are occasionally mutually discrete (1966: 53).

Clearly, Westernization for him was a social, but largely politically neutral, process. He assumed that, with scholarly distance as his armour, the scholar could (and must) steer clear of all political issues and power biases. However, recent critical debates in sociology would find such an assumption naive and untenable (see Agger 1991, for a wide ranging sociological review). In a critical perspective, Westernization would highlight its strategies of power and control, along with a mentality which assumed the superiority of 'science and scientific objectivity' in human affairs. If it was never politically neutral, it also was *not all politics*.[12]

Today, it is a socio-political process which is neither monolithic nor conflict-free nor fail proof (e.g., Heilbroner 1974; MacIntyre 1981). I think Srinivas would also agree that if this process is desirable, complex, contingent and many-layered, it is also neither infallible nor 'gift-packed', nor a panacea. Sociologically, Westernization may first change the socially discrete and then the culturally fundamental. Either way, the process involves the introduction of alienation (and identity crises) in a host culture, by presenting 'better' (and 'correct') avenues of knowing, organizing and interpreting social reality. But such 'new' ways, as Srinivas' discussions also indicated, breed wide ranging conflicts in morality, consensual conduct, protest, justice and fairness.

Unfortunately, India still lacks sustained critical debates on and evaluations of Westernization (and of Western critiques of modernity). Indian debates should include more participants and voices from all segments of society, rather than only modern educated Indians. This is crucial when India's alternative socio-political guide for modernization—the Soviet Union and its eastern bloc—has virtually dissolved itself. Meanwhile, if anthropology in independent India has offered theories of conflict, cooperation, resiliency, or compartmentalization to explain how traditional India adapts to the ever desirable modernity (e.g., Srinivas' studies; Singer 1972), its explanations still remain timid, and are often a prisoner of uncritical sociological assumptions. In such approaches, one usually values India for its passivity, docility and 'adaptability' for *accepting*, one way or another, the desirability of modern Western social assumptions and values. A critical, ground

---

[12] Critical postmodern theories sometimes stress this point to the exclusion of other substantive issues of knowledge and inquiry. I do not. But nor do I dismiss the significance of witting or unwitting politics in human knowledge and its persuasive communication and acceptance (Khare 1992; see also note 11). In response to the critical non-Western reviews of their political strategies of dominating knowledge, the Western intellectual now either vehemently protests the criticism or charges the critic with an untenable and harmful demand for 'political correctness', or dismisses the whole debate as a red herring. In America, there is already a battlecry to return to the Eurocentric knowledge 'core' and its conservative agenda.

With his flair for 'only the substantive, reliable and authoritative knowledge', the Indian sociologist would easily tend to *dismiss* the whole critical debate as 'another passing fad' of the West. Without conducting its own independent exercise, such a sociology could readily accept the same conclusion that its uncritical Western counterpart has.

level examination of that modernity which modern Indians profess and protect is virtually unheard. Many scholarly efforts may not consider the issue worthy of central concern (for a recent internal debate in the West, see Heilbroner 1974; Erickson 1974; Dumont 1977; Lears 1981; MacIntyre 1981). But they should.

Though Srinivas' work exhibits mild scepticism toward Westernization and modernization in India, it is hardly sufficient for a critical debate. Engaged in establishing a major 'center of sociological studies' in Delhi, Srinivas, it seems, had shared all the controlling premises of Anglo-American social science and anthropology. His sociology unfortunately seldom stopped to examine either the Western critiques of Western modernity or the scant critical works of such pioneering (but so remote as to be almost mysterious) Indian sociologists as D. P. Mukerji (1958) and A. K. Saran (1963).[13]

To address the subject with substance, one must design such sociological and anthropological studies which put us in touch (and in dialogue) with clamouring Indian life and its intensifying conflicts and voices of protest. Our ad hoc, usually West launched, and exclusive (and excluding) theories can wait, unless they help raise new and different questions. For social anthropology and Indian sociology, it means an increased role for *dialogical* fieldwork and *reciprocal* ethnographic accounts (where one includes the specialist's and the informant's discussions of each other). Such accounts may help increase the investigator's awareness as much of himself and his 'science' as

---

[13] The purpose of such a critique obviously is *not* to confuse the politically 'right' and 'left' camps in Indian sociological studies. Rather it is to challenge the basic significance and productivity of such a simple ideological division under Indian sociocultural conditions. It is also to propose that now (at the end of the twentieth century) we should juxtapose the works of Mukerji and Saran (in themselves wide apart) to those of Srinivas and Dumont to see how their sociological and philosophical assumptions on India and its tradition and modernity would enhance our understanding of the intellectual history of Indian sociology. We may note that Saran particularly tried to 'apply' early on India selected strands of Western critical philosophy, with vague connections to nondualist Indian philosophy. But his mystifying brevity was his worst enemy.

Throughout this essay, I have also referred to shifts of perspective occurring in an investigator's career. I have shown how these shifts occurred in the cases of Srinivas, Dumont and Marriott. Though working with a smaller scholarly credit, I am also subject to such a shift. After describing, under 'scholarly distance', for decades North Indian brahmins and Untouchables for their diverse structures of social actions and meanings, I am now increasingly inclined toward critical debates on contested ideals and representations in India (vis-à-vis the West). Perhaps it is as much a sign of my changing self-awareness as of social times and conditions in India.

of the people he studies. For him, ethnography would be at once a science, an art, and a 'reading' of diverse languages and intentions of his own and of those he studies.

Here the ethnographer discusses the real, the metaphoric, the unequal, the unsaid, and even the surreal (see Clifford 1981: 539–64). He grapples with not only the structurally 'opposed' values in India, but also the culturally negotiable between the rational and the nonrational, the cooperating and the conflicting, and the 'seen' and the 'unseen'. The Indian ethnographer learns to make the familiar 'strange' so that he can systematize and explain consciously what is explicit and orderly, and contingent and chaotic. Thus, as Clifford (1981: 548) had observed while summarizing Mauss' view, 'Ethnographic truth... was restlessly subversive of surface realities. Its principal task was to discover—in a famous phrase—the many *'lunes mortes'*, pale moons in the 'firmament of reason'. The ethnographer concerns himself with 'cultural impurities and disturbing syncretisms' (Clifford 1981: 549–50). Quoting Marcel Griaule, as Clifford notes, 'Ethnography is suspicious, too, of itself...'.

Srinivas' *The Remembered Village* sometimes turns in the direction of the contingent, but it hesitates and returns to familiar ethnographic descriptions of everyday (and power neutral) 'reality' (cf. Clifford 1981: 553). Even such an ethnography, once in stride, is neither simply 'objective' nor 'subjective', but both in such a way that it enhances our ability to question the given and the dominant, and listen to the unrepresented and the remote. It amplifies the significance of what makes most cultural sense for society (cf. Agar 1982: 783). It also addresses the wider philosophical question: What is the nature and range of reality that ethnography should seek to study and communicate? One position is that 'the aims of ethnography in this regard are vague and the philosophical assumptions behind those aims poorly understood' (Jarvie 1983: 313; 1967). The other position argues that ethnography must become increasingly self-aware, socially responsible and even handed toward 'other peoples and cultures'.

Supported by recent developments in symbolic and interpretive anthropology, new ethnography questions the theoretically accepted and explores the socially neglected. *The Remembered Village* subtly moves in such a direction. It resonates with diverse cultural messages from a diverse, vibrant and sensible rural India. However, if this India of the 1940s depicts controlled social conflicts and aversions, we now see how violent alterity, alienation and antagonism increasingly churn the same culture, demanding a commensurate change in an ethnographer's assumptions, explorations, tools and descriptions.

Marcus (1980: 508) rightly observes that the analytic significance of fieldwork and ethnography has greatly increased in anthropology in recent years, especially as symbology, phenomenology and hermeneutics have opened up new and different vantage points. In evidence is the rapidly expanding literature on the topic (see initial references in Rabinow 1977; Marcus 1980; Clifford 1981; Agar 1982; for a later summary, Manganaro 1990). Such accounts examine their own discourse forming and knowledge controlling strategies, recognizing that no ethnographic representation can remain free of intentional biases and what is called the 'discourse politics'.

The issue matters whether one goes to study a distant people or one's own, or conducts government sponsored nationally 'relevant research' (cf. Colson 1982: 253–62). Whether Western or non-Western, an ethnographer's cultural location (along with his personal biases) affects the conduct and profile of his study. Similarly, the ethnographer cannot overlook the issues of cultural distance, social differences and power conflicts in favour of his structural theories of 'order' or 'system', particularly if the people point us the other way. If the ethnographer becomes professionally responsible for an adequate and appropriate comprehension, description and analysis of such situations, then he must also introduce his self-critical cultural debates into anthropology's disciplinary history and practice (Asad 1975; 1982: 284–87).

A re-reading of Srinivas' work in the above context makes us aware of some major 'shifts' since the 1970s in anthropology and in Indian sociology. One now rarely devotes, for instance, a whole study to describe only a caste, a village or an aspect of social change. But why not? The works of Dumont and Marriott partially answer such a question by their 'theoretical quests'. These may have altered the value and place of Indian 'social change' studies. We may also ask: What does the downgrading of social change studies mean for India, a developing country?[14]

---

[14] Within anthropology and sociology, there has been a general decline in the intellectual value of social change studies. Several reasons may explain such a decline. For some scholars, the theoretical interest in the West has shifted from function and adaptation to structures and meanings. Others link this change to the post-colonial 'refocus' of the Western world and its intellectuals. To still others, structuralism helped establish *the* 'universal' supremacy of the rational order.

The question makes us return to the changing conceptual role and criticism of modernity in the West. These concern anthropology as much as sociology. In many ways this changing debate *frames and informs* all that Srinivas, Dumont and Marriott, separately and together, include or exclude as they sociologically describe and explain India. Located in a distinct frame of modernity, these three scholars bring to India their own preferred modern (read 'scientific') intellectual concerns, methods and analytical perspectives. Though they studied India from 'within', only Srinivas, it seems, freely admitted those socially diverse contexts and values which the mid-twentieth century India demanded. In comparison, Dumont preferred India to be simply ideologically opposed to modernity, while Marriott eschewed the tradition–modernity issue by focusing on India's 'paradigms' of selected classical transactional essences (or substances).

But to pursue a critical cultural perspective, among other things, one must now show how India, over the last two centuries, has developed its own distinct versions of cultural, political and economic modernity, just as it has done by 'indigenizing' English, science and technology—the 'languages of progress' (e.g., on English language, colonialism and India, see Viswanathan 1989). With English as a language of foreign domination, internal revolt, cultural and scientific regeneration, and political movements, India, I would argue, has had a direct handle on examining, rebutting and transforming modernity—in all aspects, and with difficulty—for its own purposes. Our commentaries need to reveal both—the receiving and the responding—sides of such exchanges in India.

REFERENCES

AGAR, MICHAEL H. 1982. 'Toward an Ethnographic Language', *American Anthropologist*, 84, 4: 779–95.

The attention thus shifted from the socio-cultural 'development' of a society (a model on which Srinivas worked) to locating fundamental cultural constituents, categories and meanings, irrespective of whether a society was 'developing' or 'developed'. As a logical consequence of the interest in abstract relational models, ideological principles were found to encapsulate the most, and the most crucial. To study social norms, therefore, meant to grapple with the 'core reality', while the content up for social change would, by implication, be superficial.

However, the paradox of this situation is especially evident to anthropologists and sociologists from developing countries. Everyday social experience and its conflicts rebel against abstract schemes and theories.

AGGER, BEN. 1991. 'Critical Theory, Poststructuralism and Postmodernism: Their Sociological Relevance', *Annual Review of Sociology*, 17: 105–31.

ASAD, TALAL. 1975. *Anthropology and the Colonial Encounter*. New York: Humanities Press.

——. 1982. 'A Comment on the Idea of Non-Western Anthropology'. In Hussein Fahim (Ed.), *Indigenous Anthropology in Non-Western Countries*. Durham: Carolina Academic Press.

CLIFFORD, JAMES. 1981. 'On Ethnographic Surrealism', *Comparative Studies in Society and History*, 23, 4.

COLSON, ELIZABETH. 1982. 'Anthropological Dilemmas in the Late Twentieth Century'. In Hussein Fahim (Ed.), *Indigenous Anthropology in Non-Western Countries*. Durham: Carolina Academic Press.

DOUGLAS, MARY. 1980. *Evans-Pritchard*. Glasgow: Fontana Paperbacks.

DUMONT, JEAN-PAUL. 1978. *The Headman and I: Ambiguity and Ambivalence in the Fieldwork Experience*. Austin: University of Texas Press.

DUMONT, LOUIS. 1975. 'Preface to the French Edition of the Nuer' (tr. Mary and James Douglas). In J. H. M. Beattie and R. G. Lienhardt (Eds.), *Studies in Social Anthropology*. Oxford: Clarendon Press.

——. 1977. *From Mandeville to Marx*. Chicago: The University of Chicago Press.

——. 1980. *Homo Hierarchicus* (complete revised English edition). Chicago: The University of Chicago Press.

ERICKSON, ERIK. 1974. *Dimensions of a New Identity*. New York: Norton.

GEERTZ, CLIFFORD. 1973. *The Interpretation of Cultures*. New York: Basic Books.

——. 1983. *Local Knowledge: Further Essays in Interpretive Anthropology*. New York: Basic Books.

GUHA, RANAJIT (Ed.). 1989. *Subaltern Studies IV: Writings on South Asian History and Society*. Delhi: Oxford University Press.

HEILBRONER, ROBERT. 1974. *Reflections on the Human Prospect*. New York: Norton.

JARVIE, I. C. 1967. 'On the Theory of Fieldwork and the Scientific Character of Social Anthropology', *Philosophy of Science*, 34: 223–43.

——. 1983. 'The Problem of the Ethnographic Real', *Current Anthropology*, 24, 3: 313–24.

KHARE, R. S. 1983. 'Between Being Near and Distant: Reflections on the Initial Approaches and Experiences of an Indian Anthropologist'. In Robert Lawless and Vinson H. Sutlive, Jr. (Eds.), *Fieldwork: The Human Experience*. New York: Gordon & Breach.

——. 1983. *Normative Culture and Kinship*. Delhi: Vikas.

——. 1984. *The Untouchable As Himself*. New York: Cambridge University Press.

——. 1985. *Culture and Democracy: Anthropological Reflections on Modern India*. Baltimore: University Press of America.

——. 1990. 'Indian Sociology and the Cultural Other', *Contributions to Indian Sociology*, n.s., 24, 2: 177–99.

——. 1992. 'The Other's Double—The Anthropologist's Bracketed Self: Notes on Cultural Representation and Privileged Discourse', *New Literary History*, 23, 1: 1–23.

LEARS, JACKSON. 1981. *No Place of Grace: Antimodernism and the Transformation of American Culture*. New York: Pantheon.

McGILVARY, D. B. (Ed.). 1982. *Caste Ideology and Interaction*. New York: Cambridge University Press.

MACINTYRE, ALASDAIR. 1981. *After Virtue*. Notre Dame: University of Notre Dame.

MADAN, T. N. 1978. 'A Review Symposium on M.N. Srinivas's, *The Remembered Village*', *Contributions to Indian Sociology*, 12, 1.

MANGANARO, MARC. 1990. 'Introduction'. In Marc Manganaro (Ed.), *Modernist Anthropology: From Fieldwork to Text*. Princeton: Princeton University Press.

MARCUS, GEORGE E. 1980. 'Rhetoric and the Ethnographic Genre in Anthropological Research', *Current Anthropology*, 21, 4: 507–10.

MARRIOTT, McKIM. 1959. 'Interactional and Attributional Theories of Caste Ranking', *Man in India*, 39, 2: 92–107.

———. 1976. 'Hindu Transactions: Diversity without Dualism'. In B. Kapferer (Ed.), *Transaction and Meaning*. Philadelphia: Institute for the Study of Human Issues.

———. 1989. 'Constructing an Indian Ethnosociology', *Contributions to Indian Sociology*, n.s., 23, 1: 1–39.

MUKERJI, D. P. 1958. *Diversities*. New Delhi: People's Publishing House.

POCOCK, DAVID. 1971. *Social Anthropology*. London: Sheed & Ward.

RABINOW, PAUL. 1977. *Reflections on Fieldwork in Morocco*. Berkeley: University of California Press.

SARAN, A. K. 1963. 'Hinduism and Economic Development in India', *Archives de sociologie des religions*, 15: 87–94.

SINGER, MILTON. 1972. *When a Great Tradition Modernizes: An Anthropological Approach to Indian Civilization*. New York: Praeger.

SRINIVAS, M. N. 1952. *Religion and Society among the Coorgs of South India*. Oxford: Oxford University Press.

———. 1966. *Social Change in Modern India*. Berkeley: University of California Press.

———. 1975. 'The Indian Village: Myth and Reality'. In J. H. M. Beattie and R. G. Lienhardt (Eds.), *Studies in Social Anthropology*. Oxford: Clarendon Press.

———. 1976. *The Remembered Village*. Berkeley: University of California Press.

VISWANATHAN, GAURI. 1989. *Masks of Conquest: Literary Study and British Rule in India*. New York: Columbia University Press.

3

THE WESTERN EDUCATED ELITES AND SOCIAL CHANGE IN INDIA*

I. P. DESAI

This article is the outcome of an exercise in re-reading M. N. Srinivas' book, *Social Change in Modern India* (1966), though not a review of it. The attempt is to seek validity and relevance of the concepts of Westernization and Sanskritization, 17 years after the publication of Srinivas' views. It is, therefore, necessary to outline the context then and now. To begin with, the reader's perspective is presented. This is followed by a re-reading and reflection on the elites. This discussion ends with a concluding note in the final section.

I

Ram Krishna Mukherjee writes:

> While there were a few others helping to bring about a change in the overall trend of Indian Sociology away from that of the 1950s,

* An earlier version of this paper appeared in *Economic and Political Weekly*, 14 April 1984: 639–47.

Srinivas was the foremost in this. Certainly he did not forsake his basic approach to sociology, but the changes in his orientation in attempting to unravel social reality are clearly visible in his writings in successive period todate. Because of his devotion and consistent endeavour to promote the accumulation of sociological knowledge, there is still much to be gained from him by Indian Sociology (1979: 70).

Mukherjee particularly mentions Srinivas' *Religion and Society among the Coorgs of South India* (1952), *India's Villages* (1955), *Caste in Modern India and Other Essays* (1962), *Social Change in Modern India* (1966), 'Itineraries of an Indian Social Anthropologist' (1973), and 'Village Studies, Participant Observation and Social Science Research in India' (1975). *The Remembered Village* (1976) was probably not accessible to Mukherjee when he wrote *Sociology of Indian Sociology* (1979). Srinivas has also written several other articles—long and short—on a variety of topics. It is difficult to cover all of them in this article. I shall therefore confine myself to a single topic, namely, that of the elites, and that too from a single book on social change.

Apart from the fact that the topic is of personal interest to me, it is also a problem facing India today. Fortunately, Srinivas deals with many issues of methodological interest with considerable competence. This factor raises the problem of limiting my choice of points for concentration in the present article. Srinivas comes to my succour with the clarity in thinking and writing which I envy as a friend. He writes,

The subject of social change in modern India is vast and complex and an adequate understanding of it will require the collaboration, for many years, of a number of scholars in such diverse fields as economics, social and cultural history, law, politics, education, religion, demography and sociology. It will have to take account of regional, linguistic and other differences. My aim, however, is much limited. I shall try to consider here somewhat more systematically than before, two concepts, Sanskritization and Westernization, a discussion of which I put forward some years ago *to explain some features of religious, cultural, and social change* in India (1966: 1, emphasis mine).

My concern in this article will be to discuss these two concepts and the allied category 'elites' which Srinivas has used in the book.

In the history of socialist thought, Marx and Engels distinguished their socialism from utopian socialism. Irrespective of their aims, they were demolishing not so much the utopian picture of future human society as the illusionary type of thinking. In fact, their thinking had an element of 'what is the future, desirable type of society'. Even an idealist would say that what is good must also be socially possible. But Marx and Engels were concerned not merely with the desirable type of society but also with bringing it about, as were many others who believed in the unity of thought and action. Their emphasis was on activity. Thought unrelated to activity they labelled contemplative thought. My present line of thinking is in that direction. My perception of Indian intellectuals and academicians is that they are indulging in contemplative type of thinking. I include in this category (*a*) all those who call themselves empirical or dialectical materialists, (*b*) those influenced by the different varieties of Marxism and leftism, and (*c*) a variety of sociologists who are opposed to Marxism and whose ideology I consider as that type of materialism which believes in the idea of 'my country: right or wrong'. Marx and Engels went to the root of activity, namely, the activity that human beings had to undertake in relation to nature. However, they emphasized the activity not of the individual *per se* but of the individual in relation with other individuals.

Society, according to this line of thought, begins in and with material activity. Along with that, or thereafter, thinking begins. Thought, therefore, cannot be divorced from material production, though assigning one priority over the other would vary according to the states of development of humanity and to the specific situations. Thus, man's activity in relation to nature is linked to human society. Here the argument begins as to whether the idea of pot was first or a particular material pot was first. This question may be good enough for a question paper in an examination. But it is irrelevant at the present stage of development of human society in as much as it is divided into two desirable types of future society with their variations and aberrations. One is based on private ownership of means of production and the other on societal ownership. The question for sociologists is: Which of the two types, or a third one, if in view, should they strive for? The activity consists in striving for any one of these types of society and their thinking should be directed toward achieving it. There exists a large body of literature on this issue in the world. However, I have not been able to keep pace with it. But clearly it is related to activities either for maintaining the *status quo* of the given type of society, or for changing it. While this general world development is to be kept in mind, the specificities of a given society should become our primary concern, i.e., of Indian society in our case.

The situation in India is not dissimilar to that in the rest of the world. I use the word 'situation' with reference to Indian social reality and its comprehension and appraisal by Indian sociologists as part of Indian intellectuals. (My former profession was sociology.) One such intellectual effort as regards Indian sociology on which I rely is Ram Krishna Mukherjee's *Sociology of Indian Sociology* (1979). I am not concerned with the kind of history of the subject he has written. I am referring to him only to provide the context for an appraisal of Indian social reality in Srinivas' *Social Change in Modern India* (1966). I shall first deal with what Mukherjee calls the 'what' and 'how' of Indian social reality as it obtains in Srinivas' book and then comment on it.

The book gives a very good account of Indian society from the point of view of Srinivas' sociology as it obtained till 1966 when the book was published. I must also mention his short work entitled *India: Social Structure* (1980), which was published originally as a chapter in *The Gazetteer of India* (1965). It is an excellent introduction for one who is not acquainted with India at all, as most of us are not. It practically summarizes *Social Change in Modern India*, without dealing with 'Sanskritization', 'Westernization', 'Dominant Caste' and 'Secularization' as explanatory concepts, though not eschewing them. Even today the description would stand, of course, with amendments and modifications due to the developments—social, economic, religious and political—during the last 15 years or so. That is the value of both of these books—not a small value. Nevertheless, a question arises: What is the significance of the use of the above mentioned concepts and others such as 'modernization' and 'traditionalization', either to describe (i.e., analyse) or to explain social change in India?

Here a point about the situation in Indian sociology may help us in answering this question. Mukherjee writes that there was a phase in the development of Indian sociology in which the contacts of Indian sociologists were overwhelmingly with the West: at first with Britain but increasingly with the USA. After mentioning some of these contacts, he writes (1979: 49–50):

To be sure, there were also other western sociologists who found India an appropriate field in which to conduct their researches. They pursued an eclectic approach or were structural functionalists who were not confined to parochial frame of reference and they were not unmindful of the negative components of the 'what' and 'how' questions (e.g., Dumont, Dumont and Pocock, Bailey, and Epstein). Moreover, a few western sociologists of a Marxist persuasion worked in India during this period, and for them examination of positive and negative components of the 'what' and 'how' questions was of paramount importance in order to answer the 'why' question. They were either engaged in micro-studies of the peasantry, etc. (e.g., Gough) or a macroscopic appreciation of some of India's sociological issues (Thorner, Bottomore, Gough). In any case, the dominant group of western scholars could communicate with their counterparts in India on the same wave length and, accordingly, presented them to the world in general as the representatives of Indian sociology. This led to two kinds of lacunae in the perception of sociology in India and a somewhat distorted image of Indian sociology abroad.

Imbibed with pragmatism, which was predominant feature of social science research in India in those days, theory formation was hardly of concern to the modernisers of Indian sociology. They chose to appraise reality in the light of theories handed down from their teachers and colleagues abroad. The most able among them moulded these theories to suit local conditions and evolved some nativistic concepts to describe 'social change in modern India'. Others merely subscribed to the imported theories to interpret India's changing reality.

Thus, the indigenous concepts of social change prevailing among the sociologists in the 1950s and to a large extent also in the 1960s, were formulated by M. N. Srinivas under the labels 'Sanskritisation' and 'Westernisation' which he regarded as linked processes in modern India and it is not possible to understand one without the other.

My concern in this article is not to examine Srinivas' these and other concepts. Having examined their place in Indian sociological thought, my concern will be to determine the direction in which we can proceed from there.

II

The similar processes of Sanskritization and Westernization were observable all over the country and in all religious communities. A number of sub-processes had also arisen. One can draw a long list of them, but it will complicate matters. So, I am primarily concerned with one numerically small group though big in terms of its role and influence in society. It comprises persons in whose thought and action the two processes of Sanskritization and Westernization can be observed. Srinivas writes, 'one of the results, then, of prolonged contact with the West is the rise of an elite whose attitude to the West is ambivalent' (1966: 5). This point has great relevance in India today. It needs to be considered in its own right.[1] It is necessary to understand this 'ambivalence'. The various points in life at which Srinivas observes this ambivalence are significant both in view of his ideology and methodology and they are discussed in the following.

Referring to Lerner—whose area of observation is the Middle East—in the context of preference for the term Westernization or modernization, Srinivas writes:

The allergy to 'Westernisation' is the result of Middle Eastern 'ethnocentrism, expressed politically in extreme nationalism, psychologically in passionate xenophobia. The hatred sown by anti-colonialism is harvested in the rejection of every appearance of foreign tutelage. Wanted are modern institutions but not modern ideologies, modern power but not modern purposes, modern wealth but not modern wisdom, modern commodities but not modern cant'. The passionate urge to repudiate the west prompts some middle eastern leaders to ignore 'certain behavioural and institutional com-

---

[1] When we talk of 'elite' we understand each other, or rather agree or disagree without understanding each other. That solves the problem at a particular moment. However, there are 'ungentlemanly' persons. A friend who read this article in manuscript form made the following comments. 'This term bothers me, especially as you put so much theoretical weight on it. What does it mean? Any one who has been through the university? Morarji Desai? Vinoba Bhave? Aurobindo Ghosh?' He made this remark at the point where the term 'Westernized elite' is used. However, appreciating his ungentlemanliness I tried to open the lid of my brain. But I closed it immediately after opening it by a hair's breadth. I saw the snakes inside. I decided to meet his point by this note.

I became a little mean with a friend who was to attend an international conference on ethnicity or ethnic something. I asked him casually: 'What is this "ethnic"?' He proved one better than I. He replied, 'You tell me', and thus shut me up. I had written a page referring to ethnicity in the present article. When Srinivas read the manuscript of this article he suggested that I refer to the papers of the conference in which he had also participated. I dropped the whole page from the present article. But I cannot drop this article itself. I have to do a friendly turn to the organizers of this volume.

pulsions common to all (Europe, America and Russia)' countries which have achieved modernisation, and to try 'instead new routes and risky by-passes' (1966: 51).

It is a matter of public knowledge that in the Arab countries and in India, too, the supporters of fundamentalism (both Hindu and Muslim) today belong to a section of the Western educated elite. Probably the opposition to fundamentalism comes from another section of the same elite, although I do not have much information on this. It is still less known what the anti-fundamentalist section stands for. But it appears that they have no guts to oppose the fundamentalists at least openly and actively. Does anti-fundamentalism come from another type of appeal, namely, communist ideology? Srinivas considers it also as a source of hostility to the West.

At a more general level Srinivas says:

One reason for the enormous appeal of communism to non-western countries is its hostility to the west, expressed in communistic anti-imperialism and anti-capitalism. Communism is seen as a humanitarian creed in its espousal of the cause of the underdogs, the workers and the subject nations; and its forecast that capitalism and imperialism are doomed to disappear and give way to a classless society wears the mask of science. It also enables the non-western intellectual to reject, in the name of science and humanity, not only the aggressive west but also his own society and its traditions. It enables him to identify himself with the future, with progress, science, and humanitarianism (1966: 51).

Communism—a product of the West—is viewed as the result of hostility to the West, wearing the mask of progress, science and humanitarianism.[2] Communism is not merely ethnocentrism, expressed politically in extreme nationalism, psychologically in passionate xenophobia. It has an ideological affiliation. This is, in turn, embedded in the idea of what may be called future social structure. This idea is based on the structure largely of the Western society but not unmindful of the Asiatic societies in the past. The point here is to show the relationship between ideology and social structure. Srinivas is not

[2] A point can be made here that communism may lead to political but not cultural hostility to the West.

unaware of this relationship. In fact he deals with it, as we shall see in what follows, though he gives more emphasis to caste, kinship, language and religion, which is understandable when one is dealing with a society like India and when one considers Srinivas' own ideological and academic background.

Nearer home in India, Srinivas states:

The work of western-inspired scholars resulted in providing a new and objective perspective for Indian civilization; it was a civilization that went back in time to the third millenium B.C., and it was astonishingly versatile. Thus the new elite were given a sense of pride in their country, and its rich and ancient culture. This enabled them to stand up to the western colossus, and was continual source of strength in their longing to become a nation, independent, sovereign, and equal to others. The discovery of the past was not, however, without its pitfalls and dangers. It produced a certain amount of paleocentrism in all educated Indians and, as is well known, a great past can be either energiser or opiate. In the main, however, it acted as an energiser, and has provided modern India with a mystique for national identity as well as development (1966: 79).

Thus, according to Srinivas, Westernization[3] emerges here as the energizer of nationalism and development through the Western educated Indians, though influenced by, if not imbued with, palaeocentrism. Srinivas further states:

The first response on the part of the new elite was to agitate for the removal of the glaring social evils of contemporary India. The nationalist urge gained gradually in strength in the latter half of the nineteenth century, so much so, that in the nineties the question was sharply posed as to whether reform should have priority over freedom or vice versa (1966: 84).

This, in my view, is a very important point though in a different context from that of Sanskritization and Westernization. It has great relevance for Indian social and political movements today.

---

[3] Again a point may be raised here. Is it Westernization, or the Western impact, or the contact with the West? This question cannot be dealt with in this article. The point implies more than mere difference in expression.

But where has all this led Indian society to? Srinivas writes:

In a country segmented along the lines of caste, language, and religion, heightened national selfawareness necessarily implied heightened selfawareness at every level of social structure from the highest to the lowest—the one could not be without the other. The existence of a considerable degree of overlap between the old and the new elites and the consequent exclusion of traditionally under-privileged groups from the new benefits—along with the presence of an alien and powerful ruler who not unnaturally took advantage of the deep divisions in society—resulted in the division of sub-continent into India and Pakistan (1966: 89).

This division does not seem to follow from Srinivas' analysis which has all along presumed the Hindu society—even when the word India is used—and not the relations between religious groups. However, what he says about independent India is very significant:

Independent India is forced, in the interest of her survival, to commit herself to a policy of quick elimination of traditional and hereditary inequalities, and in particular, of untouchability. The impulse toward equality has resulted in a policy of protective discrimination—discrimination in reverse—towards tribals, Hari-jans and backward castes to enable them to catch up with the advanced groups.

Finally in the case of sects and religions, self-awareness has resulted in the reinterpretation of traditions, 'communalism', and even revivalism. Revivalist movements such as Arya Samaj, the Sanatan Dharma Sabha, and the Ramkrishna Movement, have founded educational institutions imparting modern knowledge, pro-vided hostels, and so on. This has produced in the course of time a body of men with western knowledge but who also emphasize the distinctness and superiority of their particular sect or religion. Between them and the nationalists there was an irreconcilable conflict, which has resulted not only in the creation of India and Pakistan, but has provided each country with certain built-in threats to its own survival and development (1966: 87–88).

We have cited these lengthy quotations from Srinivas to illustrate that the terms Sanskritization and Westernization, though used for heuristic purposes, are not irrelevant or meaningless. They raise a number of problems which need to be addressed. For example, in 1959 I wrote:

This section (the new elite) is politically more dangerous than the revivalist section of our intellectuals because it is nearer the seat of political power. Because of the very character of their intellectualism their policy will be devoid of the understanding of the problems and state of mind of their people; and they are blind to the capacities and incapacities of their people. The only way open to them to make their policies succeed is to get the people to submit to them. The form of the force will be 'democratic'. The bureaucracy in a parliamentary democracy eminently suited to their feudal origin and feudal heritage. Their idea of democracy is as fake as that of Westernisation and cosmopolitanism. They have democratic slogans but their actions are undemocratic. Democracy as a way of life is foreign to their social nature and nurture.

Notwithstanding all that Srinivas has said in favour of the elites, I do not think I need to change my views about them which I expressed 20 years ago. Some amendments (see also notes 1 and 7) may be necessary regarding the distinction I made between the new elite and the revivalists. The categorization of revivalists among the Hindus, in the sense of Sanatanists or in the sense of those who among the Arya Samajists were in favour of the Gurukula system of education as distinguished from those in favour of the Anglo-Vernacular system, does not seem to be valid today. The Bharatiya Janata Party (BJP) seems to be concerned more with defending the Hindus than Hinduism. Its volunteer force, the Rashtriya Swayam-Sevak Sangh (RSS), does show some concern for Hinduism, more than the BJP does. There are rumours of differences within the RSS but what exactly are the ideological differences is not known. One section is said to maintain that they should be more secular and support the similar faction in the BJP. But one thing is certain that both the BJP and the RSS are becoming more 'secular', in the sense that they are seeking political power. The number of their followers is increasing, and the number of their sympathisers is increasing even more, both among the Hindu population and among different political parties. The section of educated persons in the Hindu middle classes which supports them overtly or covertly today is much wider than at any time in the past.

Islamic fundamentalism is similarly increasing among the educated Muslims. It should be noted that the proportion of the educated capable of holding bureaucratic positions among them is increasing, although compared to Hindus either in terms of their gross number or in terms of their percentage of the total population, they lag behind Hindus. In the Islamic Shia sect of the Dowudi Bohras of Gujarat the number and probably the percentage of the educated to their total population is higher than among the Sunnis. But fundamentalism still holds its sway over the Bohras.

. There are similar divisions between the reformers or progressives and the orthodox among the Parsis. The latter are a type of fundamentalists though possibly not of the staunch or rigid variety. The percentage of degree holders among the Parsis is very high. Similar divisions exist among the Christians and Sikhs in India.

This is the situation at the level of climate of thought in practically all the religious communities all over India, and the Western educated elite is the 'energizer' of fundamentalism in all of them. These elite are closer to political and economic power today than they were about 20 years ago, and the threat to Indian society from their ideology is not less, if not greater, today.[4] This is not to deny the fact that there is another section of the educated in all these communities which believes in secular and democratic ideals. But it cannot also be denied that they are not more effective than the fundamentalists.

The reverse of liberalism[5] seems to have taken place among the elites. In the 1920s the Liberal Party became weak with the rise of the Indian National Congress under Gandhi, but political liberalism did not die. In the political field it expressed itself as Swarajists who were arch-rivals of the no-changers in the Indian National Congress. In the social field Gandhi's constructive programme achieved what the liberals were preaching. Even with Gandhi's 'direct action' in both

---

[4] The difficulties with the term 'elite' have been discussed earlier in note 1. Here it may be possible to be a little more specific. They are definitely those who have gone through university after 1947 and also some before 1947. Among them are employable unemployed, professionals, businessmen, journalists and political leaders. They feel discriminated in their fields. They offer arguments in the contemporary world to the traditional Mullas, Maulvis, Swamis, Sants, Sandhus, Maharajas and others who are emerging in large numbers.

[5] Liberalism is another term requiring clarification. Its referents vary from political institutions, social institutions and attitudes, and rules of the game in politics, to the general view and way of life.

policy and practice, what was aimed at all along was the constitutional and peaceful transfer of power. That transfer of power automatically gave power to high caste Hindus both at the centre and in the states notwithstanding adult franchise. With the creation of Pakistan the Muslims became a religious, economically weaker, and less educated political minority. Provision was made in the Constitution for the Scheduled Castes and Tribes to catch up with the advanced groups, i.e., Hindus, by what has been called the policy of protective discrimination. If Srinivas was writing today he would have had to deal with the conflict between liberalism and illiberalism in the political as well as social fields brought about by these post-independence developments.

It is not that Srinivas believed in a smooth transition to secular beliefs, ideas and practices. He writes, 'Inter-dining among castes is slightly more liberal than before, but only slightly. All the "touchable" castes will unite against Harijans who want to exercise their constitutional right of entering temples and drawing water from village wells' (1966: 138). What is important is that the 'touchables' are uniting not only against the Harijans but also against Muslims and tribals.

The violence against the ex-untouchables, tribals and Muslims appears to be becoming endemic along with the ideological emphasis on efficiency, merit and injustice to the higher castes. It is significant that in the clashes which break out on the streets periodically there is direct involvement of the youth and that some of them are educated. The ideological support on both the sides comes definitely from the university educated class, including bureaucrats. Consider along with that the fact that fundamentalism is supported by the university educated among all religious communities. Further, since religious fundamentalism of some sort has percolated down to all the political parties such as the Congress-I, the Janata, the BJP and the Lok Dal, one thing common to all of them is that they want to maintain the *status quo*. That is to say, they do not want to bring about change in the direction of the desired type of society as envisaged in the directive principles of the Constitution of 1950 notwithstanding their verbal support to it as and when it suits them. This Constitution was the work of the liberal Western educated elite, but the same elite is actively engaged against it. That is the dominant trend of thought and action in India today. Notwithstanding the support of all parties in Parliament to 'reservations' or protective discrimination, the followers of some of these parties in Parliament and in the State legislature were actually engaged in the recent agitation and rioting against reservations in Gujarat. The situation is not different in other states.

As mentioned earlier, there is also a trend opposed to the one just described, but it has still not crystallized in both thought and organization. Among the established political parties, the two communist parties can be cited as an illustration. There are also several Naxalite and non-Gandhian groups influenced by Marxism. Contributing to the above trend are Gandhians who believe in action against political authority but at the same time in voting at elections and thus recognizing the role of political authority in society. This split among Gandhians occurred in 1976 when Jaya Prakash Narayan launched his movement. The other section among Gandhians—the followers of the late Vinoba Bhave—are organizing themselves separately, but they are non-political in the sense that they are neither in favour of voting at elections nor opposing the present political authority. In any case they need to be watched.

Then there are activists practically in every state who are motivated by a sense of justice, feelings of sympathy for the oppressed, and believing in action in accordance with their feelings. There are some Christian groups too among them. All these are localized groups in terms of their influence over people and may also be regional in terms of their influence on thought. These groups believe in the role of political authority in society and in influencing it, but they distrust the various political parties.

If all of these ideologically liberal—in the sense of being pro-oppressed—parties and groups can agree to launch a movement for achieving a society based on the principles of equality, and against the discrimination of caste, class, sex and religion, they may be able to draw into such a movement some elements from other parties that also believe in such an ideology. The question is: What position would the university educated elite take if such a movement is launched? Will they assume the leadership in organizing it, and if they do not organize it, will they support it?

The question is relevant in the present situation, because Srinivas believed that the work of Western and Western-inspired scholars, who provided on the one hand new and objective perspectives on Indian civilization and on the other a certain amount of palaeocentrism in the educated Indians, has in the main acted as an energizer. The rise of fundamentalism of the Indian variety, though unanticipated, comes as no surprise if we agree with Srinivas.

A number of questions arise in this context. Was there something wrong with the perspective provided by the new elite? Or, was there something wrong in our understanding of the character and role of the new elite? How does a certain degree of palaeocentrism still persist among large numbers of university educated persons? Was our understanding of palaeocentrism incorrect? Or, does it persist because it performs some functions in the situation developing after the middle half of the 1960s? If, in the past the new elites were the energizers of change, do we expect them to perform the same function of providing direction of change today?

Srinivas read the first draft of the present article and permitted me to add the following clarification regarding what he meant by palaeocentrism.

Palaeocentrism has a two fold aspect, one energising, and the other, an opiate. Energising palaeocentrism is again two fold. It may make possible the introduction of changes in the society to accommodate new forces while maintaining the fiction that the changes only mean a movement into a purer past, or it may become mere revivalism. Revivalism, it must be stressed, involves action while opiate does not. It rests content with glorification of the past.

Srinivas thus does not support revivalism in the sense of reproducing or replicating the past. It is also wrong to presume that he is not in favour of making an effort to change the situation. As we shall see later, he approves the participation of social scientists in the process of planning.

It has been mentioned earlier that revivalism in the sense of replicating or reproducing the past does not exist in India today, except among Muslim fundamentalists and very feebly among followers of Shankaracharya. But both revivalism and the opiate aspects of palaeocentrism involve glorifying the past. I will reiterate that reconstructing society to accommodate new forces while refashioning traditions is a more dangerous aspect than the opiate aspect of palaeocentrism with regard to the direction and path of change. The energizing of palaeocentrism is being done by the 'educated' in contemporary India. Insofar as these educated persons are concerned, the terms Sanskritization and Westernization do not have much relevance in the sense in which they are understood generally or by Srinivas. Both these processes and the categories of persons involved in them do not exist today as they existed in the late nineteenth century. The present-day activists among the educated persons are found in different activist groups. Most of these groups are openly political and others claiming to be cultural or religious are either the front organizations or unofficial affiliates of political organizations. Thus, educated persons are affiliated with such groups either after deliberation or without deliberation.

These parties and groups either represent or are affiliated with not only economic interests but also social (i.e., caste) or religious interests. These interests in the final analysis can be traced to material conditions in general and to relations of production in particular. Thus there is only energizing and no opiate and it does not exist in a neutral glass container. It guides actions towards short-term goals and long-term ends. Are these goals and ends refashioning the old traditions to accommodate new forces, or are they creating new rival traditions? I support the latter view. These traditions belong to the type of society called capitalist. Though, in India, it is in the developing stage, the direction is clear. It can be observed even in the refashioning of old traditions to accommodate new forces. It may be called Westernization, because capitalism is as much a product of the West as communism is. What justification is there for us to use concepts such as Westernization, Sanskritization, modernization for the direction of change rather than the concept of type of society? Once we accept that a certain type of society—in this case, capitalist society—should be our referent for future development, the characterization of the new elite and their role in future development will be different.

The role of the elite is summed up in the following words by a like-minded friend[6] who read an earlier draft of this article:

> The so called 'modern' educated are accepting 'modernization' only so far as it materially benefits them (at the expense of the large majority). Otherwise they join forces with the 'old' to preserve and strengthen their privilege and property.
>
> The new power elite of rural, peasant origin has enormously reinforced this regressive trend in the post-1947 period. (The young educated peasants are not different.—I.P. Desai)

[6] These comments are from late A.R. Kamat. He expired on 9 July 1983. I had a typed copy of the final version of the article ready on 14 August. I was to send it to him for perusal with the hope that he would be satisfied. But that was not to be. I read his obituary on 18 August. I was not prepared for this shock. He was taken to the hospital from the midst of a discussion, never to return.

Srinivas and men like him (*a*) have faith in the 'limited' modernisation; they believe that India and other underdeveloped countries will travel by the same road as that of the developed countries of the west, and (*b*) do not have in mind the large deprived majority at all in this process of 'modernisation'; (*c*) in that sense they have forsaken even liberalism, particularly radical liberalism.

III

Let us now discuss Srinivas' understanding of the situation in developing countries, which has great relevance for us.

The developing countries are today arenas for conflict between the old and the new. The old order is no longer able to meet the new forces, nor the new wants and aspirations of the people, but neither is it moribund—in fact it is still very much alive. The conflict produces much unseemly argument, discord, confusion and, on occasion, even bloodshed. Under the circumstances, it is tempting for the sociologist to look for the good old peaceful days in sheer nostalgia. But a moment's reflection should convince him that the old order was not conflict free and that it perpetrated inhuman cruelties on vast sections of the population. A theoretical approach that regards conflict as abnormal, or that invests equilibrium with a special value in the name of science, can be a handicap in developing societies (1966: 159–60).

After quoting Leach regarding the consequences of preoccupation with 'structural equilibrium', 'functional integration', 'cultural uniformity' and 'social solidarity', Srinivas writes, 'conflict ought to be seen as inhering in social life everywhere' (1966: 160). After pointing out that it is necessary to distinguish between forms of conflict that can be resolved by the existing institutional mechanisms, and more fundamental conflicts that threaten the entire social order, Srinivas says, 'The developing countries are characterised by the existence of leaders who are determined to bring about radical changes in traditional life and culture, and these leaders both reflect and guide the aspirations, hopes and ideals of their followers' (1966: 160). A question arises here: Do the so-called 'modern' educated elites really do it, and can they do it? I believe that they do not and cannot do it today, whatever they might have done in the past. Nevertheless, we have to do it and, more importantly, for us. By 'we' and 'us' I mean Indians in general and intellectuals in particular. Indian academicians will have to consider themselves as part of Indians and, more importantly, not above them.[7]

In Srinivas' view,

Under the circumstances a return to the old order would only mean starvation and misery for millions. Sociologists from developing countries are therefore forced to take a positive attitude toward social change. Some are also actively involved in the process of development and an increasing number are likely to be thus involved in the future as these countries become committed to programmes of planned development (1966: 161).

Srinivas wrote this in 1966 when the prospects appeared bright for achieving the new order by resolving conflicts with the help of the

---

[7] My view is that in the late nineteenth and early twentieth century the educated person, the social reformer and the political person were all rolled into one. Probably from the first decade of the twentieth century onwards social reformers and political reformers began to be differentiated—say, from the time the venues and pandals of the Indian National Congress and the Social Reform Conference were deliberately separated. The terms moderate and extremists have their origin in this process. In the second phase, political activists and educated persons were separated. This occurred with dubbing those educated in administration as part of the 'steel frame'. They were called the instrument or handle of the foreign rulers by Gandhi. By that time the number of university educated and of professionals such as lawyers and doctors among them had increased. Also, Indian businessmen and industrialists were growing both in influence and numbers. A section of the educated favoured Gandhi's action programme at the ideological level. They formed the extremist (Jahal) section in politics. 'Social reformers' and also political reformers (i.e., those who wanted to sever ties with the British slowly and gradually) came to be known as 'moderates' (Maval). After the failure of the 1920–21 Satyagraha by Gandhi the 'moderate' section in the Indian National Congress emerged as Swarajists, or changers in policy as distinguished from non-changers. This also had consequences for the split among the 'educated'. These divisions are an interesting subject to pursue in relation to the present distribution of population over different activities for earning an livelihood. Social differentiations and the growth of secular vested interests occurred at a rapid rate after independence and we have the educated elite as the vested interest distributed over different areas of life. If this distribution is viewed in relation to the growth of industry and business, changes in agriculture, growth of government and administration, and growth of education at the top level, we may be able to examine the growth of experts, specialists and researchers, etc. and their role. I have not formulated a research project; I am merely expressing my thoughts.

existing institutional mechanisms. Probably many others would have also thought that way then. I do not know what Srinivas thinks now. But taking his theoretical position from what he said then, he could not be thinking otherwise:

> Modernisation thus involves the 'rationalization of ends' according to Bellah, which means that the goals chosen by a society should be 'rational' and the subject of discussion. It needs to be pointed out, however, that social goals are in the final analysis the expression of value preferences, and therefore, non-rational. The public discussion of goals can in no way guarantee their rationality. Rationality can only be predicted of the means but not of the ends of social action (1966: 52).

Accepting the definition of rationalism as given in the *Encyclopedia of Social Sciences*, he writes:

> Another essential element in secularization is rationalism, a comprehensive expression applied to various theoretical and practical tendencies which aim to interpret the universe purely in terms of thought, or which aims to regulate individual and social life in accordance with the principles of reason and to eliminate as far as possible or to relegate to the background everything irrational. Rationalism involves, among other things, the replacement of traditional beliefs and ideas by modern knowledge (1966: 119).

Do those theoretical and practical tendencies which aim to interpret the universe purely in terms of thought have any relation to the other aim of rationalism, namely, to regulate individual and social life? It should be noted that in the first case rationalism is an interpretation and that too purely in terms of thought. Alternatively, it is also understood to regulate, that is, to become a guide to action, for individual and social life. Obviously, thought is presumed to have some relation to action. Srinivas' understanding of that relation is clear from his statement: 'Rationalism involves, among other things, the replacement of traditional beliefs and ideas by modern knowledge.' The problem facing Indian society is that of building up social relations, i.e., relations between man and man, on the basis of modern knowledge. Therefore, if we know how these ideas and beliefs operate in relation to social relations we can also understand change in social relations.

Thus, the basic task of the sociologist is to unfold the implications of social relations with the help of knowledge. Srinivas' emphasis on social structure can be understood in this way. Also, since modern knowledge is based on observation it is necessary to observe the social structure, i.e., parts of a society as they are related to one another, and see how a change in one part brings about a change in others, contributing to the maintenance of equilibrium at a given point of time. As we have seen earlier, Srinivas does not subscribe to that view inasmuch as he does not believe in investing 'equilibrium with a special value in the name of science'. He believes that conflict is not abnormal. All structural–functionalists do not believe that parts are always related to the whole in such a way as to contribute to its maintenance, and the concept of dysfunction is also put forth. But there is another question. If equilibrium is disturbed, does a society tend to remain in a permanent state of disequilibrium or of continuous change, or does it seek another state of equilibrium, i.e., another state of relationships? Since conflict is as much normal as are cooperation and consensus, the new state of equilibrium must also be disturbed. If that is so, we assume a state of permanent change or a state of flux rather than a state of equilibrium. The Greek philosopher Heraclitus is attributed to have said that we never swim twice in the same river. Srinivas anticipates such a situation and mentions the distinction between conflict that can be resolved by the existing mechanisms and more fundamental conflicts that 'threaten the entire social order'. He also believes that conflict in Indian society may be of the latter type when he says, 'Developing countries are today arenas for conflict between the old and the new.'

In view of all this, the correct question would have been: What is 'new' in the direction in which India is moving? My contention is that Srinivas could not ask this question as he was then imbued with 'empiricism' and 'positivism'. He therefore views the present 'planned development' as the direction of social change, notes with satisfaction the 'involvement of sociologists in the process of development', and discusses the pros and cons of such participation for the academic sociologist. It was relevant to have raised the question of direction of change, particularly the characterization of the new, when he said that there is 'conflict between the old and the new'. If 'development' is taken as something new, if the social processes of Sanskritization and Westernization are seen in relation to one another, and if secularization is viewed as part of that new, are we or are we not entitled to question the nature of that development, and the direction in which it is moving. Srinivas rightly says that one of the functions of Sanskritization was to 'bridge the gap between secular and ritual rank' (1966: 28). But that question implies characterization of the whole. Srinivas probably doubts if societies exist as wholes. In keeping with that doubt, he goes by parts and is concerned largely with the issue of how that development is taking place.

Mukherjee considers Srinivas as the foremost of the modernizers of Indian sociology. He makes the following observation about modernizers:

> Moreover, they hardly ever looked beyond the societal characteristics which were clearly observable, and thus failed to consider systematically the 'what', 'how', 'why', 'what will it be' and 'what should it be' questions within the total framework of society. For the 'fact' of social change, value-laden as we have seen it to be, was built into their ideological make up: change was not a matter requiring theoretical comprehension and, correspondingly, nor were methodological distinctions needed with which to characterise a social space as comprising *infinite but enumerable facts* of change or no change, and containing desired or undesired course of change (1979: 52).

I agree with Mukherjee that the mode of thinking of those whom he calls modernizers of Indian sociology did not permit them to raise the question of direction of change in terms of characterization of the whole. But a question may be posed to Mukherjee and to all those who agree to comprehend the changing Indian social reality and its direction of change: Is it also not logically essential to provide an answer to the question as to how to work for, and in the direction of, that desired direction of change and also to work against the undesired direction of change? If we do not provide an answer, we are welcome to remain at the contemplative level and to consider action as out of bounds for academics. Of course, it will suit our social origins and academic nurture to keep action out of bound, to emphasize 'free' and 'pure' thought and knowledge for its own sake and to maintain our position as impartial and 'objective' observers and delineators of the process of change.

However, a legitimate and valid question arises: Are we not required to think before we act? Should our action be thoughtless? Are we not required to decide 'what should it be' before we act? The answer to this question is related to the answer to the question 'what will it be' and the series of questions raised by Mukherjee regarding what, how and why. It is necessary to mention here that our response regarding the way of thinking before acting will differ from answers given by those, for instance, who believe in what is known as social engineering, economic planning, and other such planning. It is obvious that I have gone a long way with Mukherjee up to the last question to which we are seeking an answer. For both of us, one direction in which we seek the answer is clear. It must bear relation to the answer to the question 'what will it be?' and to answers to questions preceding it. The amendment I wish to make to Mukherjee's last question is, to add the words 'for which we should strive'. The question would then read 'What should it be for which we should strive?'. Is it only a verbal amendment, or does it lead to any substantive difference in thinking and acting? I am inclined to say 'yes' to the latter part of the question. What substantial difference it makes is the next legitimate and valid question. I am not sure of the answer in detail, though I feel committed to the direction given by Marx: 'Philosophers have only interpreted the world; our task, however, is to change it.'

Mukherjee has tried to relate theory and research—a form of action. Though that issue deserves our consideration, I am not referring to it in the sense of what Srinivas says: 'the entire social order.' He also suggests the point at which action can be taken for changing it, i.e., the type of conflicts 'which threaten it.' I believe that this is no minor issue for sociological thinking in India. We need to discuss the points arising from Srinivas in detail. If we do not, we shall commit the same error that the 'modernizers' committed—the error of overlooking the contribution of pioneers. Srinivas has been quiet for some time now. We should remind him that Indian sociology has much to learn from him.

IV

We began with viewing Sanskritization and Westernization as concepts to explain the religious, cultural and social change in India and the role of the new elites in bringing about that change. My first difference is with the understanding of change. I have understood change as the complete transformation of society. My focus has been on social change and not on cultural and religious change. Once we accept change as the problem, several questions arise: What is the direction of change? How is that direction decided? Does that change take place on its own, without the activity or intervention of human beings? What is the role of academicians in bringing about that change?

It is not that Srinivas has not given thought to these questions. He sees change in the direction of what he understands by Westernization, with the Western educated elites both as carriers and agents of change. He sees conflict between them and the agents of what he calls Sanskritization. Not only that but he also believes that conflict ought to be seen as inherent in social life everywhere. He perceives conflict in all developing countries as the conflict between the old and the new. This was the general trend of his thinking till 1966. I would not like to join issues with him on these points.

However, the comments by a young friend are relevant here:

> It's all very well for you to agree with Srinivas on 'conflict', 'disequilibrium', etc. But where has he dealt with violence and repression, as processes of social change? And why not? There was enough of it even when he was very prolific. 'Conflict' is a nice bloodless category; broken heads, huts ablaze, rape, torture, and terror are very bloody indeed.
>
> I suspect that at bottom what's disabling our 'elite' is aversion to the very datum of legal and extra-legal repression—killing, raping, maiming, wounding people. In their greenhouses, the dichotomies and taxonomies are well preserved like orchids. Violence is *not* a phenomenon for the Indian social scientist. It can't be encapsulated in well manicured generalizations. That's why they are not stirred to action of any kind. Social scientists are unable, despite the emergency, to ever imagine that they might also be at the receiving end of the stick!

There are certain tendencies in Srinivas' thinking which need to be pointed out. First, there is the tendency to emphasize the empirical, so much so that it might lead to the trend of his becoming an empiricist—someone might add if he is not already one. His tendency to emphasize the 'what' and 'how' of an enquiry need not be deplored. I would only like it to be seen with reference to the future type of society to be envisaged. Some do not consider that question within the purview of science. But my point is: how we arrive at it can be controversial and there can be more than one view of the desired type of society, but if we go on observing 'what is' and 'how' without reference to the future we shall be saying only that this is happening. But our quest should be: does what is happening lead us to the type of society desired by us? The desired thus also becomes the desirable. Srinivas views government and society as it obtained till 1966 as the desired one. He talks of the undesirable things happening then with reference to the same. (Not that he is satisfied with what is happening now.)

My view is that the society envisaged by the directive principles given in the Constitution of 1950 should be the society desired by us. All our movements should be motivated by that end. However, an examination of what is happening around indicates that most political parties do not want to move in that direction. They are busy manipulating alliances and mergers for winning the next elections whenever they are held. They have programmes, but neither the parties nor the people take them seriously. But there is one significant common factor in all these manoeuvres. They do not want to include the communist parties of all hues in their alliance, on the ground that they draw their inspiration from foreign sources. In any case, there is no reference to the future type of society, much less to the one guided by the directive principles of the Constitution. The Western educated elite which is believed to have framed the Constitution, does not want to defend it. That is not surprising if we know what they are. The following excerpt from Owen Lynch clearly reveals what they are.

In the U.S.A. today there is an organisation called A.I.A., Association of Indians in America. This organisation is arguing that Indian immigrants to the U.S.A. should be counted in the U.S. Census under the special category, Indians of Asian descent. Although they are the most technically trained immigrant group to enter the U.S.A. todate and are financially well off, they seek separate classification in the census as a part of the strategy to claim financial and other benefits meant for the poor and disadvantaged minorities in the U.S.A. It is ironic these come from the very class which would deny the benefits of protective discrimination to untouchables in India (1982: vii–viii).

The behaviour of this class may appear ironical to a third party like Lynch. We in India know that it is the very material of which this class is made. This attitude they derive from their mentors, the Indian bourgeoisie, which itself is brought up under the guidance of European and American bourgeoisie. And now they are being guided by multinational bourgeoisie, including the Arabs and a category called 'foreign nationals of Indian origin'. They are always afraid that they may lose their patronage.

The friend mentioned earlier makes the following comments:

I see a little inconsistency in your position. On the one hand, the direction of capitalistic development you accurately identified *exists*. On the other, you rely on Part IV of the Constitution. The society identified in Part IV—the aspirational model—is broadly 'socialistic'. (What kind of 'socialism' is another question. Incidentally, when people begin to talk of Gandhian 'socialism' we lose all meaning of that form.) Page 93 says that capitalistic form of society 'should be referent for our future type of society'; page 101 says that 'our immediate or short term goal should be the movement to achieve the society' envisaged by Part IV. It also says: 'The desired thus also becomes the desirable.'

The Constitution mirrors contradictions in the ideologies of the ruling bourgeoisie. May be, what you suggest amounts to a call for sharpening and reinforcing these contradictions. May be, Part IV is conducive to capitalism in so far as state capitalism is conducive to corporate/monopoly capitalism. In this sense, Part IV is an ally of capitalist form of development, contrary to its 'socialistic' pretensions.

It also meets, in my opinion, the legitimation needs of the ruling coalitions against (*a*) pre-capitalistic formations (merchant capital etc.) and (*b*) fractions of capital in conflict *inter se*. It also provides an ideological apparatus of coercion.

In that sense, you may be right. But it has got to be made explicit.

I think my friend has done the job for me. I thank him.

REFERENCES

DESAI, I.P. 1959. 'The New Elite', *The Economic Weekly*, XI, 28–30: 913–16. Reprinted in I. P. Desai, *The Craft of Sociology and Other Essays*. Delhi: Ajanta, 1981.

LYNCH, OWEN. 1982. 'Foreword'. In Barbara Joshi, *Democracy in Search of Equality*. Delhi: Hindustan.

MUKHERJEE, RAM KRISHNA. 1979. *Sociology of Indian Sociology*. Delhi: Allied.

SRINIVAS, M. N. 1952. *Religion and Society among the Coorgs of South India*. Oxford: Clarendon Press.

SRINIVAS, M. N. (Ed.). 1955. *India's Villages*. Calcutta: Government Press.
——. 1962. *Caste in Modern India and Other Essays*. Bombay: Asia.
——. 1965. 'Social Structure'. In *The Gazetteer of India*, Vol. I. Delhi: Publications Division, Government of India. Reprinted as *India: Social Structure*. Delhi: Hindustan, 1980.
——. 1966. *Social Change in Modern India*. Berkeley: University of California Press.
——. 1973. 'Itineraries of an Indian Social Anthropologist', *International Social Science Journal*, XXV, 1–2: 129–48.
——. 1975. 'Village Studies, Participant Observation and Social Science Research in India', *Economic and Political Weekly*, X, Annual Number: 1387–94.
——. 1976. *The Remembered Village*. Delhi: Oxford University Press.

4

THE THERAPY OF METHODOLOGICAL REVERSAL

J. V. FERREIRA

There is mounting evidence to suggest that the state of the sciences in India, both natural and social, is far from healthy and flourishing. In spite of adequate personnel and a developed infrastructure, the output, when compared with Europe and America, is evidently poor. And yet, it can be taken for granted that not many natural and social scientists in the country will hasten to acknowledge this fact.[1] On the contrary, critics of the established order or of the prevailing state of affairs, whose numbers are of course few, are often dismissed as malcontented and disruptive of the peace, and their indictments are allowed to perish for want of nourishment or gathering support. This may be due at one level to the fact that the generality prefer the effortless task of drifting

---

[1] In her doctoral dissertation Radhika Ramasubban (1977) shows that the Mertonian norms making for efficiency in science such as rewards and recognition, organized scepticism and originality do not appear to be operative in the CSIR and ICAR laboratories. As far as social sciences are concerned, indictments exposing the near total absence of originality among social scientists in India have appeared in newspapers and journals occasionally.

with the tide; but at a deeper level it may be due to a psychic-ontological stasis—a state of inactivity caused by opposing forces.

Professor M. N. Srinivas' life work has been largely dedicated to the objective of documenting the relative strengths of these opposing forces and the consequences of their confrontation. Many other social scientists have also followed in his footsteps and sought to do likewise, using his framework or other frameworks of interpretation or explanation. What is the net result of all these efforts at gauging the situation in the country? The result is, it seems, a blurred picture. Neither has modernity succeeded in wiping out tradition, nor has tradition succeeded in arresting the progress of modernity. On the surface the progress of the one is easily noticeable; in depths the hold of the other seems firm. Compromises, too, have been observed and duly noted. It is, however, to this tenacity-in-depth that we can perhaps trace the recrudescence of a militant palaeo-Hinduism, the resurgence of a proselytizing neo-Hinduism and the petrifaction of our scientific endeavours.

One of the basic problems that we, therefore, confront is how to make our scientific endeavours less sterile. In tackling this problem, what is needed is not a more diligent apeing of the West but, first and foremost, a methodological reversal in the social science disciplines which should and can be engineered by the force of self-assertion. This is so because the adoption of the outward trappings does not ensure the transfer of the spirit behind the scientific enterprise of the West; and without the spirit there is neither root nor fruit. Is, however, a methodological reversal possible without shaking the foundations and toppling the edifice? And what of the unity of scientific method—a doctrine so strongly held and so staunchly defended till recent times?[2]

At any rate, a foreshadowing of such a reversal (with success writ large in its pages) is evidenced by Srinivas' *The Remembered Village* (1976)—an ethnography which, as is widely known, was 'composed' under unusual circumstances. The measure of its success can be gauged from the fact that it has been much discussed,[3] and also, its

[2] The positivist doctrine of the unity of scientific method has been considerably eroded by the emergence of new directions in the philosophy of science represented by Karl Popper, Thomas Kuhn, Imre Lakatos and Paul Feyerabend. In earlier decades scholars like Jacques Maritain continued to hold the opposite standpoint. See, for example, Maritain (1937).

[3] See, for instance, *Contributions to Indian Sociology*, 12, 1: January–June 1978, dedicated entirely to a discussion of *The Remembered Village*.

ethnographic material, or what was remembered of it after a disastrous fire had destroyed the notebooks containing it, has been transmuted by the memory and aesthetic intelligence of the ethnographer into a work of art. One sees that on the face of it the ethnographer is seemingly engaged in this book in doing what all ethnographers are supposed to do, that is to say, to give a faithful account of the life of the tribe or village concerned in the ethnographic present.

Srinivas begins by telling us about the trials and tribulations, the consolations and ecstasies which he experienced in the course of his fieldwork and the task of processing his garnered data. He then goes on to discuss the leading men in the village and to describe the universe of agriculture, since agriculture is the dominant activity in the village. Noting the attributes of the activity, the distinctions which characterize it, and the concomitants which go along with it, the ethnographer then discusses the sexes and the household. The household, the sexual division of labour, the modes in which the sexual appetite is satisfied and the characteristics of the male dominated village society are presented fluently and flowingly, the ethnographer commenting with some asperity that men have a profound sense of private property not only in their ancestral lands but also in the genital organs of their wives. The narrative, we perceive in passing, is occasionally interspersed with phrases which have the piquancy of paprika.

From the household we move on to relations between castes and note the fact that the villager's relations with other human beings are mediated through caste, and not so much through the all-India category of *varna* as through the small endogamous groups called *jatis*. The members of a caste follow the traditional occupation and are proud of their skill in it. While occupational specialization has led to the interdependence of castes, hierarchy which is omnipresent separates them from one another. Notions of purity and pollution maintain structural distance. Since ranking is uncertain, mobility is possible within the caste system, and ambitious castes try to adopt the customs and lifestyles of the higher castes in their efforts at moving upwards on the hierarchical social ladder and in circumventing the obstructions of the locally dominant caste.

As art has its chiaroscuro, so society has its factions and disputes. Thus, Srinivas points out that the villagers have an aesthetic as well as an intellectual interest in disputes which arise from time to time in their midst. Turning, thereafter, to the changing village, he sketches its main aspects, and then proceeds to consider the quality of social relations through concepts like reciprocity, hierarchy, face, friendship, enmity, gossip, envy and sense of humour. As if to highlight the ethnography, he turns to religion in his penultimate chapter. In the final chapter he bids farewell to his friends, the gracious villagers who had helped him in his ethnographic endeavours. And as he moves out and away from the village, he has, as he puts it poetically, brief and tantalizing glimpses of the shimmering Kaveri flowing in the distance.

If we have tarried over the contents of this book, it is to demonstrate in the first instance that there is nothing extraordinary about them. In fact, much of what Srinivas has to report here has not only been reported by him before, but has also been reported by others of other villages in India. And yet the book stands out, gripping one's attention to the very end, holding the mind captive through its significant form.

Thus, the trajectory of Srinivas' scholarly life has moved upwards from the descriptive–diffusionist ethnography of his first phase with Ghurye as his guide, to the analytical ethnography of his second phase under the influence of Radcliffe-Brown, and finally to social anthropology as art, if not as historiography, of his third phase in the light perhaps of Evans-Pritchard's affirmations to this effect.

From this trajectory emerges a moral. The moral is that we should not allow the accidents of history to dictate our understanding of the nature of science or the methods by which we acquire 'scientific' knowledge—at the very least in the sphere of the social sciences.[4] Instead, we should follow our deepest inclinations and the pressures of our cultural conditioning and look for support in quarters in which more or less corresponding ideas and orientations have been developed. The accidents of history brought the British to our shores and before long, whether through the pull of a vacuum or for other reasons, they became the overlords of the subcontinent. The schism in the soul which this gave rise to engendered, among other things, a mimetic urge. By the magic of mimesis we hoped to reach the level of our alien superiors; and so, forgetting or ignoring our roots, we followed blindly in the footsteps of a rigorous British empiricism, and, therefore, adopted the positive methods as primary and science as understood in the West till recently as our guiding star.

---

[4] From the outflow of books on the subject authored, among others, by Lawrence LeShan, Fritjof Capra, Gary Zukav, Michael Talbot and Amaury de Riencourt, it would appear that micro-physics has been moving closer to Oriental mysticism in its interpretations of the microreality it studies. But it is too early to say where all this will finally lead.

The nature of our philosophic–social heritage and the cultural conditioning which followed from it point in a different direction. As Surendranath Dasgupta, the historian of Indian philosophy, tells us:

The old civilisation of India was a concrete unity of many-sided developments in art, architecture, literature, religion, morals, and science so far as it was understood in those days. But the most important achievement of Indian thought was philosophy. It was regarded as the goal of all the highest practical and theoretical activities, and it indicated the point of unity amidst all the apparent diversities which the complex growth of culture over a vast area inhabited by different peoples produced. It is not in the history of foreign invasions, in the rise of independent kingdoms at different times, in the empires of this or that great monarch that the unity of India is to be sought. It is essentially one of spiritual aspirations and obedience to the law of the spirit, which were regarded as superior to everything else, and it has outlived all the political changes through which India passed (1975: vii).

With the exception of the Carvaka materialists, all the other systems of Indian philosophy, Dasgupta further adds, agree on the fundamental points of importance, on the summum bonum of life, on the postulates, aims and conditions for the realization of the religious purpose of life. More specifically, the points of agreement are the *karma* theory, the doctrines of *mukti* and of the soul, and a pessimistic attitude towards the world. It is true that some interpreters have ascribed the intellectual stagnation of contemporary India to this pessimistic attitude or the widely pervasive concept of fatalism; and it would be erroneous to deny all truth to such an ascription. But this is exactly why the methodological reversal in social sciences to which we have adverted already must be made not merely in terms of our deepest inclinations and our cultural conditioning but also in terms of the basically similar orientations in the German-speaking countries[5] and elsewhere in the

[5] It is true that some Hindu scholars have strongly appreciated German oriental scholarship. As Agehananda Bharati says: 'Hindu scholars (particularly Sanskrit professionals) who have not been exposed to the liberal, analytical, or administration-oriented atmosphere of Britain or Westernized India have entertained an intensely appreciative attitude toward Germany or Germans (particularly their oriental scholarship, actual or putative)' (1982: 44). In calling, however, for a methodological reversal, one does not at all intend to add fuel to smouldering fascist fires, but to liberate creativity which, when ascendant, has a powerful, positive multiplier effect.

West. Only then can the substitution of the pessimistic attitude by an optimistic confidence in one's own self and ultimate destiny be transferred from the terminal points at which it occurs in India to the whole of life in all its mundane and developmental dimensions.

As is well known, in the German-speaking countries a host of thinkers raised and defended counter-affirmations against the encroachments of the positivism of the natural sciences into the cultural disciplines as they are called there or social sciences as they are known in the English-speaking world. From Herder to Meinecke, German historians affirmed the autonomy of history and denied that the positivist quest for causal laws could be applied to the realms of nature and history alike. They were close to the spiritual domain of romanticism. For instance, Leopold von Ranke, the great German historian, who was noted for his meticulous research methods, showed affinities with the romanticists in the categories of his thought. 'Like them', says H. Stuart Hughes, 'he dealt in spiritual entities that were "intuited" and "contemplated" in semi-mystical fashion, rather than in firm concepts, empirically tested or logically analyzed. And in these procedures, Ranke's method was typical of German Idealism' (1967: 186).

The neo-romanticists, who also revolted against positivism, were deeply interested in the non-rational motivations of human behaviour. Having re-discovered the world of the non-logical, the non-civilized and the mysterious, they became obsessed or even intoxicated by it. They turned towards the subjective and applied the values of the imagination in their efforts at understanding and describing its manifestations. Thus romanticism and German idealism were closely related. The romanticists separated the phenomenal and the noumenal, as Kant had done, and went on to assert a radical cleavage between the natural sciences and human activities or between the *Naturwissenschaften* and *Geisteswissenschaften*. The aim of the cultural sciences, it was claimed, was not to strive after general laws but seek detailed and concrete historical descriptions on which the philosophers of history could reflect. Therefore, the concept which idealism associated with such studies was the concept of *Geist* in its particularities, individualities or the specificities of cultural totalities; and the method by which these totalities could be interpreted was the method of inner understanding or *Verstehen*.

These affirmations were more systematically developed by Wilhelm Dilthey and by the neo-Kantians. According to Dilthey, the poetic approach to life was an authentic interpretation of it. This was the basic insight which he utilized in interpreting almost all the spiritual endeavours of mankind. Profoundly concerned with the future of Western culture and the place of science in it, Dilthey took up as his main task the vindication of the autonomy of the cultural sciences against the imperialist claims of the natural sciences. In this task he was perhaps aided by the fact that the German word *Wissenschaft* was broader in its denotation than the English word 'science'. The English word 'science' had come to acquire the more restricted meanings which were associated with the natural sciences and finally became almost indistinguishable from those narrower meanings; whereas the German word *Wissenschaft* includes both the natural and cultural sciences and does not discriminate against the latter.

Paying tribute to Hegel, Goethe, Schleiermacher, Lessing, Novalis and Hoelderlin, Dilthey realized that he was in conflict with the tendencies of his time and decided to dedicate his energies to overcoming it. Adopting the historical approach because it regarded the life of the mind as a historical product, Dilthey insisted that human studies had to develop a methodology of their own, and, therefore, felt it necessary to write a critique of historical reason, even as Kant had formulated a critique of pure and practical reason. As a philosopher of history, Dilthey viewed it as a deep and comprehensive flowering of life; life not so much as a biological phenomenon but as a psychological one which embraces all the mental processes, particularly the creative ones. Interpreting history in terms of a feeling for life, of a world picture (*Weltbild*) and of a world-view (*Weltanschauung*), Dilthey propagated the view that history deals with individuals. Accordingly, it was necessary to study the inner workings of the individual mind in its totality.

A scientific understanding of these mental totalities could be secured through the method of empathic intuition or *Verstehen* (or indwelling, as Michael Polanyi has recently called it). Through this method an objective knowledge of another individual consciousness could be acquired because it made possible the reliving and emulation of the spiritual life of another person. In this way we grasped its significance. As Gerhard Masur says, 'What we encounter in the act of understanding is not only the stream of consciousness flowing through another life; it is much more, something which Dilthey at the end of his life called *Bedeutung*, or signification' (1961: 167). The hermeneutic idea on which Dilthey focused is, therefore, the imaginative recovery of other men's thoughts and the interpretation of the multiple creative forms of the human spirit or the decipherment of their hidden significance. Later in life Dilthey tended to follow Edmund Husserl in the latter's radical rejection of psychologism.

The relationship between positivism and human studies was also dealt with by the neo-Kantians, Wilhelm Windelband and Heinrich Rickert. Discarding Dilthey's earlier psychologism, Windelband suggested that the difference between the natural and cultural sciences lay not so much in their objects of study as in their methods. The natural sciences were nomothetic, while the cultural sciences were idiographic. The nomothetic sciences aimed at the discovery of laws; the idiographic sciences pursued unique or particular descriptions. Rickert, who was Windelband's pupil, sought to absolutize the validity of the historian's system of values, but was denounced by the positivists for his inability in achieving independence from a metaphysic which, they felt, was superfluous. Nevertheless, affirming that history was basically a science of culture, Rickert preferred the term *Kulturwissenschaft* to Dilthey's *Geisteswissenschaft*. He viewed the opposition between culture and nature on both logical and objective grounds, and then distinguished the scientific approaches to them after the manner of Dilthey and Windelband.

As we know, Max Weber, eminent German sociologist, also made significant contributions to the methodological debate. Weber was influenced by both Dilthey and Rickert, but finally concluded that their work was unsatisfactory in several directions. Finding that idealism was lapsing into excessive relativism or intuitionism, while positivism was uncritical in its pursuit of facts, Weber undertook the task of mediating between the two and of transcending their 'sterile' opposition. He accepted the validity of *Verstehen*, but felt that this was only one side of the picture. The picture could be completed by the addition of empirical-causal studies. Values, it is true, were relative, as Dilthey had maintained, but in social studies the scientist must adopt an attitude of value neutrality. That is to say, one must carefully discriminate between the categories of 'is' and 'ought', if sociology is ever to become objective in its task of clarifying issues and conditions relating to social choices. Sociology, Weber believed, could not and should not tell men how to lead their lives. As is well known, he also showed how religious factors may outweigh economic ones in the dynamics of social and economic development.

The credit of bringing together a number of streams in German thought goes to Werner Pelz whose sociology has as its highlights the concepts of subjectivity and inter-subjectivity, of *Verstehen* and *Besinnung*, of history, of dialectics, of hermeneutics, of phenomenology and of art. It is a sociology of life-abounding. As Pelz (1974: ix) says, 'facts' are becoming increasingly problematic in the social and humanistic disciplines, and social sciences have not told us what they are but have evaded the issue. By imitating the manipulative methodology of the natural sciences, social scientists only succeed in making themselves and others into manipulable objects. In the process they forget that they themselves are behind their observations, and that their values, viewpoints, theoretical orientations or, more widely and deeply, their subjectivity, play a significant part in their activities. In spite of Weber's advocacy, it is impossible to be value free. To exaggerate reason is to destroy it, as is exemplified in the thought systems of Durkheim, Freud and Marx. 'Rationality for its own sake', says Pelz in a telling phrase, 'is reason's cannibalism' (1974: 74).

It, therefore, follows that any sociology for our times must begin by recognizing the fundamental significance of subjectivity and inter-subjectivity. The subject-and-his-consciousness is characterized by intentionality and intensionality, the first signifying that consciousness is consciousness-of-an-object and the second that it is purposeful directedness. As the subject is a totality, he is steeped, according to Gabriel Marcel, in the mystery of being. In its undifferentiated, primal state, this subjective totality encompassed all our feelings of helplessness, despair, terror, joy, peace, rage and power and in their kaleidoscopic transformations and interactions. The onset of verbal thought introduced a cleavage into this undifferentiated state; but the mystical state of ecstasy, as Martin Heidegger claims, still points to it (quoted in Pelz 1974: 19).

However, verbal thought does not succeed in eliminating the primal state which continues to subsist in us, especially in the depths of our psyche from where it reveals its strength, its fertility in rationalizations, its capacity for hidden changes and interconnections, and its restless drive towards its lost wholeness, expressing itself through a poetic-mystic vision, through falling in love, and through orgiastic, communal, Dionysian ecstasies, all of them with their intimations of omnipotence. Of this subjective totality, Ernst Bloch points out, hopefulness is an important constitutive element. In other words, what is there is *Dasein*, and *Dasein*, as Heidegger indicated, is transcendence-in-immanence and being-unto-death. The subject is open to the a-rational and to metareality; he is a knower and as such tries to know himself, and in the process transforms the earth into his world, a world of image, gesture, word, concept and instrument. In an attempt to understand Hindu philosophy, Pelz views the network of *maya* as being woven from the guilt and errors of the self which refuses to recognize itself for what it is. As the lost self goes in search of itself, it recognizes reality as an illusion. It is only the subject's full acceptance of its subjectivity that can destroy the belief in the fixity of reality.

If, then, subjectivity is fundamental, the social is the stuff of inter-subjectivity, and society is the interplay of subjective totalities. Human reality is essentially communication, communion, intercourse which bring together and join that which has been sundered. The meeting point of the individual and society is the psyche which projects itself into the social world and introjects the social world into itself. It does so in order to re-establish the primal at-one-ment between I and thou and I and it, as Martin Buber (1949), elucidating the idea of a dialogue, pointed out. Thus, the aim of sociology is an integral one—the relating of the part to the whole in a reality which is fluid. Fluidity subordinates the objective to inter-subjectivity.

This is the essence of history. Pelz recognizes Dilthey's services in establishing the importance of history, Kant's contribution in under-lining *das Ding-an-sich* and the German historians' work in perceiving the value of values and the reason of unreason in human affairs and in thinking of history as an attempt in aesthetically understanding the manifestations of each historical phase in its particularity. As all knowledge is historical, sociological considerations cannot be separated from historical ones.

From history so considered it is a short step to dialectics and dialogue, and the way to the latter is through the thought of Hegel, Marx and Buber. In particular the prime justification for dialectics and dialogue is the task of unifying I and thou and I and it without reducing I to it. In this task the negative dialectics of Horkheimer and Adorno can also be seen as playing a role in so far as by its means the hardening of abstractions and obstructions can be prevented and the path can thus be cleared for the free flow of human creativity. Jurgen Habermas' interests also contribute to this end.

Dialectics is not so much a matter of argument as of realization. Its claims are deep and wide. Life and knowledge can only be advanced through 'the a-rational confrontation of rationally irreconcilable rationalizations' (Pelz 1974: 111), and human development, as Hegel and Marx saw it, is the consequence of extreme contradictions. Furthermore, dialectics is concerned with the mutual relations between the knower and the known or the to-be-known; and unlike realism and positivism, dialectics does not absolutize the status quo but reflects on it and fluidizes it. This is so because a basic assumption of dialectical thinking is that reality ever eludes every idea, thought, concept, method and system. In focusing on the thinker the dialecticians affirm that without reflection there can be no theory and without theory there can be no facts. Looking at the totality they, therefore, try to arrive at an understanding of it, wherein it is both more and less than the sum of its parts and is different from them. The individual is also considered similarly. Since dialectics floats in the air, so to say, it can cast an unbiased gaze on the prevailing circumstances. It can thus perceive the interrelations between reason and interest; but in doing so, avoiding Freud's scientific causal interpretation and Marx's economic ones and ranging into the tangled depths of the psyche.

Pelz recommends that dialectics should initiate a dialogue with phenomenology, and in order to illuminate his theme he takes steps in that direction. Phenomenology emerged as a reaction against the scientific-philosophical thought of the late nineteenth century and its atomistic sensationalism. Its founder Edmund Husserl bridged the separation between value and science. Intending, willing and desiring were seen in the late nineteenth century as self-contained and autonomous constellations of meanings. But the basic forms of perception through which scientific knowledge establishes itself are closely related to the act of valuing which is necessary for the preservation of life and its delight in itself. Facts are shaped by values and are tailored for a purpose; and all statements, whether relating to facts or values, are intentional. Phenomenology, therefore, takes the subjective intellect as a fundamental fact. That is why it refuses to acknowledge the paramountcy of reason. Despite, however, Husserl's pretensions towards making phenomenology into an exact science, he continued to believe in the ancient philosophical tradition which took as its aim the clarification and consummation of that innocence in which self-understanding becomes self-evident.

What of hermeneutics? From auto-gnosis or consciousness of one's self which is the basis of philosophy, one proceeds in the Diltheyan manner to hermeneutics or the interpretation of other lives and thence to the interpretation of history. For Heidegger, ontology is only possible as phenomenology, and philosophy which is universal phenomenological ontology begins with the hermeneutics of *Dasein*. Thus, the central problem of hermeneutics brings it close to Pelz's central concerns. Pelz sees this central problem as an attempt to understand a human being and his work in relation to his age, his problems, the controversies in which he is involved and the presuppositions and predispositions which influence his life. A human being is subject to many influences. These influences shape him and his thoughts, he and his thoughts in turn act upon and transform these influences. Since his thoughts do not passively reflect the influences but go beyond them, the individual is in a position to make a contribution of his own. Thus, individuality and social conditioning come together in intricate patterns, and hermeneutics, as Pelz looks at it, endeavours to reach the individual's contribution by a careful consideration of the intricate patterns in which it emerges and in which it is involved.

So far as the concept of *Verstehen* is concerned, Pelz acknowledges his debt to German philosophers and sociologists who, unlike their Anglo-Saxon and French colleagues, have continued to concern themselves with problems relating to it because any attempt at understanding persons is an attempt at self-understanding. An observer of society is a part of that which he observes, and his understanding as well as that of those whom he observes is totally involved in the interrelations between projection and introjection. They interpenetrate each other. In conversing with those whom he observes, the observer, therefore, acquires an understanding of them and of himself. That is why it is not the intellect detached from the intercourse, but the intercourse which constitutes understanding. If one examines the psyche, one sees that rationality is a part of the whole and that it suffuses all of the psyche just as all of the psyche suffuses it. Hence reason 'is the rhythm without which there is no music and which apart from the music is nothing' (Pelz 1974: 35). It is form. It is the individual. It does not claim to know with certainty, but tries time and again to understand. Reason so understood is understanding.

In order to emancipate the social sciences from their thralldom to the natural sciences and their positivist methodology, one must accordingly apply this concept of reason to them. Indeed, the need of the day is to extend the scope of understanding and to draw out its implications more fully, since the encroachments of scientism have considerably eroded the concept. In the light of this fuller concept of

Verstehen, truth would reside 'in scholarly antiphons, in the dance of contradictory and complementary insights and apprehensions' (Pelz 1974: 207). The commitment to truth would mean understanding reality as a Heracleitian flux; for truth dwells in the fluidity of all things. Thus, if it is true that slow changes occur in the psychic structure, understanding can validly view economics, politics and sociology as the epiphenomena of those inner changes. In this way understanding would strive to bring together Hegel and Marx, Lukacs and Freud, Heidegger and Adorno, psychology and sociology, epistemology and economics, philosophy and poetry, the *Geisteswissenschaften* and religion and mysticism. The end to which it should aspire is a growth in sensitivity, sensibility and sensuousness. Understanding is an operation which engenders insights into the motivational flow of individuals which may comprise the most rational and purposeful elements and the most irrational, instinctive or asocial ones. As the Canadian philosopher Bernard Lonergan (1957) puts it, the social sciences aim at gaining and imparting insight into the insights of others. The task of *Verstehen* is, therefore, to perceive the individual in all his totality and complexity within the intricate network of social interdependencies.

What is *Besinnung*? It concerns the meaning or significance of reality. It is a kind of brooding, a permitting of sense to reveal itself. It is contemplation. A basic error of Western civilization is, as Heidegger points out, the quest for certainty; and, as Blaise Pascal said long ago, too much clarity darkens. *Besinnung*, according to Pelz,

> is ready to listen to all kinds of voices, from Einstein to the Hindu Guru, from Freud to Reich, to exoteric and esoteric religions, to advertisements and astrology, and the claims made for extra-sensory perception. Above all, *Besinnung* will listen to the poet and artist, will wish to compare art with life, desire with reality, the ideal with the actual, and all this without prejudice (1974: 100–1).

This is the reason the aim of philosophy, sociology and education should be *Besinnung* and not *Bildung*, contemplation and not formation. It is an 'intellective–emotive compound' consisting of the senses and feelings, of 'seeing-hearing-smelling-tasting-and-feeling.' As such, contemplative thinking stands in sharp contrast to manipulative thinking which it must complement if not subordinate.

Contemplation, thus broadly considered, and art are obviously related. Art penetrates more deeply than science. It brings man face-to-face with his hidden identity, with his actuality and his potentialities. In doing so, a work of art acquires a life of its own, a vitality which speaks for itself. This is because it expresses transcendence-in-immanence. Its significance lies in the fact that it is at one and the same time beyond itself and yet itself. It is ex-stasis. It is life enhancing without losing any of its own life. Accordingly, in expressing his individuality fully, the artist achieves universality.

If sociology is to expand and deepen the scope of its understanding, it must take on the lineaments of art like an inspired documentary film or television programme. What is the secret of the radiant power which such documentaries or programmes possess? Evidently, it is their imaginative, pointed and interested mode of presentation. It is from such a presentation that sociology can learn and so come alive. In other words, just as the success of a work of imagination depends on the extent to which its producer remains faithful to and understands the passions involved in the situation which is sought to be represented, so also the sociologist can unveil the significance of a social complex by doing likewise. This is necessary because reality is extremely complex and of high density—it is so complex and dense that James Joyce, for instance, devoted 400 pages to the dreams of a single man in a single night in one of his works. Therefore, Pelz lauds the writings of the anthropologist Oscar Lewis and of the sociologist Ferdinand Zweig because they have tried to recapture imaginatively, artistically, the nuances and the mind and heart of the situations that they studied. Hence, the scope of understanding in sociology is well illustrated in their works.

Finally, according to Pelz, love and mysticism are transcendental, and because of this they alone can generate a hierarchy of meanings and values. Our reality has been wrenched out of that which cannot be conceived, a metareality which substantiates it. Although he raises what he calls the fascinating question of religion, Pelz, however, does not make an attempt to examine it in width or in depth.

Thus the most seminal ideas in countering the encroachments of positivism and in strengthening the humanistic approach in social sciences have arisen in the German-speaking countries; and from there they have diffused to England and America, influencing the struggle against positivism in those countries. We shall consider some of these efforts here.

In England Anthony Giddens, seeking to break the positivist spell that Durkheim cast on sociology and social anthropology through his

The Rules of Sociological Method (first published in 1895) and other writings, considers the interpretative sociologies sympathetically and constructively in his book *New Rules of Sociological Method* (1979). Giddens abandons the concept of function altogether and maintains that social theory must concentrate on 'action as rationalized conduct ordered reflexively by human agents, and must grasp the significance of language as the practical medium whereby this is made possible' (1979: 8). From the positivist standpoint, Giddens adds, social science is clearly a failure; theories are not merely meaning frames but also constitute moral interventions in social life. As for understanding or *Verstehen*, 'it is the very ontological condition of human life in society as such' (1979: 157). Therefore, the social sciences must move beyond the baleful influence of the natural sciences and turn to existential phenomenology, ordinary language philosophy, the later Wittgenstein and the like, since meaning and action are central to them. Examining the ideas connected with these orientations and with the orientations of a host of other more or less like-minded thinkers such as Heidegger, Mead, Schutz, Gadamer, Winch, Apel, Ricoeur, Habermas, Garfinkel, Cicourel, Popper, Kuhn, Lakatos and Feyerabend, he points out that the influences and interconnections among them are complicated but that Schutz relies on Husserl whom he combines with Weber and is accordingly indirectly related to the tradition of the *Geisteswissenschaften*. Garfinkel in turn was influenced by Schutz and related his ideas to those of Wittgenstein and Austin, and so it goes on.

Giddens' standpoint has been described by Ricoeur as 'a Kantianism without a transcendental subject' (quoted in Giddens 1979: 119) and Giddens agrees with this description. According to him, the nine rules which he formulates in his conclusion are merely 'a skeletal statement of some of the themes of the study as a whole' (1979: 159). They are, however, a clear proof of his anti-positivist orientation and sympathetic assimilation of much in the interpretative sociologies, and also of his cautious Kantianism. He views the primary tasks of sociological analysis as consisting of, first, 'The hermeneutic explication and mediation of divergent forms of life within descriptive meta-languages of social science', and second, 'Explication of the production and reproduction of society as the accomplished outcome of human agency' (1979: 162).

In America the *Methodenstreit* has waxed strong in recent decades, giving rise to the impression that the new humanistic paradigm is gaining strength rapidly. We shall refer to two or three representatives of the emergent orientation.

The first of these is Robert F. Murphy who stresses the dialectics[6] of social life. Reacting against positivism and the over-socialized view of human personality and the over-integration of society in the Parsonian system, Murphy supports the more fluid dialectical approach to them. Dialectical reason is both ancient and ubiquitous and far more broad and loose than the limited Marxist version of it. Although largely ignored in the social sciences till recently, it has continued to make itself felt as a recurrent minor theme in them and is now gaining ground as a result of favourable circumstances. Dialectical thinking is critical of received truth and established fact and is concerned with the alienation of man. It is oriented towards wholeness, continuity and movement and endeavours to surmount the discontinuities, limitations and fixities which a positivistic social science tends to encourage. It is in tune with phenomenology. Epistemologically the subject, as dialectical reason sees it, constitutes the object, since its objectivity arises in the mind. Mind realizes itself in history and society through the resolution of the contradictions which follow from the oppositions between finite entities and their otherness. In the dialectical process will and passion are the motive forces, and ideas the ingredients and results. Thus, that which was not or something new comes into existence. The method of dialectics is embodied in the process of negation, since reality is fluid and things are in a continual state of transition into other forms of themselves. Dialectical reason thus destroys the static reality of commonsense and affirms a time-conditioned reality of relationships and processes, of becoming and transformation. 'What is important to us,' adds Murphy, 'is the mood and spirit of dialectical discourse' (1971: 97).

How does an analyst of society, seeking to apply the dialectical method, go about his task? Without going into a detailed exposition of Murphy's persuasive and book-length attempt at justifying the application of dialectics to sociology and social anthropology, we will quote his response to the above question. He says:

> The dialectical exercise is simple in the extreme, for it requires only that the analyst of society question everything that he sees and hears, examine phenomena fully and from every angle, seek and evaluate the contradiction of any proposition, and consider every

---

[6] Recently Topitsch (1982) has directed a critique against dialectical reason. The critique, however, seems one-sided and polemical.

category from the viewpoint of its noncontents as well as its positive attributes. It requires us to look also for paradox as much as complementarity, for opposition as much as accommodation. It portrays a universe of dissonance underlying apparent order and seeks deeper orders beyond the dissonance. It urges the critical examination, in the light of ongoing social activity, of those common-sense guidelines to behaviour and common-sense interpretations of reality that lie at the core of our cultural systems. It enjoins us to query the obvious and given truths of both our culture and our science. The result of all this may fall short of revelation and the discovery of general social laws, but it will at least impel us to ask new and fresh questions. And the measure of a science lies as much in the questions it asks as in the answers it obtains (1971: 117).

Dilating on a poetic for sociology, Richard H. Brown (1977) attempts to discover concepts by which interpretative procedures will become more rigorous as a method of knowledge and thus subsume the epistemology of positive sociology under them. He calls his attempt cognitive aesthetics or a critical poetic and bases it, among other things, on phenomenology, hermeneutics, dialectics and, above all, symbolic realism. As he sees it, science, art and human studies depend on metaphoric thinking, both analogic and iconic, as their logic of discovery. Hence, it is perceivable that aesthetic criteria such as economy, originality, perspicacity, concinnity, elegance, cogency and form apply to all three of them. If this is indeed so, then cognitive aesthetics offers us knowledge of ourselves and society which is simultaneously objective and subjective and both scientifically valid and significantly humane.

A fundamental postulate of such an outlook is that all symbolic systems are equally real and that rationality is to be understood aesthetically. Accordingly, works of art also offer a kind of knowledge, even as scientific theories call for aesthetic adequacy. Therefore, sociology as a symbolic form has the attributes of both a natural science and a fine art. If all ways of knowing, as modern philosophy tends to suggest, are both symbolic and perspectival, both science and art generate their own realms of application. But in a successful scientific theory or a work of art the internal and external dimensions are elements of a single structural system. In other words, there is no basic difference in the manner in which science and art allow us to articulate the world. Thus, symbolic realism goes beyond scientific realism and romantic idealism. Indeed, symbolic realism views the debate between the positivists and the romanticists as sterile, since an adequate social theory must be meaningful in both objective and subjective terms. That is to say, an adequate social theory must provide an understanding of the consciousness of persons as well as an explanation of social forces beyond their immediate control.

A dialectical, symbolic, realist theory of knowledge, therefore, seeks generalized explanations of the natural as well as the human world, together with subjectivity but without a materialist bias. In such an orientation all knowledge is symbolic construction, and symbolization, irrespective of its particular mode of expression, must be valued in accordance with how far it enhances our perception and understanding. Existential reality speaks to us through innumerable symbolic forms, thus requiring frequent interpretation or transcoding from one to the other. As Brown says:

> There is perhaps something unsettling in this notion that not only theories within a scientific discipline, but the very subject matter of these disciplines, and indeed the disciplines themselves, are 'merely' symbolic constructs. Yet a cognitive aesthetic—a dialectical hermeneutic that recaptures the fuller meaning of a thesis by transcoding it and thereby transcending its partiality—may be an appropriate way of knowledge in a world where we have abandoned fixed objective realities. To transcode the vocabularies of Being is to recognize that all of our world is objectification—at once an expression and alienation of reality. To accept the necessity of such disguises, of such a 'tragedy of culture' is not to make oneself at home in our world. But it is a step toward building a science through which we can understand it (1978: 48).

Having presented the fundamentals of his position, Brown proceeds to demonstrate the usefulness of a poetic for sociology through a discussion of point of view, metaphor and irony in sociological theory. If social order is a construction, cognitive aesthetics, as Brown and Lyman affirm in the introduction to *Structure, Consciousness and History*, 'invites us to actively reconstruct our worlds' (1978: 9).

However, to be able to actively reconstruct our worlds we should first understand them or, at any rate, both understanding and reconstructing should proceed together or should reinforce each other. But how is understanding to be achieved? Some general responses to this question have already been indicated earlier. A somewhat more specific inventory of tools is offered by Roger Poole in the following words:

> Personal commitment, ethical concern, desire to treat of the totality, necessity of taking account of the reality of perspectival variation and distortion, necessity of taking account of variations in operative criteria, the use of strange and unquantifiable collocations of evidence or information (such as sheaves and profiles), comparison, inter-relation, description, as well as sympathy, empathy and antipathy (1972: 125).

Poole himself thinks that these tools are 'a strange lot', but believes nevertheless that they can deal with complex problems effectively than more objective ones.

A more detailed demonstration of methods in qualitative sociology has been offered by American sociologists Howard Schwartz and Jerry Jacobs (1979) despite the fact that qualitative sociologists try to avoid standardization of methods since research is an art form, since, therefore, it necessitates a large variety of different tools, and since the researcher, considering the nature of his task, is impelled to improvise concepts and methods in order to deal effectively with a novel situation. In reconstructing the reality of a social scene researchers, for instance, have played the role of participant observers, have conducted interviews, have studied personal accounts and have recorded life histories. The object of the research is to gain access to the insider's view of the reality in which he is involved. For some qualitative sociologists, this access is the end which they pursue; but for others it is the basis for more technical dimensions of the qualitative approach. The question, however, arises: Since there is no science of subjectivity, what is the status of the qualitative sociologist's endeavours? Trying to be objective about the subjective, Schwartz and Jacobs (1979) point out that many sociologists like to apply the term science to their activities in order to legitimize them, but this application has rendered the term problematic. For, the qualitative sociologist aims at grasping that which by its very nature is not amenable to science, and if he attempts to render it so amenable it ceases to be what it is. It is precisely for this reason that *Verstehen* lays stress on indwelling, intuition, empathic identification; and is not intuition the core of all successful scientific theorizing? In their book Schwartz and Jacobs have stated the case for qualitative sociology fairly; and they have fortified their descriptions of methods by adding relevant case studies. More than this cannot be demanded from them—certainly not an open sesame or Alladin's lamp.

It is important to recall at this juncture that if Europe and America have not been swept into limbo by the strong surface currents of unidimensional ideologies and thought systems, it is because the concept of the person in which their societies and the psyches of their peoples have been steeped for centuries has exercised a steadying undertow. It is, therefore, pertinent to note that in the realm of sociology Anthony Giddens affirms the person or acting self as the proper unit of reference for an analysis of action and accordingly distinguishes between agent causality and event causality.

Man as a person has his own ontological reality and is not identical with the Ultimate Being although oriented in that direction. He is the centre of movement, intention and agency and the source of all knowing and affirming. He is, therefore, not a stagnant entity, but is to be understood, as the British philosopher P. F. Strawson (1967) puts it, 'as that which relates to,' or, in other words, man as a person is not a closed being but is open to all of being. He is capable of ecstasy and communion, that is, of moving beyond the narrow confines of his petty ego and of intimately integrating himself to the totality in a paradoxical movement which is a merging and not a submerging one. This paradoxical movement arises from the very nature of personhood which is of necessity 'a relating to' by reason of its finitude, but not 'a dissolving in' by reason of its uniqueness and non-repeatability. Further, man as a finite person is driven by an insatiable urge towards self-transcendence—upwards, downwards or in a horizontal direction. But the main danger which emerges from this insatiable nisus is the danger of unidimensionality. Because man as a person is the centre of intentional action, he is genuinely creative; and the ontological basis of creativity is a contemplative-active bringing forth, out of nothing, through the agency of one's personhood.

In the current revulsion against positivism and the dehumanization and automatization of man, it is therefore noteworthy that the new appreciation of the unique value of the human being has begun to play a fundamental role once again in the present-day culture of the West. As Joseph L. Roche says: 'In almost every field of activity, but especially in the fine arts, literature, philosophy and current theology, there is constant reference to the person as the ultimate source and end of all meaningful activity' (1970: 103–4). In India also at this moment of its contemporary history, an injection of a similar person-alist philosophy into the bloodstream of its hoary ideological orien-tation would no doubt act remedially against the action neutralizing metaphysical impersonality and fatalism which have pervaded the life of the mind of the people. It would no doubt also help in unleashing creativity in the social sciences.

The propositions which we have been trying to justify in this essay can now be summarized as follows:

1. As the state of the sciences in India is far from a healthy and flourishing one, what is needed to rid ourselves of this sterility is a methodological reversal from a literal dependence on the positive methods and a positivistic version of science.[7] This reversal should and can be brought about by force of self-assertion.[8]
2. The justification for such a reversal arises from the nature of our philosophic-social heritage and the cultural conditioning which follows from it.
3. The methodological reversal should also seek to actualize itself in terms of similar orientations in the German-speaking countries and elsewhere in the West. This is necessary to curb and control the vices of our virtues.
4. Such curbing and controlling can best be done through the assimilation of a personalist philosophy which has acted as a ballast or steadying and balancing force in the West.
5. When one considers the interpretative or qualitative orientations in the German-speaking countries and elsewhere in the West, one finds that they are basically oriented towards an under-standing of totalities through a unified or aesthetic awareness. (This is also the basic orientation in India, as Richard Lannoy and many others[9] have elaborated upon.)

[7] Uberoi (1978: 56) says: 'The philosophy of the future that would overthrow the positivist regime as a whole will have to open an alternative road to science as well as politics. Perhaps it will be a religious philosophy of unity in variety.'

[8] I am inclined to believe that methodological oscillations have their main roots in a subjective dialectic of the self as finite and the self as self-sufficient. Therefore, meth-odological reversals by force of self-assertion are not impossible. For an elaboration of this point see 'Introduction' in Ferreira and Momin (1986).

[9] See, among other books and papers, Ferreira (1979).

6. The interpretative or qualitative orientations tend to be of two types. Reacting strongly against positivism, the first type tends to swing towards the other extreme of deep subjectivity and sees all of reality through subjective spectacles. The second type takes an intermediate position, conceding an equal or subordinate role to scientific or objective reality.

7. For dialectical reasons India's interests, both in the social sciences and the general life of the country, would be best served in terms of a phased movement of methodological reversal. The first phase will involve a movement towards an extreme subjectivist standpoint. The second phase, basing itself on the concept of the person, will adopt an intermediate position.

The net result of such a phased methodological reversal, let us add by way of conclusion, is very likely the eventuation of a heightened creativity in the social sciences. From there it will probably diffuse or percolate into other walks of life in India. Creativity, stemming as it does from the centre of a person's intentional life, has, as is well known, a multiplier effect of incalculable proportions. It is to the emancipation of such a heightened creativity in this country that this essay is dedicated.

REFERENCES

ARON, RAYMOND. 1957. *German Sociology*. London: Heinemann.

BHARATI, AGEHANANDA. 1982. 'Hindu Scholars, Germany, and the Third Reich', *Update*, 6, 3: 44–52.

BIDDISS, MICHAEL D. 1977. *The Age of the Masses: Ideas and Society in Europe since 1870*. Harmondsworth: Penguin.

BROWN, RICHARD H. 1977. *A Poetic for Sociology: Toward a Logic of Discovery for the Human Sciences*. Cambridge: Cambridge University Press.

BROWN, RICHARD H. and LYMAN, STANFORD M. (Eds.). 1978. *Structure, Consciousness, and History*. Cambridge: Cambridge University Press.

BUBER, MARTIN. 1949. *Paths in Utopia*. Boston: Beacon Press.

DASGUPTA, SURENDRANATH. 1975. *A History of Indian Philosophy*, Vol. I. Delhi: Motilal Banarsidass.

DURKHEIM, EMILE. 1938. *The Rules of Sociological Method*. Glencoe, Illinois: Free Press.

FERREIRA, J.V. 1979. 'The Anthropology of Unified Awareness', *Tribal Research Bulletin*, 1, 1: 1–4.

FERREIRA, J.V. and MOMIN, A.R. (Eds.). 1986. *Nemesis: Critical Perspectives on Modernization*. Bombay: Ramrakhiani.

GIDDENS, ANTHONY. 1979. *New Rules of Sociological Method: A Positive Critique of Interpretative Sociologies*. London: Hutchinson.

LANNOY, RICHARD. 1971. *The Speaking Tree: A Study of Indian Culture and Society.*
London: Oxford University Press.

LONERGAN, BERNARD J.F. 1957. *Insight: A Study of Human Understanding.* London:
Longmans, Green.

MARITAIN, JACQUES. 1937. *The Degrees of Knowledge.* London: Geoffrey Bles.

MASUR, GERHARD. 1961. *Prophets of Yesterday: Studies in European Culture.* New York:
Harper and Row.

MURPHY, ROBERT F. 1971. *The Dialectics of Social Life: Alarms and Excursions in
Anthropological Theory.* London: Allen and Unwin.

PELZ, WERNER. 1974. *The Scope of Understanding in Sociology: Towards a More Radical
Re-Orientation in the Social and Humanistic Sciences.* London: Routledge and
Kegan Paul.

POOLE, ROGER. 1972. *Towards Deep Subjectivity.* London: Allen Lane.

RAMASUBBAN, RADHIKA. 1977. 'Science and Society: A Sociological Analysis of Science
and Technology in India'. Unpublished doctoral dissertation, University of Bombay.

ROCHE, JOSEPH L. 1970. 'The Human Person in Contemporary Philosophy', *Philippine
Studies*, 18, 1: 103–46.

SCHWARTZ, HOWARD and JACOBS, JERRY. 1979. *Qualitative Sociology: A Method to the
Madness.* New York: The Free Press.

SRINIVAS, M.N. 1976. *The Remembered Village.* Delhi: Oxford University Press.

STRAWSON, P.F. 1967. *Philosophical Logic.* London: Oxford University Press.

STUART HUGHES, H. 1967. *Consciousness and Society: Re-Orientation of European
Social Thought.* London: McGibbon and Kee.

TOPITSCH, ERNST. 1982. 'How Enlightened is "Dialectical Reason"?', *Encounter*, VLIII,
5: 45–55.

TOURNIER, PAUL. 1957. *The Meaning of Persons.* New York: Harper and Row.

UBEROI, J.P.S. 1978. *Science and Culture.* Delhi: Oxford University Press.

5

THE REMEMBERED VILLAGE: INSIGHTS INTO AN AGRARIAN CIVILIZATION[1]

P. C. JOSHI

INTRODUCTION

The issue of understanding India's traditional social institutions and values as part of understanding the specifics of Indian civilization had acquired an urgency in the context of India's transition to a colonial society, economy and polity. The rediscovery of India by the Indian intelligentsia meant essentially the understanding of the nature of Indian social institutions and values and the changes introduced therein by the impact of British colonialism. It is in this historical

---

[1] This is a revised version of my article, '*The Remembered Village*: A Bridge Between Old and New Anthropology', in 'A Review Symposium on M. N. Srinivas' *The Remembered Village*', *Contributions to Indian Sociology*, n.s., 12, 1, January–June 1978: 75–89.

context that Indian sociology emerged as an academic discipline by taking up in right earnest the enquiry into religion, family, caste and village as the basic institutions of traditional Indian society. If in the early phase of Indian sociological studies the enquiry into the Indian social structure was dominated by a reliance on Indian religious scriptures as the basic source of information on Indian society, in the more mature phase of Indian sociology such studies were pursued by a reliance on fact-finding and intensive fieldwork at the grass-roots of Indian social life.

M. N. Srinivas' name is associated with the transition of Indian sociology from the first to the second phase—from reconstruction of the 'book-view' of Indian society to reconstruction of the 'field-view' of Indian social institutions, especially, religion, caste and village. Very few scholars are as gifted as Srinivas to be able to communicate their basic sociological insights and findings in a manner that is comprehensible to the wider intelligentsia than merely to a small minority of academic specialists.

Among Srinivas' writings, *The Remembered Village* (1976)[2] has as much the rigour of a sociological study as the charm of a novel which is appreciated both by specialists and non-specialists alike. It helps to bring the urban educated intellectual closer to an understanding of the social realities and processes of rural India. Even though *TRV* has its roots in a specific social milieu of a region in South India, it captures certain basic aspects of an Indian village so as to make it relevant for an understanding of rural India as a whole. Above all, it stimulates scholars in other regions to contribute similar studies covering different parts of the Indian subcontinent.

HUMAN ELEMENT IN COMMUNITY STUDIES

The erosion of 'the human element'[3] in social sciences poses a grave threat to the developing countries, for here the need for responding to the challenge of social and economic transition, and reducing its human cost, makes great demands on them. A dehumanized social science is least suited to play this role. In this context, the work of

---

[2] Citations from the *The Remembered Village* (hereafter *TRV*) are identified by page numbers only, without the usual identification of the source by the year of its publication.

[3] 'What is it that seems to dictate the appearance of history? It is the appearance of the human element' (Bloch 1954: 25).

social anthropologists becomes significant because they accord far greater value to first-hand knowledge of people and their institutions than do economists.

Among Indian social anthropologists, Srinivas has expressed great concern at the emergence of a 'completely instrumentalist view of social science which seems to be axiomatic among economists if not social scientists in India' (1975: 1389). He has contributed a number of studies of India which are the outcome of his fieldwork among people in rural areas and which therefore have the human element in abundant measure. *TRV*, describing his work on the village of Rampura, is an intensely human document. The earlier works on Rampura had the freshness of a first impact of fieldwork. This work is marked by maturity born of prolonged reflection over facts observed 35 years ago.

The outstanding quality of *TRV* is its success in combining professional competence with communicability so that it appeals to both specialists as well as non-specialists. It arouses in the reader a deep interest in rural people. By the time one has finished reading the book one gets so deeply engrossed in the human characters and affairs of Rampura that one feels as if one had personally lived in the village and known its people directly.

It is hoped that works such as *TRV* will exercise a humanizing influence on urban politicians, planners and administrators who are often ignorant about rural communities but play such an important role in the decisions affecting them. It is not the villager alone who needs to be re-educated. The urban planner, the policy maker and the scholar also need to be re-educated through close interaction with the people. From this point of view *TRV* also illustrates the growth of Srinivas as a social scientist. He began by applying his moral and intellectual resources derived from his brahmanical culture and Western education to the field study of a village. But contact with rural people helped him to shake off many, though not all, pre-conceived ideas and prejudices about them that he had acquired as a brahmin and as a Westernized, urban intellectual.

VIEW FROM THE TOP AND
VIEW FROM THE BOTTOM

The fieldwork experience in Rampura gave Srinivas an insight into the rural–urban hiatus and the distortions caused by it in policy-making and its implementation. He has noted how the urban elite create a make-believe world of their own about rural people and how a wide gulf exists between the view from the top and the reality below. In the past the elite often functioned under the belief that 'the rural masses are ignorant, tradition-bound and resistant to economic progress', and 'people are like dough in the hands of planners and the government', and that 'the government is able to change the lives of citizens in any manner it wants to' (Srinivas 1975: 1389).

What distinguishes Srinivas' approach from that of a conventional economist or planner is his emphasis on understanding people and their behaviour. He has emphasized that

> it would be more fruitful and interesting to look at the development programmes as responses of human beings with certain resources, values and aims to the policies and programmes of a powerful government acting through its officials who not only wish to achieve certain targets but have a culture of their own...(1975: 1390).

Further, 'over the millenia they [the people] have evolved an outlook and strategies which have enabled them to survive a variety of predators such as tax collectors, landowners, village headmen, accountants, moneylenders, marauders and the like' (1975: 1389).

According to Srinivas, 'the annoyance of the elite with the peasant for not making choices which they want him to make ignores the fact that choices are linked to structural, economic and cultural factors' (1975: 1389).

Further,

> change is much more serious and pervasive in small and stable societies where the same people are involved with each other in a number of relationships, than in huge, industrial societies where the different aspects of social life do not form as closely knit a whole and where relationships between individuals are specialized and disparate (Srinivas 1962: 127).

Attempts at changing only one element in the total system may have repercussions for the entire system quite contrary to the intentions of the rural elite.[4] It should be clarified that nowhere does Srinivas

---

[4] For an analysis of land policy and its unintended consequences, see Joshi (1975).

categorically adopt the position of opposing the 'concept of sponsored rural change' or 'rural planning'. What he seems to be questioning is the concept of planning and intervention from above without a grasp of the problems and processes at the village level.

This question of intervention of exogenous forces in the village society raises a number of questions relating to the basic premises and assumptions of social anthropology in the past. It should be pointed out that social anthropology, perhaps because of its emergence under colonialism, has primarily been concerned with the cost of change for the tribal and peasant communities exposed to colonialism or modern industrialization. It has been far less concerned with the cost of stagnation or status quo for these communities. Social anthropology, therefore, had a 'minimum intervention' bias in relation to these communities. It included an implicit, if not an explicit, assumption that what exists is rational and any drastic interference in it is a departure from rationality. It had, therefore, not attempted to identify social institutions which had become obsolete and had become impediments to social and economic change.

Moreover, the basic tools of social anthropology were originally evolved in the context of pre-market primitive societies untouched by the forces of modern civilization. With increasing exposure of the primitive and peasant societies to these forces and with their increasing integration into a wider social framework, a great tension was created between the old concepts and tools on the one hand and the changing structure of these communities on the other. A break from the inherited premises and assumptions of social anthropology was therefore necessary, if it was to serve as a tool of understanding the problems of primitive and peasant communities in the context of the emergence of the nation-state following the end of colonial rule and the programmes of economic development and social change sponsored by the nation-state.

Srinivas' contribution lies not only in presenting new insights into the changing village in *TRV* but also in his effort to reorient the anthropological perspective to the new phase beginning with the end of colonial rule. More accurately, his work assumes significance if it is understood as a bridge between the old anthropology which originated under colonialism and the new anthropology which began to emerge following the collapse of the colonial regime. Before discussing the insights into the village offered by Srinivas in his works, it is useful to present the basic elements of the new anthropological perspective which he evolved during his long career as a social anthropologist.

THE ANTHROPOLOGICAL PERSPECTIVE

Srinivas regards the study of village communities on the basis of participant observation as the basic contribution of a social anthropologist, which distinguishes him from other social scientists. In Srinivas' opinion the fruitfulness of such a study lies in highlighting the great hiatus between the 'book-view' of Indian society as derived from ancient texts and the 'field-view' as derived from direct observation. The field-view provides 'an antidote to the "book-view"' (1962: 140). The conception of this dichotomy used by him for an understanding of the caste system could be successfully employed for an understanding of other important institutions, e.g., the agrarian social structure. Moreover, the 'book-view' may be interpreted more broadly as including the view of society embodied not only in the scriptural texts but also in all *a priori*, logical models of society developed by social scientists. More specifically, I would like to draw attention to the contrast between a 'harmonic' view of society on the one hand and the 'disharmonic' field-view on the other. This is a promising area of enquiry and a beginning towards this has been made by Srinivas himself in *TRV*.

Srinivas attaches great importance to the study of a small community in so far as it brings out, as nothing else does, the importance of viewing 'particular phenomena in their social and cultural context to ascertain properly their meaning' (1975: 1392). This is in marked contrast to the strategy of treating social facts 'as though they are pebbles which can be lifted from a heap', which is characteristic of macro surveys. This is a significant methodological point. On this basis the economist who studies the rural economy in isolation from caste or religion is as much open to criticism as a social anthropologist who studies caste without reference to its political or economic basis. Srinivas' earlier work was not free from such criticism, with its neglect of the economic basis of caste. But *TRV* provides a refreshing break by throwing more light on caste and the economy.

It should be stressed here that the idea of the holistic study of a small community to which Srinivas attaches great importance does not so far mark any significant break with social anthropology as practised in the colonial era. New elements are introduced by Srinivas

(1962: 134) when he asserts that 'the villages are invaluable observation centres where he [the social anthropologist] can study in detail social processes and problems, occurring in many parts of India, if not in a great part of the world'. It is clear that here Srinivas broadens the scope of social anthropology by including in it not only the stable primitive communities but also the changing rural communities.

The new perspective finds a clear expression in an essay (1966: 147–63) in which Srinivas grapples with 'methodological issues which stem out of the study of one's society, particularly when that society is undergoing rapid transformation' (1966: 147). In the post-colonial context he clearly emphasizes the dual commitment of a social anthropologist—to scientific study on the one hand and to development on the other (1966: 163). Today, the concerns of an anthropologist are very different from those of an anthropologist of the colonial era, who was an ethnographer of societies and cultures disintegrating under the impact of colonialism. The anthropologist is now expected to study his own society which is making a break from the colonial past and embarking on a new future shaped by the efforts and strivings of its people. He is, therefore, 'forced to develop a positive attitude towards social change' (1966: 161). Srinivas adds: 'The study of one's own society while it is changing rapidly…poses challenge that calls for the mobilization of all the moral and intellectual resources of the sociologist' (1966: 159).

This redefinition of the scope of social anthropology has another important consequence. It has drawn sociology and social anthropology together. The study of post-colonial rural India necessitated a greater interaction between the sociologist dealing with the larger society and the social anthropologist dealing with small rural communities. In fact, as in the case of Srinivas himself, the social anthropologist had to be his own sociologist. If *Social Change in Modern India* (1966) is Srinivas' important work at the macro level, *TRV* is his major work at the micro level. This micro level enquiry provides insights which could be explored further at the macro level. The latter raises questions which give direction and focus to the former. Generalizing from his own experience, Srinivas (1966: 2) observes: 'Micro-studies provide insights while macro-studies yield perspectives, and movement from one to the other is essential.' Srinivas has been able to use his fieldwork experience much more creatively than many other anthropologists because of the cross-fertilization of micro insights and macro perspectives. The creative potential of many other anthropologists has remained untapped as a result of their over-reliance on fieldwork itself and their inability to draw upon macro theory. It must, however, be pointed out that Srinivas himself has not explored the full potential of blending macro theory and micro observation. In his work he has not drawn fully upon macro level general concepts (such as class, colonialism, feudalism, capitalism and market economy) and upon historical and politico-economic approaches to the understanding of Indian society.

Perhaps the most significant theoretical advance made by Srinivas is his positive attitude to social conflict. He assigns a central role to the study of conflict when he says that 'conflict as such is an inescapable part of social existence, and should be of serious concern to the sociologist' (1966: 160). What is still more important is his distinction 'between forms of conflict that can be resolved by existing institutional mechanisms, and more fundamental conflicts that threaten the social order' (1966). All this marks a departure from the 'integrationist' model of society. This shift in Srinivas' approach has led him to assign an important place to conflict in *TRV*. But in so far as this recognition of the role of conflict is more an intuitive than a theoretical advance, the full promise of the analysis of conflict is yet to be realized.

We have tried to indicate briefly how Srinivas' anthropological perspective has broadened from the time that he did his fieldwork in Rampura in 1948 and 1952. What distinguishes a good social scientist from a mediocre one is that the former is all the time critically evaluating his own work: he is his own best critic. The same applies to Srinivas who has given ample indication of the change in his orientation between the time he did his fieldwork and when he wrote *TRV*. He writes that when he was doing fieldwork he concentrated on reconstructing the traditional social structure and this made him less sensitive to the factors making for change (p. 247). Further, since he lived in a high caste area and his friends and companions were all peasants and Lingayats, his was 'a high caste view of village society' lacking an intimate view of the Harijans and the Muslims (pp. 197–98).

It is obvious that at the time when Srinivas did his fieldwork in Rampura he was oriented primarily towards exploring and emphasizing the stability of the traditional social system as expressed in the interdependence of groups and the unity and solidarity of the village. But in *TRV* he has tried to identify elements of change at the economic, social, technological and ideological levels, and has shown much greater awareness of the conflicts growing within the social system. This shift in outlook between the two points of time is borne out by the contrast between 'The Social System of a Mysore Village' (1955a: 1–36) and *TRV*. It is extremely important to note that Srinivas' view of the same social reality undergoes a marked change during this period resulting in a reorganization and reinterpretation of his data.

It appears to me that in Srinivas' case the reorientation of perspective—from an over-emphasis on continuity and integration to a recognition of processes of change and conflict—has come about not through the theoretical but through the empirical and intuitive route. The strengths and weaknesses of advance through the empirical route will be discussed later. First, an attempt will be made to highlight the progress achieved in the understanding of social reality between the two points of time.

RAMPURA REDISCOVERED

If one keeps in mind the view of Rampura as presented in Srinivas' essay (1955a), one feels that *TRV* could appropriately be called 'Rampura Rediscovered' because of its sharper focus not only on the traditional system, as in the earlier paper, but also on the processes of change. It shows how the system is in a flux due to the powerful attack on its very foundations by new forces from both outside and inside the village. This contrast between the old and the new may be understood in terms of the following five themes.

RAMPURA AN ISOLATE OR A PART OF THE WIDER SOCIETY

The 1955 view of Rampura (see Srinivas 1955a; 1955b) does not throw much light on its links with the larger society. The village is treated almost as an isolate, as if undisturbed except occasionally by outside forces. *TRV* by contrast introduces the perspective of rural–urban integration. It introduces a new element in the analysis—the gradual loss of rural distinctiveness and the rapid urbanization of the village. Srinivas dramatizes this change by his pithy observation: 'It looks as though the day was not far off when Rampura would be a dormitory of Mysore' (p. 233).

What are the forces propelling Rampura in the direction of modernity? The shift from bullock-cart to bus and motorcycle as means of transport (pp. 236–37); the introduction of electric power (p. 238); the education of village youth in schools and colleges and the rise of a rural middle class (p. 232); the break from traditional agriculture; the greater circulation of money (p. 240) and the increasing cash nexus; the plunge into the world of commerce and industry by village entrepreneurs resulting in new asset preferences (p. 105); the demands for new technical and organizational skills (p. 237); the increasing penetration in the village of urban officials and the rise of village politicians; the increasing impact of market forces making the fortunes of village people dependent not only on 'gods and the government' (p. 212) but also on outside economic forces, such as through price changes (p. 240); the bulldozer and the tractor symbolizing the miracle working powers of modern technology (p. 238); the declining influence of traditional customs and practices as in regard to age at marriage (p. 316); changes in the religious world-view (p. 320)—all these and many more factors were impinging on the village and pulling it in a new direction. The most significant indication of the fact that the pull of the village was rapidly yielding to the pull of the town was that

> the richer youth did not want to look after ancestral farms but enter the new and challenging world of trade, commerce and industry. The more educated youth dreamed to becoming members of the state legislatures, and, in fact, even ministers in the Cabinet. They had come a long way from the world of their fathers and grandfathers (p. 237).

In short, Rampura was acquiring the way of life and the look of an urbanized village; it was moving in the direction of becoming an extension of the town.

It goes to the credit of Srinivas that, instead of trying to reconstruct the picture of a traditional social structure as he did earlier, he moved forward towards perceiving and recording the elements and processes of change. But to present social facts pointing towards change is one thing; it is quite another thing to assess the extent of change and to interpret its full significance. What is happening to the village as a distinct form of social and economic organization? What are the scope and limits of social anthropology in understanding these processes of change and the emerging patterns of social and economic organization which pose a threat to the very structure of the Indian village? Though

TRV raises such basic questions Srinivas has not pursued them at a theoretical level in his writings.

CHANGING ECONOMY

An understanding of the changing economy is basic insofar as the village was distinguished by a certain type of economy which has been undergoing rapid change. The dominance of monsoon-fed agriculture, based on bullock power and on traditional techniques of cultivation; the pursuit of agriculture as a way of life rather than as a commercial activity; relations between landowners on the one hand and artisans and labouring groups on the other, based on custom rather than contract; investment of economic surplus from cultivation in purchase of land, moneylending, jewellery and conspicuous consumption by the rural rich; perennial scarcity of goods over-shadowing rural life—this was the typical land-based rural economy since ancient times. Srinivas has presented evidence to show how this picture is already a thing of the past in Rampura. He shows how traditional activities like agriculture are pursued in a new way by an increasing number of people. The building of the dam which 'constituted a landmark in the development of agriculture' has made agriculture 'more predictable' (p. 121). This led to a chain reaction by creating the scope for converting agriculture itself into a commercial venture. The change from the aristocratic ways of the headman's father to the acquisitive and dynamic spirit of the headman is part of this chain reaction. The introduction of the tractor, the bulldozer, the rice mill, the huller, electricity, etc. are also part of the same process. New techniques and forms of economic activity compelled a restructuring of social relations as well as the introduction of cash nexus, economic bargaining, and conflict over share of increasing agricultural produce.

Moreover, new economic opportunities in commerce and industry eroded the traditional dominance of agriculture. It is noteworthy that

> those who were moving into new enterprise were really inhabiting two economic and social universes. Thus a landowner obliged a candidate standing for elective office, or a bureaucrat, and obtained in return a permit to start a bus service or rice mill. Such men were shrewd, acquisitive and competitive (p. 130).

Instead of the traditional urge to buy 'more and more land' (p. 233) the rural rich sought new avenues which linked them with the town economy. The rural rich thus ceased to be merely rural. A new class of the rich was emerging which enjoyed both the rural and the urban worlds. Another important aspect was that the 'new opportunities' which enhanced 'the power and resources of the wealthy made possible the more effective exploitation of the poor' (p. 255).

This trend of economic transformation made it increasingly difficult to view the rural economy in terms of old concepts, as a land- and caste-based economy. Srinivas' basic observation that 'if the Rampura villager's relation with the external environment was mediated through agriculture his relation with other human beings was mediated through caste' (p. 164) cannot be sustained by the changes highlighted by him. The new economic processes also weaken the explanatory power of the concept of 'dominant caste' which Srinivas had offered in his 1955 view of Rampura.

DOMINANT CASTE VS NEW CLASS

With the village ceasing to be an isolate and with the connexion between caste and landownership being weakened, it may not be unreasonable to expect the dominance of caste being increasingly substituted by the dominance of a new class. Since the process of upward mobility is facilitated by new opportunities than by old privileges and connexions, the rise of this new class may be based on recruitment from many castes. It may, therefore, be associated with the weakening of the dominant caste. So long as the pace of change was slow, the village existed in isolation, and upward mobility was an exception rather than the rule, the new elements were keen to legitimize their position within the caste order. However, with the pace of change accelerating, the village and the town getting reintegrated, new opportunities, apart from broadening the scope of upward mobility, also enlarged the scope of economic disparity between members of the dominant caste. The new rich in this context, belonging both to the rural and the urban worlds, emerged as a new class, thus losing the attributes of a dominant caste. Even as a mode of their self-identification or of identification by other members of the village, the dominant caste could no longer serve as a meaningful concept.

Srinivas, as a keen observer of the village, takes note of the emergence of the new class from 'the richer, influential and better-informed households' (p. 255). He also notes the tension between the bigger and the smaller landowners (pp. 230–31), the increasing matrimonial alliances among the rich cementing their cohesion as well as serving their business interests (pp. 99, 231), the conflicts among the rich as indicated by 'the rice mill episode', and the conflicts between the rich and the poor as indicated by the 'incident of the transformation of the bull into the bullock' (p. 255), etc.

Srinivas, however, does not raise the question whether these new pressures and challenges could be accommodated within the framework of the dominant caste. His observation 'that the entrepreneurs gave jobs to their kinfolks, caste folks and fellow villagers and this had the effect of drawing more people to them' gives the impression that these reinforce rather than erode caste dominance. But it is pertinent to ask whether both as a result of changes in the external environment and in the minds of people the concept of 'dominant caste' has not lost much of its relevance. The same questions can be asked concerning the 'patron–client' relationship as the traditional mechanism of reducing the rich–poor cleavage.

HARMONY *VS* CONFLICT

In *TRV* Srinivas reveals an awareness of forces which make for conflict rather than for harmony. There is first the phenomenon of rural–urban conflict. Srinivas uses the term 'villagers' quite often, implying certain interests which the entire village has in common. In a remarkable passage he sums up the rural–urban contrast:

> Misfortunes were only too frequent in village India. The villager's pitiful resources, economic and intellectual, and his continuous struggle with the forces, natural and human, ranged against him, made him a frequent victim of disaster. The lack of any medical attention coupled with the total ignorance of the rules of sanitation made child-birth hazardous and the frequent epidemics which carried off large numbers of people gave a chancy character to life. If to this were added undependable rains and insects and other pests, and vermin, extortionate landowners, usurious moneylenders and corrupt officials, we get an idea of the risks faced by farmers in growing a crop and the demands he had to meet. It was indeed a miracle that he managed to survive (p. 291).

One of the gaps in Srinivas' account, however, is that he does not explicitly mention the emergence of a dual society within the village itself—the co-existence of an urbanized and prosperous world of the rich and the non-urbanized and backward world of the poor. In the world of the rich the rural–urban contrast was getting reduced while in the world of the poor this contrast was still sharp.

Srinivas shows how the conflict between the rich and the poor arises from three sources: (a) the inconsistency between the changing world-view of the poor and the innate conservatism and class prejudice of the rich (pp. 95, 197); (b) the effort at economic planning within the highly stratified society in which the people lived (p. 255); and (c) the new ways of exploiting the poor created by new economic and political opportunities. He makes an interesting point that the new educated class in the village was a champion of equality in relation to castes above them and a defender of inequality in relation to Harijans below them (p. 196).

The new rebelliousness of the Harijan youth is articulated by Pijja 'who represented the winds of change that were blowing in the wider society': who was not only in conflict with the power elite of the village but also with the 'conservative elders of his own caste' for being afraid of 'the power wielded by landowners' (p. 203). Old and degrading practices like 'beating the tom-tom on festive occasions, removing the leaves on which higher castes had dined at collective occasions and removing the carcasses of domestic animals from their houses' came into sharp conflict with the Harijans' newly aroused sense of dignity and self-respect as human beings. Srinivas' observation that the Harijans were 'caught between the forces of oppression and liberation, the former firmly in the saddle while the latter was then only a hope' (p. 201) sums up very aptly the explosive social situation of the village.

The several instances of clash of interest between the rich and the poor are very telling. The most basic cleavage was between the interests of the landed class and those of the tenants and the landless. The process of development was increasingly enlarging the scope of this clash. Some glaring cases may be mentioned. For instance, the government's programme to change the distribution of land in favour of the rural poor through land reforms was effectively resisted by the landlords. Similarly, 'the government's efforts to have tiled instead of thatched roofs for the Harijans' huts were foiled by the manner in which the headman dispersed grants' (p. 255). The headman's enthusiasm for electric power and bulldozer contrasted with his hostility to the very idea of constructing a new building for a 'complete' middle school because of his fear of losing 'the supply of cheap and obedient labour' (p. 64). There was tremendous opposition from the high castes to the entry of Harijans into the temple (p. 197) or to their drawing water from caste Hindu wells (p. 316). 'A rich man was able to escape punishment for his wrong deeds while the poor man did not' (p. 314). Further, 'two sanctions were available to the poor against the rich: one was to curse and the other to run away' (p. 268).

One last point on the issue of the changing world-view of the poorer classes with which the question of intensity of conflicts between the rich and the poor is closely related. Chapter III, 'Three Important Men' (one of the best in the book), deals with men from dominant castes. Srinivas admits that he saw the village 'principally through them and their activities' (p. 53). In the absence of an opportunity or an attempt to see the village reality through the eyes of the Harijans or the poorer sections of the dominant caste itself, the existing picture, or prognosis, of conflict remains partial.

Even though Srinivas has opened in this work a new area of enquiry, namely, that of conflict, he has refrained from posing the basic question of the significance of conflict for the social system as a whole. Does the system continue to be a 'harmonic' one or has it become 'disharmonic'? In view of the radical changes at the normative level from inequality to equality and the continuance of an inegalitarian economic and social system, conflicts provide a potential for revolutionary change. He does not, however, look beyond the immediate.

It sometimes appears as if Srinivas has not entirely given up the old way of looking at things. For instance, his concluding observation on the headman is that 'under his leadership the village had climbed from poverty to prosperity or at least that is how many villagers saw the situation.' This implies that the prosperity of the headman and of the villagers were identical. Srinivas' own work, however, has demonstrated in unmistakable terms the erosion of this harmony of interest between the haves and the have-nots.

CONTINUITY _VS_ CHANGE

Srinivas has remarked that the Rampurians are 'creatures of two worlds' (p. 114). They are pulled both by forces of continuity and of change.

Whether any social fact denotes continuity or change is a complicated issue. The village may have the appearance of continuity, hiding the break from the past. Or, it may have the appearance of change, disguising the fact of continuity. Anthropologists generally believe that it is easier to distinguish between the form and the substance in smaller than in bigger communities. In the former, direct contact with the people who experience continuity or change and embody it in their way of life is possible while in the latter such contact is not possible. But, precisely for this reason of closeness to people, change may go undetected in smaller than in larger communities. Caste, for instance, is such a basic and old institution having its ramifications in all spheres of life that it is not easy to detect changes in it. It may assume new roles and functions while its outward appearance may continue to be traditional. Methodologically speaking, it appears to me that caste cannot be understood by itself. Whether it exhibits continuity or change cannot be assessed by observing caste alone.

Insights into continuity or change can be gained if changes in other vital spheres like productive forces, production relations, belief system and power structure are investigated. In a large part of the anthropological literature the continuity of caste has been overplayed because of the lack of an in-depth study of the economic system.

In this context, the Marxian view that the understanding of relations between man and man—caste being one such relation—will always remain illusory or partial without an understanding of man's interaction with nature, has a substantial grain of truth. The understanding of caste in the Indian context has been largely obscured by the tendency to view it in isolation from economic activity and organization. In my view, Srinivas' work, though far more his earlier work than *TRV*, suffers from this failure to attach due importance to economic organization.

One would like to draw Srinivas' attention to the distinction between 'natural' and 'man-made' inequality. The caste of yesterday was an institution of 'natural' inequality as it combined paternalism with exploitation. But caste in an acquisitive and market-oriented village economy shakes off paternalism and accentuates exploitation. It thus transforms itself increasingly into an institution of 'man-made' inequality. Caste is consciously buttressed and utilized now by the richer classes as a mechanism of social and economic exploitation. *TRV* illustrates in a telling manner the ambidextrous character of the emerging class of entrepreneurs in Rampura which utilizes the traditional institutional forms (e.g., caste) as well as modern organizations (e.g., the political party) for their purposes. It, therefore, brings out new attributes and functions of caste which denote a sharp break with the past. But the ideology and idiom of caste conceal this discontinuity. This use of caste for new forms of exploitation by commercially motivated dominant groups is a metamorphosis of caste. Srinivas, however, has not laid adequate emphasis on this growing approximation of caste to class. It would be unfair to say that the new features of castes have gone unobserved by Srinivas. The point is not the observation of facts, but the interpretation of the significance of these facts from a theoretical point of view. Are these facts indicators of continuity or of change? That is the question.

Sometimes change may go unobserved if social facts are not assessed from a historical perspective. In the case of Rampura a lot of information is available but not a total view of what the village was like before the peasants became the dominant caste, or its way of life before the introduction of bus and motorcycle as a means of transport, or a discussion of the pattern of agriculture before the construction of the dam as a new source of irrigation. It is by comparing the facts of today with the facts of yesterday in all these respects that one can generalize what changes have occurred.

It is also important to ask how the villagers themselves view the phenomenon of change. The myths arising out of memories and recollections of the people are sometimes more 'real' than the facts of history.

Change also needs to be appraised from the normative perspective. The gap between the normative principles of the social system (equality and classless society) and the actual conditions of existence (hierarchy and exploitation) is itself a motive force for change. Srinivas shows that the new normative principles have acquired legitimacy. For instance, the educated young men 'were dissatisfied with the existing state of affairs' and 'wanted change' (p. 250) in terms of the normative principles. There was the 'young Harijan', who was defiant and 'who refused to be pushed around by the high caste landowners' (p. 195). But a complete understanding of the potential and motive forces for change has suffered because of the lack of close contact with Harijans and other low caste people. However, the analysis of 'Three Important Men' does convey a good idea of the possibilities and limits of change which is so far spearheaded by the 'pillars of the old society'. Their enthusiasm for economic and political change which increased their wealth and power contrasted sharply with their deep 'conservatism in social and religious matters' (pp. 54, 93). This is an eloquent commentary on how change was a contradictory process, combining a break with the past in one sphere with the status quo in other spheres. Considering that these men were now a part of the power structure of the larger society, it was very unlikely that the transition would be a smooth and peaceful process.

The normative evaluation of change may also be interpreted in another way. Should we assume that change is by definition desirable and continuity undesirable? The cost of change is an important question for enquiry. Srinivas is aware of this but has not explored it in TRV.

To sum up, TRV is an outstanding work which shows the full possibilities of the anthropologist's craft. Being the work of a master of this craft, it also shows its limits. It throws up, however, a number of important questions which should be taken up by anthropologists in collaboration with other social scientists. As Bloch (1966: xxiv) has argued:

It should, after all, be common ground that in a scientific subject every positive statement is simply a hypothesis. When the time comes for my own work to be superseded by studies of deeper penetration, I shall feel rewarded if confrontation with my false conjectures has made history learn the truth about herself.

CONCLUSION

From the foregoing account it is obvious that the Indian village has entered a new era where the forces of change have a much greater pull than the forces of continuity; and the forces originating from outside the village act as far more powerful agents of change than forces emanating from within the village. In such a qualitatively altered social context, perhaps the theoretical premises and postulates which underline TRV need to be reconsidered and reformulated; and new theoretical premises and postulates must form the basis of new types of enquiries into the Indian village in different parts of the country. In this way a new generation of social scientists who stand over the shoulders of sociologists like M. N. Srinivas must carry forward the tradition of rural studies beyond the theoretical limits within which Srinivas' generation thought and did fieldwork. This is the only way to assimilate the heritage of Srinivas' generation and then to supersede it.

REFERENCES

BLOCH, MARC. 1954. *The Historian's Craft.* Manchester: Manchester University Press.
———. 1966. *French Rural History.* Berkeley: University of California Press.
JOSHI, P. C. 1975. *Land Reforms in India.* Delhi: Allied.
SRINIVAS, M. N. 1955a. 'The Social System of a Mysore Village'. In McKim Marriott (Ed.), *Village India.* Delhi: Asia, pp. 1–36.
———. (Ed.). 1955b. *India's Villages.* Delhi: Asia.
———. 1962. *Caste in Modern India and Other Essays.* Bombay: Asia.
———. 1966. *Social Change in Modern India.* Delhi: Allied.
———. 1973. 'Itineraries of an Indian Social Anthropologist', *International Social Science Journal*, 25, 1–2: 129–48.
———. 1975. 'Village Studies, Participant Observation and Social Science Research in India', *Economic and Political Weekly*, 10, 33–35: 1387–94.
———. 1976. *The Remembered Village.* Delhi: Oxford University Press.

6

WESTERNIZATION: AN ESSAY ON INDIAN AND JAPANESE RESPONSES

T. N. MADAN

Magnificent! Magnificent!
No one knows the final word.
                    Fumon (1302–69)

During the 1950s and 1960s Professor M. N. Srinivas made many
seminal contributions to the sociology of India. Among the thematic
areas in which he stimulated research interest, the process of

Acknowledgement: This essay is a revised and expanded version of a lecture I
delivered at the centennial symposium of the Kokugakuin University in Tokyo in 1983
(see Madan 1983). I am grateful to the University for their invitation and to them as
well as the Japan Foundation for their hospitality. I also owe the warmest thanks to
Professors Chie Nakane and Yoshiya Abe for their many acts of kindness.

I am indebted to Professor Savitri Vishwanathan for pointing out some factual errors
in the first draft of this essay and to Professor David Plath for his unfailing encouragement and the insights of his own excellent work on Japan. The inadequacies that remain
are, of course, my own fault.

Westernization as a form of social mobility was particularly noteworthy. He first published an essay on this subject in 1956 in *The Far Eastern Quarterly*, exploring the historical linkages between Sanskritization (or endogenous social mobility) and Westernization (or exogenous social mobility) (see Srinivas 1962: 42–62). He then returned to it for a more elaborate statement in his Tagore Lectures at the University of California at Berkeley in 1963 (see Srinivas 1966: 46–88 *et passim*).

Srinivas traced the roots of Westernization to India's encounter with the West in the form of British rule which he considered responsible for laying 'the foundation of a modern state' in the subcontinent and for other 'radical and lasting changes in Indian society and culture' (1966: 46). These changes were in his judgement 'profound, many-sided and fruitful', embracing 'technology, institutions, ideology, values' (1966: 47). He further maintained that 'implicit in Westernization are certain value preferences', among which he made particular mention of 'humanitarianism', including in its ambit equalitarianism and secularism (1966: 48). The fact that religious beliefs and social customs had now to meet the challenges of 'reason and humanity' emanating from the 'British–Western' attack on the traditional culture led to a 'reinterpretation of Hinduism at both ideological and institutional levels' (1966: 49, 50). Apart from the good that ensued, however, certain 'pathologies of modernization' also became manifest, but these were held by Srinivas to be the result of 'partial or disturbed modernization itself' (1966: 52). He concluded: 'The Westernization of India produced in Indians an urge to change their traditional society, but in the course of time it came to occupy a secondary place beside the even more powerful, in fact almost elemental, urge to freedom' (1966: 87). This urge too was inspired by Western political ideals and quickened, perhaps ironically, by the very same British rule.

In sum, Srinivas's assessment of the processes of Westernization in India was largely, and by implication in principle, favourable. In this respect his views reflect the mood of optimism about the future of the so-called modernizing societies that prevailed among India's political leaders and intellectuals during the early years after independence in 1947. This mood was born of faith in social intervention for the solution of socio-economic problems and encouraged a confident view of the course and outcome of the process of modernization of traditional societies. It would seem that Srinivas did not quite share the ambivalent attitudes of some sections of the intelligentsia towards Westernization, which, he wrote, had resulted from prolonged contact with the West.

This ambivalence, he pointed out, was characterized by a curious mixture of ' 'self-criticism'—even 'self-debasement'—and 'paleocentrism', of 'crude caricaturing of Western life' and 'Xenophilia' (1966: 79). It is obvious that Srinivas' own viewpoint not only recorded the existence of this ambivalence but was itself incorporated in it.

II

Now, as is well-known, many Indian intellectuals have, over the last 200 years or so, borne evidence in their life and work of this split in consciousness. Rammohan Roy (1772–1883) in Bengal was perhaps the first outstanding intellectual to articulate it: and he has been generally acclaimed as the first modern Indian. While he thanked Providence for the blessings which the British presence in India seemed to him to promise in many fields, including administration, education, and the moral life of the people, at the same time he endeavoured to evolve a synthesis between diverse cultural heritages—Vedantic, Islamic and Christian.

The concern with a Vedantic foundation for the new world-view he endeavoured to shape remained prominent in the midst of efforts to broaden and enliven the intellect, and reform and refine the social order. In a famous letter addressed to Lord Amherst, the British Governor-General, in 1823, he protested against the establishment of yet another Sanskrit College, for he wanted Indians to learn the rational sciences of the West and not be engrossed in Sanskrit grammar and Indian metaphysics. He favoured Westernization, using in his writings and speeches emotive words such as 'enlightenment', 'amelioration', 'improvement', 'benefit' and 'happiness' to describe its expected results. Above all, he laid great stress on the superiority of the moral principles in the teachings of Jesus.

This ambivalence, or the desire for synthesis, whichever one prefers to call it, has remained with us ever since and to this day. A couple of generations after Rammohan Roy, Mahadev Govind Ranade (1842–1901) in Maharashtra gave expression to almost identical sentiments concerning the providential nature of the good that was part of the dispensation under British rule. He, however, added: 'We could not break with the past if we would. We must not break with it if we could' (quoted in Ganguli 1975: 5).

In the twentieth century no one has given more poignant expression to the ambivalence and the desire for the synthesis we are talking about than Jawaharlal Nehru (1889–1964). He wrote in his autobiography: 'I have become a queer mixture of the East and the West, out of place everywhere, at home nowhere. Perhaps my thoughts and approach to life are more akin to what is called Western than Eastern, but India clings to me...in innumerable ways' (1941: 341). Apropos British rule, while he held it responsible for the political subjugation and the economic exploitation of India, and castigated the British for obstructing social change except when it suited their imperial interests, yet he paid a tribute to the 'inspiration' of Western socio-political thought and institutions.

Nehru's assessment of the Indian middle classes, who were supposedly moved by this inspiration more than others, is, however, very negative. Writing about the time when Mahatma Gandhi (1869–1948) assumed the leadership of the national movement (c.1915), Nehru observed:

Incompletely developed and frustrated, they [the middle classes] did not know where to look, for neither the old nor the new offered them any hope. There was no adjustment to social purpose, no satisfaction of doing something worthwhile, even though suffering came in its train. Custom-ridden, they were born old, yet they were without the old culture. Modern thought attracted them, but they lacked its inner content, the modern social and scientific consciousness (1961: 379).

It was perhaps Gandhi alone, a Titan among even great men and women, who could contain in his oceanic soul many cultural streams without feeling uprooted, torn apart, or burdened. He too, it may be recalled, combined a denunciation of the 'satanic' British rule and of the evil embodied in Western industrial civilization with an admiration for the moral precepts of Jesus (most notably the Sermon on the Mount) and an approbation of the teachings of modern Western savants such as Emerson, Ruskin, Thoreau and Tolstoy. Similarly, he was deeply concerned with reforming Hindu society—his life-long crusade against untouchability being the best-known example—without abandoning his allegiance to it. In a famous and oft-quoted statement he said that he wanted to keep all the doors and windows open, to let the winds blow in from all directions, while remaining firmly seated in his own house.

While one may not easily associate ambivalence with Gandhi's personality, it is undeniable'that he too was in search of a new, forward-looking synthesis, but this was qualitatively different from the liberal nationalist and Hindu reformist exercises. The point that I am trying to make here is that by the twentieth century, Westernization had indeed become an integral part of India's historical consciousness, and its political implications had acquired increasing importance since Roy's time. Not to speak of Nehru, even Gandhi's response to the West carried a political load far heavier than what Roy experienced.

The ambivalence and uncertainty of the middle classes in their pursuit of Westernization is, of course, nothing peculiar to India, and is general in the non-Western countries. The most confident of modernizers have been afflicted by it, often resulting in the kind of dullness of thought and paralysis of action for which they have been reviled, and not by Third World 'radicals' such as Frantz Fanon alone. But it is also instructive to recall that the middle classes have 'success stories' to their credit in some places and at certain times, the most notable in our own times being the Japanese success story.

A comparison of Indian and Japanese responses to Westernization would be very instructive because, as we all know, Japan is the only non-Western country which has not only successfully Westernized (or modernized) itself but, in fact, turned the tables on the West, so that Western intellectuals and managers (if this combination of human types appears strange, one has only to be reminded that the role of managers in modern society today is no less important than that of intellectuals) are writing about what their countries could now learn from Japan, which has been simply judged as 'number one' by the Harvard Japanologist, Professor Ezra Vogel (1979). As another Western scholar puts it, at the beginning of the era of Westernization in the late nineteenth century, the slogan was 'Japanese spirit and Western techniques' (*Wakon Yosai*), but now 'it would make as much sense to turn it around and for Europeans to talk of "Japanese techniques and Western spirit" (*Wasai Yokon*)' (Wilkinson 1982: 170).

By its success at mastering the game of Western science and technology, and at the same time claiming to remain Japanese in its social organization and aesthetic and moral sensibilities, Japan delivered a deadly blow to the arrogance and smugness of the tradition-versus-modernity view of the contemporary world in a much more convincing manner than India would be judged to have done. It is of some interest to recall here that one of the first scholars to point this out was the American sociologist Joseph Gusfield (1967). But then, as long ago as 1938, Japanese intellectual Nyozekan Hasegawa had observed that, not only did the traditional and the modern go hand in hand in Japan, but also that 'in an extremely modern period, something extraordinarily traditional always begins to revive' (1982: 59). This view is endorsed by many Japanese intellectuals today.

The whole issue of demonstrating that traditional cultures are not incapable of Westernization (*seiyoka*) or modernization (*kindaika*), if the two processes are differentiated sharply, which seemed so essential for the self-confidence of the non-Western nations soon after they attained independence, is today seen as dangerously misleading: it imposes upon all cultures of the world a single paradigm of modernization (see Madan 1983). These reservations notwithstanding, or perhaps because of them, a comparison between the responses of India and Japan to Westernization seems very worthwhile. More specifically, have the Japanese too suffered from uncertainties as to how to respond to Western culture as we have in India?

III

Japan's contacts with the West began in the sixteenth century just as they did in India, and as in the Indian case it was the missionaries and the merchants who sought her shores. St Francis Xavier, one of the original members of the Society of Jesus, visited Japan in 1549, just as he came to India, and for the same purpose—to reclaim for Christ the Asian heathen peoples—and he rests in peace in Goa. In Japan, Christianity was eventually proscribed by Tokugawa Ieyasu in 1614. The Shogunate also shut out all foreigners from the country in 1639 except some Chinese and Dutch merchant traders who were confined to the small island of Dejima at Nagasaki. What is more, no Japanese were allowed to travel abroad. This policy of *sakoku* ('no in-come, no out-go') lasted until modern times. But neither could the Shogun's edict exterminate wholly the Christians nor could Western influence be kept out completely: thus Western knowledge and techniques in the fields of astronomy and medicine did seep into Japan. This contrasts with the continuously ramifying influence of Western culture during the same period in India.

By the early nineteenth century a consciousness of domestic weakness and foreign threat (*gaikan*) developed in Japan and the same was confirmed by the unequal treaties which the Western powers imposed upon it beginning with the treaty dictated by Commodore Perry of the US Navy in 1854. The sense of being imposed upon generated a most urgent need to learn about the Western powers and the sources of their strength. In a characteristically pragmatic move the Japanese government established in 1856 an Institute of Barbarian Letters, giving expression both to their contempt and hatred for the Westerners (who were actually called the southern barbarians, *nanbanjin*) and to their determination to learn *even from barbarians* in order to fight them back.

What strikes me as remarkable is the rapidity of the response and not merely its narrowness. As a contemporary Indian historian puts it, 'The Indian mind ... does not respond to new ideas and events promptly, for as a result of centuries of civilized history, we have acquired a highly discerning mind which refuses to be overwhelmed or hustled by any new idea or any new evidence' (Mookerjee 1967:1). I quote Mookerjee not because I find his argument wholly convincing but because it exemplifies a smugness of attitude and a sloth of mind—a Brahmanical superiority—which contrasts sharply with the Japanese alacrity to change mentioned above.

We are perhaps doing here no more than recalling a distinction made by Hajime Nakamura between the 'passive' or 'contemplative attitude' of the Indian people which, he thought, makes them adaptive, forbearing and averse to activism (1960: 58), and the 'fluid way of thinking' of the Japanese which produces 'an emphasis upon activism' and 'this-worldliness' (1960: 414, 540 *et passim*). Regrettably, due to constraints of space this contrast cannot be examined in detail here. Suffice it to say, these broad characterizations of national dispositions do seem to contain a kernel of truth.

After the Meiji Restoration in 1868 the rigid dualism of *Wakon Yosai* (Japanese spirit, Western techniques) was abandoned in favour of the state policy of 'reverence the Emperor, open the country' (*sononu kaikoku*). The earlier policy of 'reverence the Emperor, expel the barbarian' (*sononu joi*) had, in fact, been abandoned even before the Restoration when the country's weakness *apropos* Western military powers had become apparent in the 1850s. For the next two to three decades the attitude of Japanese leadership to the West remained clear and coherent: the West was considered the source of all the self-improvement of which it was in need and also capable. Without Westernization national survival was considered highly problematic: the unequal treaties had to be repealed or renegotiated, and to achieve this one had to be as powerful and efficient as the Westerners themselves. In these circumstances, as Jansen rightly puts it,

'Westernization was a device as well as a policy': Whether as sincere admiration or crafty tactic, the Meiji policies of Westernization clearly reflected the overwhelming importance of the West in the latter half of the nineteenth century' (1965: 69–70).

One of the intellectual leaders of the policy of out-and-out Westernization was Yukichi Fukuzawa (1835–1901). In some ways he was like Rammohan Roy, in others totally unlike him. He read extensively about the West and went to Europe and America on historic diplomatic missions the purpose of which was to find out what Japan could obtain or copy from there. His short book, *Conditions in the West* (*Seiyo jijo*, 1886) became modern Japan's first best-seller; 25,000 copies were sold in the first year. While his enthusiasm for the West was as great as Roy's, his approach was basically different, reflecting Japanese pragmatism in contrast to the Indian's preoccupation with fundamentals. This comes out dramatically in their attitudes to Christianity. Roy's reverence for the moral content of Christianity has been mentioned earlier. Fukuzawa was hardly concerned with the moral impact of the teachings of Jesus; he was rather interested in the practical politico-economic advantages that could be derived from Christianity. Hence he advised: 'We do not propose that a majority of our people should become Christians, a small proportion would be enough. All that is necessary is to accept the name of a Christian country' (quoted in Sansom 1950: 457f).

Some others went to further extremes. It has been recorded that Arinori Mori (1847–89), who was mainly responsible for the reformulation of the post-Meiji educational system, had 'privately' reached the conclusion that, if Japan was to have a strong, effective, modern educational system, the Japanese language would have to be replaced by German or English. This set off quite a lively debate (see Miller 1982: 108). (It may be added here *en passant* that a similar plea for the abandonment of the Japanese language was made by some intellectuals at the end of the Second World War.) These pleas about changes of religion and language reflected pragmatism, but for the Japanese it was soul-stirring pragmatism, for they are a people highly sensitive to situational pressures and, therefore, their responses to them are context-specific. In another book, *An Outline of a Theory of Civilization* (1875), Fukuzawa observed:

> Foreign countries are not only novel and exotic for us Japanese, everything we see and hear about these cultures is strange and mysterious ... a blazing brand has been thrust into ice-cold water.

Not only are ripples and swells ruffling the surface of man's minds, but a massive upheaval is being stirred up at the depths of their souls (quoted in Wilkinson 1982: 116).

The Japanese might have had their souls stirred, Indians perhaps simply lost theirs. All our textbooks record that the Battle of Plassey in the plains of Bengal in 1757 laid the foundations of the British *imperium* in India. We are also taught that better guns, better goods, and better government enabled the British to conquer India militarily and economically. And yet we might suggest that for India the battle had already been lost, say in 1606, when a Jesuit missionary, Roberto de Nobili, walked the streets of the ancient Hindu city of Madurai, dressed as a Brahmin—holy thread and all—possessing knowledge of Hindu scriptures, but converting people (mostly those of the higher castes) to Christianity. He and his successors never made many converts; Christianity had, in fact, arrived in India, if we go by well-established tradition, with the apostle Thomas at the very beginning of the Christian era. What the new missionaries represented was the cultural invasion of Asia by the West. It is in this sense that Indians may be said to have lost their souls before they lost their territories or markets. Ultimately all the processes were unified. Colonized lands are always populated by colonized minds.

India modernized under the aegies of Western colonialism: it was a matter of imperial and not national policy to Westernize the country. In other words, the compulsion to modernize was external, but of a significantly different kind than that experienced by Japan. The British did in India whatever they did to serve, first and foremost, their own domestic and international interests and only then, if at all, the interests of their Indian 'subjects' who were never given the status of the 'citizens' of the British empire. In acting thus, Karl Marx pointed out in 1853, they were 'actuated by the vilest interests' and, in addition, were 'stupid' in the 'manner of enforcing them'. And yet, Marx believed that, acting as the unconscious hand of destiny, England would fulfil 'a double mission in India': 'the annihilation of old Asiatic society, and the laying of the material foundations of Western Society'.

The industries and railways, in the transformative power of which Marx placed much faith, arrived in India (just about the same time that the Meiji era of Westernization began in Japan), but the hardware, the nuts and the bolts, came from Britain, contributing more to the prosperity of the latter than the former. While in Japan Westernization brought prosperity in its wake, in India pauperization was the outcome. Neither the economy nor the administrative apparatus could be national in character as in Japan. Though men like Roy and Ranade (and many others) appreciated the establishment of *pax Britannica* in the country, and applauded the West for the values of human dignity and liberty, they were painfully aware that these came nowhere near to being realized in the life of the people of India under British rule.

It was, however, the educational system that the British introduced in India—to produce loyal and reasonably efficient servants of the Raj—which inflicted the worst cultural wounds on Indians. Before this educational system came to hideous fruition, highly gifted and self-educated Indians, such as Rammohan Roy, gave expression to the immense scope for the widening of cultural perspectives. Let us remember that Roy's search for synthesis and rationalism began with his encounter with the Muslim world and the Arabic and Persian languages before he knew anything or much about Christianity and the classical and modern European languages.

But soon after, under the impact of missionary and government educational institutions, the search for synthesis degenerated into schizophrenia. The split in the consciousness of the affected educated elite damaged the authenticity of their creative response to Western culture and stilled their spontaneity. It is amazing but startlingly true that there has been no one on the national scene in India after Roy who has mastered as many non-Indian languages as he did.

A passive acquiescence in negative Western evaluations became the hallmark of the attitude of the Indian middle classes toward their own culture. Alternatively, they sought refuge in glorified memories of the past, citing for these too the authority of Western scholarship. Thomas Babington Macaulay's disparagement of Sanskrit literature almost inevitably led to Max Mueller's panegyrics about it being imprinted, as it were, on the minds of Indian intellectuals. In the process the sense of responsibility to the past, the present and the future was seriously damaged, if not lost. The situation changed only with the emergence of the national movement, which too was a brainchild of the middle classes, towards the end of the nineteenth century.

IV

By contrast, what strikes me as an outstanding characteristic of the Japanese mode of Westernization (*seiyoka*) is the self-consciousness and confidence that marked the choices that were made. No Western power conquered Japan, which was what happened in India. The West was, as it were, dragged (or invited if you prefer) into Japan. As stated earlier, the choices that Japan's new leaders made regarding what to borrow and what to emulate pointed to practical rather than philosophical concerns. The model for the new post-Meiji Restoration constitution was Prussian, for the legal code French, for the educational system American and German, for the navy British, and so on. This eclecticism is striking both in terms of its scope and deliberateness. One has only to recall the visits to Europe, England and the USA undertaken by government officials and intellectuals—particularly the historic visit of the top leadership group in 1872. Nothing of a comparable nature happened in India. Indians' contacts were exclusively with the British and mostly on the individual plane. In fact, there was something tragically appropriate about Rammohan Roy's end-of-the-life visit to Britain and his death there rather than at home in Bengal.

The Japanese made evaluations—judgements about superiority and inferiority—and expressed fears about being overwhelmed, but there was no sense of defeat as in India. Though both the Japanese and the Indians had known foreigners—the Indians all the time over the millennia—before their encounter with the Westerners, the Japanese had evolved a pragmatic culture of adaptation and of dealing with the strangers (*tanin*), of either relating to them in emotionally positive terms to the point of being dependent on them (*amae*), or totally excluding them from their own consciousness (see Doi 1977).

The Japanese had already evolved a cultural homogeneity by the eighth century when their encounter with the mainland giant, China, occurred. It was then that they formulated the doctrine of *Wakon Kansai*, that is, Japanese spirit and Chinese knowledge. Confucianism, Buddhism, Taoism, tea, architecture, character-writing, literature, drama, and so much more, all came from the mainland, but this process of massive borrowing has always been accompanied by the insistence that foreign ideas, knowledge and techniques must be imbued with a characteristically Japanese spirit, best summed up in the ideal of 'harmony' (*wa*), which obviously is a subtler concept than 'synthesis'. Synthesis, it will be agreed, involves the reconciling of opposites dialectically, and is a strenuous process. *Per contra*, harmony typifies the containment of conflict through consensus. It is also noteworthy that the educated classes never took to the learning of English or other

European languages, thus shutting out European categories of thought *as originally expressed* and continuing to live in the thought and value worlds of the Japanese tongue. This is a defence mechanism which the Japanese use even today. Not that they have closed their minds: the works of all major European thinkers are available in translation. (A bibliography of Japanese studies on Nietzsche runs up to 300 pages.) Self-confidence may be shaken temporarily but the Japanese spirit always triumphs again—so it is claimed.

Erwin Baelz (a German doctor who worked in the Tokyo Medical School and was one of the first Europeans to give detailed impressions of Japan in its early years of modernization) wrote in 1876 (the ninth year of the Meiji era) that cultured Japanese were ashamed of their past. He recorded being told: 'We have no history; our history begins today' (quoted in Ishida 1977: 121). What is important, it would seem, is that this was a Japanese judgement about Japan and, therefore, not quite comparable to, say, Karl Marx's 1853 magisterial pronouncement that 'Indian society has no history at all, at least no known history'. What Indians thought about their history has already been described earlier in Ranade's words, which bear repetition here: 'We could not break with the past if we would. We must not break with it if we could'.

Nor did the Japanese break with their past. The enthusiasm of the early years of the Meiji era provoked misgivings about the impact of the West. Thus a project was inaugurated in 1870, just two years after the Restoration, for the compilation of national history—a fine example of the reassertion of the Japanese spirit. Westernization was indeed seen by its critics as destructive of an entire way of life, a whole national heritage and national learning (*kokugako*). Becoming gradually stronger, and using the Emperor as a major symbol of tradition, the reaction against Westernization became quite prominent towards the closing years of the century. Japan's victory over China in 1895 further strengthened the reaffirmation of tradition and weakened the obsession with the West.

The idiom of the critical Japanese response to Westernization was, however, primarily aesthetic and moral, rather than religious and political as in India. A Japanese Vivekananda would not have made historical sense if he had lived. And a movement for national liberation, too, did not have to be launched: the Meiji Restoration had fulfilled that purpose. As for the artistic and literary expressions of the critical attitude towards Western culture, let me recall here the minor English classic, *The Book of Tea* (1906) by the aesthetician Kakuzo Okakura (1862–1913).

Concerned about the lack of appreciation in the West of the traditional Asian cultures and their superiority to anything modern in the realm of art, Okakura bemoaned that 'Indian spirituality has been derided as ignorance, Chinese sobriety as stupidity, Japanese patriotism as the result of fatalism' (1906: 3). He came to India in 1902 to meet Rabindranath Tagore (1861–1941) in an obvious effort to consolidate an Asian response to the West. His essay on tea was a poignant critique of modernization through an exposition of the history and art of the tea ceremony (or 'Teaism' as he called it) as an expression of the Japanese tradition, which he held out to the West as something to admire.

Okakura's emphasis was on the positive ideal of aesthetic tranquillity, a quality of the Eastern traditions which the West found deplorable. One may recall here all the rigmarole about Eastern mysticism and quietism, about other-worldliness and lack of achievement. Okakura wrote: 'In religion the Future is behind us. In art the Present is the Eternal' (1906: 61). It will be noted that nothing is said about modernization except the fundamental criticism of it so subtly concealed in the observation about the eternal values of art, which (to borrow E.H. Gombrich's phrase) are ideals and not idols.

I would like to mention another classic, Inazo Nitobe's *Bushido: The Soul of Japan*, published in 1905. This work eulogized the samurai ethic and way of life and has continued to sell hundreds of thousands of copies since it was first published. (The copy of the book I personally possess is from the 79th edition of 1979 and 13 editions had been published in the previous ten years.) What is noteworthy here is the Japanese fascination for, if not attachment to, a medieval value system which is somehow considered by many to express the quintessence of the Japanese world-view. This could hardly be mere nostalgia or romanticism or escapism: it must give expression to something deep and vital that has always animated the Japanese soul, sometimes more intensely and at other times less, and remains largely unaffected by modernization. The historian Aida Yuji has written somewhere—not wistfully but confidently and joyously—of the ever-strengthening regression of the present-day Japanese into 'Japaneseness'. His views are echoed by many others.

Let me not, however, oversimplify the situation, for it is the complexity and the ambivalence of attitudes which is the principal concern of this essay. I will, therefore, go back to *Hagakure*, the teachings of the samurai-turned-priest Jocho Yamamoto (1659–1719), which became available to the reading public only after the Meiji Restoration, when its ethics of loyalty was linked to the nation and the nation's prime symbol, the Emperor. *Hagakure* was, however, also criticized under the impact of Westernization as supportive of feudalistic ideals and insular attitudes. During the 1930s, the book became very popular again, and was hailed as an expression of 'the unique spirit of Japaneseness' (*yamato-damashii*). *Hagakure*'s central teaching, namely, 'I found that the way of samurai is death', made it a national best-seller during the Second World War.

But in post-war Japan it was generally condemned as a jingoistic and pernicious tract, though it never lost its admirers, the most notable among them being, of course, the famous novelist Yukio Mishima, who lived by the letter and the spirit of *Hagakure* to the point of committing *hara-kiri* (or *seppuku* as it is also called). He published an adaptation and interpretation of *Hagakure*, saying that in the 'pitch darkness' in which he believed post-war Japan had become submerged under American occupation and fallen a prey to Western culture, '*Hagakure* radiates its true light' (see Sparling 1978: 5). It is very significant that Mishima confessed his quest for a book in his youth which would not only support his 'loneliness' but also 'must be a book banned by contemporary society' (1978: 6). Does not 'contemporary' here mean 'modern'?

I have written about *Hagakure* at some length to highlight the swings of the pendulum of opinion—between *sakoku* (closure) and *kaikoku* (openness)—that have characterized the response of Japanese intellectuals and opinion leaders to Westernization. Even today there are differences of opinion some of which I was privileged to hear at the centennial symposium of the Kokugakuin University in Tokyo in January 1983. While some of the senior scholars were frankly worried about their Japanese identity (*Nihonjin-ron*) and its preservation through national learning (*kokugaku*), there were others who made light of the issue saying that Westernization had been made a bogey and that whatever was new in the Japanese way of life—whether values, attitudes, or gadgets—which had not displaced something that existed earlier, could only be called modern and international, not Western. Science and technology had outgrown their historical origins and belonged to everybody, as did the values and attitudes that were a necessary accompaniment of science and technology. In this sense

Japan's prolonged search for models had finally come to an end. The impatience of youth was succinctly expressed by a young faculty member of the Kokugakuin University who exclaimed: 'I was born after the war. Please do not deify tradition. To me modernization is an unmitigated blessing, not an invader of tradition. It is a beautiful thing!'

It has been pointed out that the early 1970s witnessed a definite search for Japaneseness in the context of the country's splendid recovery from the economic and psychological ravages of the war. The Jews became a new comparison group for the Japanese and, at the same time, opinion polls also showed a reaffirmation of traditional Japanese values such as filial piety (*oyakoko*) and gratitude (*ongaeshi*). By the close of the decade radical changes of attitudes were, however, again visible. While becoming rich remained as important a guiding principle of life in 1978 as it had been in 1931, 'suiting one's taste' and 'living cheerfully' became considerably important over the same period, and 'serving society' declined equally considerably. In conformity with these trends, the feelings of reverence towards the Emperor, which had earlier been an absolute value and the supreme test of patriotism, suffered a decline. These observations have led the distinguished Japanese sociologist, Tadashi Fukutake to conclude: 'it is safe to say, at any rate, that contemporary Japanese in general live for their family and their work and are not concerned about outside society' (1982: 148).

Recalling the crucial primacy of the group (ranging from the family to the state) vis-à-vis the individual, which has so long been considered the edifice of Japanese society, and the importance of which was reaffirmed as recently as 1967 in Chie Nakane's celebrated work on personal relations in a vertical society (see Nakane 1970), the changes Fukutake reports must be judged quite revolutionary in nature. Is Japaneseness, then, being absorbed into a universal modern culture? Perhaps: Shuichi Kato, the historian of ideas, puts it thus: 'once a universal concept is created, no matter who is responsible, it belongs to everybody. We have already accepted that idea where science is concerned, and almost certainly, in the years ahead, we shall come to accept it in contemporary art as well' (1981: 208). Perhaps not: if one reads Aida Yuji rather than Shuichi Kato. The issue of Japanese responses to Westernization is not a settled one (see the Zen master Fumon's *muttio* at the beginning of this essay), but there are new winds blowing.

The Japanese are inevitably opening themselves to foreign influences in areas of life that had earlier remained quite protected. Having established themselves as one of the three top industrial nations of the world (if not yet quite number one as in Ezra Vogel's phrase), they are legitimately seeking a new place of honour and influence in the affairs of the world and not in its market place alone. The techniques and products of Japanese industry are known, admired and bought all over the world, and these now include military technology, with the USA as a buyer from 1983 onwards! The Japanese themselves are, however, still relatively less known than their goods and skills. The situation has changed dramatically though since 1974 when the Japanese government relaxed whatever restrictions on travel abroad had still remained in force. Japanese business promoters and tourists are now visible all over the world.

Equally important is what is happening in academic circles. Japanese scholars are seeking closer ties with scholars elsewhere and, as a means to this, they are learning foreign languages on an unprecedented scale. The Tokyo University of Foreign Studies is a unique institution in this respect and one of their overseas research projects in the recent past has been located in Tamil Nadu in collaboration with Madras University, and a number of publications in English have become available already. I was told in 1979 by a bright young Japanese economist, specializing on Pakistan, that he deeply regretted that a major and rather technical work on agriculture in India by a distinguished Tokyo University Professor had been published in Japanese and not in English. Now, this most certainly represents a new attitude to international communication in the field of scholarship.

This raises a question. Will this decision and drive to have an impact abroad, to communicate better, to cultivate international dialogues, to learn English and other foreign languages weaken Japaneseness? Is there a cultural identity crisis after all in the making for the Japanese?

Or, is another scenario in the making? Writing in the famous national daily newspaper *Asahi Shimbun*, a commentator, Toshio Aoki, pointed out in 1982 that Japanese was increasingly being spoken in the foreign offices and the shopping centres of the Western world. He, however, cautioned that when a 'local' language becomes an international medium, the risk of 'big-power mentality' taking shape is also present. 'Language is where big power hegemony begins', said Aoki (quoted in UNU 1982: 9). Aoki's fears may not be far-fetched. Takao Suzuki, the well-known expert on Nihongo (the Japanese language), said in 1978, in the course of a well-attended lecture in Tokyo on the teaching of Nihongo to foreigners, that a religion must be made of Nihongo, that this new religion must be spread throughout the world. He added, obviously carried away by his own rhetoric: 'It is in truth a misfortune for any member of the human race to go to the grave ignorant of the Japanese language' (quoted in Miller 1982: 255). Yet, and paradoxically, Japanese language specialists, including Suzuki himself, have long asserted, and continue to do so, that to learn Japanese you must think like the Japanese, and this is impossible (see Miller 1982: 279). Hence the interesting and subtle distinction between Nihongo, the language of Japan which the non-Japanese also may learn, and Kokugo, the national language which only the Japanese can master. Their language thus becomes an impregnable armour against cultural invasion from abroad.

Let a cultural anthropologist have the last word here on this very important issue of intercultural communication which provides the setting for the Westernization of Japan (or India for that matter) as much as for the teaching of Japanese to foreigners. Writes Eiichiro Ishida: 'Perhaps it is difficult for the Japanese to attain a complete understanding of European civilization. At the same time, we may say that for a European to achieve a real and complete understanding of Japanese culture is also difficult. However... I think we should study each other's civilizations...' (1977: 138–39). As a student of anthropology I agree that the understanding of any culture is to be obtained only through the mutual interpretation of cultures rather than in the stigmatizing terms of a one-way flow of cultural streams from the Western centres to the world-wide peripheries, such as the process of Westernization would convey, or a Eurocentric concept such as Oriental (see Said 1979) would signify.

This is imperative for whether it is Japan, or India, or any other country, a merger of cultures is a reality in today's world. The question we have to answer is, 'what are to be the nature and terms of this merger?' Judging by the Japanese example, I would say there is no single answer: there are many roads to modernity, and many definitions of it: nothing is inevitable. As for Western culture itself, it perhaps imposes dualistic modes of thought of a particular kind on other cultures, producing schismatic responses to Westernization. In turn, the West too has been bewildered by India and Japan. These aspects of the two encounters are, however, beyond the scope of this limited essay.

V

Turning back to India, we know that the problem of the merger of cultures and, therefore, of cultural identity has been with us for millennia, but it acquired a new form and content following the encounter with the West. Inevitably 'cultural synthesis' is a key concept in Indian historiography, but it has often only served as a mask for the ambiguity and uncertainty which we discussed earlier.

So much has been written, for instance, about the Hindu–Muslim cultural synthesis—not by politicians alone but also by scholars—and yet it has not been the kind of *coincidentia oppositorum* which a genuine dialectic is expected to produce. Referring to the period with which this essay is concerned, we find that the most notable leader of Indian Muslims, who wanted to lead his coreligionists towards Westernization, was Syed Ahmed Khan (1817–98). Like Rammohan Roy, he was a rationalist and had great expectations of education that institutions modelled on the Cambridge and Oxford Universities could provide to Muslims.

Accordingly, he founded a number of schools and finally in 1878 the Muhammadan Anglo–Oriental College at Aligarh. It was proposed to prepare a curriculum of which the European sciences would be as essential a core element as Oriental literature. Khan publicly denounced the Islamic sciences as worthless. He was also, to begin with, a confirmed believer in the culturally composite character of north India, the religious divide notwithstanding, and in the common political aspirations of the Indian nation. He earned the wrath of the Muslim orthodoxy for such views. Gradually, Khan changed his views on most of these matters as his contacts with the British government became thicker (see Lelyveld 1978).

This is a long and complex story and the only reason why I mention it here at all is to suggest that, even in a large and culturally diverse country such as India, the new middle class intellectuals did share many basic attitudes towards Westernization, including ambivalence, despite regional and religious differences, which it is instructive to compare with the attitudes of the Japanese leaders in the post-Meiji years of the last century.

In all these attempts the dominant concern was to Westernize without somehow losing one's cultural roots completely. Those who would like to reassure us, write of India's historic capacity for absorption and 'encapsulation'; those who take a less sanguine view of the process of synthesis, particularly in recent times, such as V.S. Naipaul, the West Indian writer of Indian origin, simply speak of 'mimicry'. I would like to suggest that ambiguity is inescapable whenever an encounter of cultures takes place. The point rather is, what do we make of it? It is in this context of cultural ambiguity that the liberal nationalist, the Hindu or Muslim reformist, and the Gandhian responses may each be judged to have failed so far to constitute an adequate response to the march of Westernization in India.

A perusal of available literature reveals three main viewpoints regarding this response in India. Limitations of space allow only the briefest mention of these.

First, there are those numerous optimists who beckon us all to come out of our caves and cells of primordial loyalties, and participate in a modern, international civic culture based on 'reason'. They hold that science and technology, and the institutions, values and attitudes of the mind associated with them, will redeem the world. They view the Japanese miracle as proof of the triumph of technology, and consider the persistence of Japanese institutions and values a kind of 'myth'.

Second, there are those who would like to be called hard-headed realists and who hold that, good or bad, there is no escape from Westernization and that it is no more than sophistry to press too far the distinction between Westernization and modernization. For them modernity is good, though perhaps not an unlimited good. I believe they too would not take seriously the mystique of Japaneseness and largely discount a thesis like that of Michio Morishima (1982) that traditional ethical attitudes, religious values and institutions (such as the bureaucracy) have played a crucial role in making Japan what it is today. There is, therefore, little for Indians to learn from Japan, for Japan itself has learnt its most crucial lessons from the West. Morishima also says that it is a 'mistake' to consider Japan as a model for other countries which lack its ethos (1982: 201).

Third, there is the small minority (to which I too would like to belong) which does not subscribe to the view that all the paths of development must lead to the same kind of culture and society, or that Western society or, for that matter Westernized Japanese society, provides the rest of the world its best or only paradigm of development. These are people who would point out that at the core of the notion of Westernization lies the notion of cultural arrogance and politico-economic power and, therefore, the so-called 'burden' of modernizing the world.

They maintain that the very 'success' of Japan highlights the fact that the time for an incisive critique of Westernization and modernization is already with us and brooks no further delay. Time is one of mankind's very scarce resources today. In this connection, it is noteworthy that a Japanese historian, Minoru Kasai, has recently pointed out that Gandhi is as relevant to Japan in its present predicament (he believes that one exists), as he has been and continues to be to India in its own predicament. In fact, Kasai emphasizes the universal import of Gandhi's vision (see Kasai 1980).

One would have liked to elaborate here the idea that the West itself has of course been changing over the last 200 years and that extremely perceptive and radical critiques of industrial society and modernization have been advanced by Western intellectuals themselves. Also, there is the important fact that the perceptions of the 'West' among nineteenth century Indian and Japanese intellectuals were not exactly the same. Limitations of space, unfortunately, preclude these discussions. From the point of view of the present essay, however, what is most noteworthy is that, though India was colonized and Japan was not (at least not formally), for the middle class leadership of both countries, Westernization largely fashioned tastes, formed mental attitudes, formulated notions of well-being, and defined the skills for achieving the same.

It would thus seem that while the successors of the liberal nationalists, representing the first two viewpoints, have reached a dead-end rather than their goal, the Hindu reformists have been inexorably overtaken by the flow of events. Together they are the orphans of nationalism. As for the seekers of alternatives, they have really yet to cut their intellectual teeth. May be Gandhi has to be retrieved from the scrap-heap and reinterpreted, but this is no easy task.

VI

The doubts, questionings and misgivings that I have tried to outline in this essay reflect at least one of the moods of the 1980s, just as M.N. Srinivas' essays on Westernization gave expression to the hopes for the future of three decades ago. His analysis and views still retain their relevance and importance, and ought to be discussed in the light of the experience that we have gained since he wrote them. It is a tribute to his intellectual leadership that his work should still serve as a point of departure for the discussion of the problems we face today.

The point to ponder is that the experienced reality is far more complex than the extant discourse on Westernization perhaps lets us recognize.

REFERENCES

DOI, TAKEO. 1977. *The Anatomy of Dependence* (tr. John Bester). Tokyo: Kodansha International.

FUKUTAKE, TADASHI. 1982. *The Japanese Social Structure: Its Evolution in the Modern Century* (tr. R.P. Dore). Tokyo: University of Tokyo Press.

GANGULI, B.N. 1975. *Concept of Equality: The Nineteenth Century Indian Debate*. Simla: Indian Institute of Advanced Study.

GUSFIELD, JOSEPH R. 1967. 'Tradition and Modernity: Misplaced Polarities in the Study of Social Change', *American Journal of Sociology*, 72, 4: 351–62.

HASEGAWA, NYOZEKAN. 1982. *The Japanese Character: A Cultural Profile* (tr. John Bester). Tokyo: Kodansha International.

ISHIDA, EIICHIRO. 1977 (1974). *Japanese Culture: A Study of Origins and Characteristics* (tr. Teruko Kachi). Tokyo: University of Tokyo Press.

JANSEN, MARIUS B. 1965. 'Changing Japanese Attitudes to Modernization'. In M.B. Jansen (Ed.), *Changing Japanese Attitudes to Modernization*. Princeton, N.J.: Princeton University Press, pp. 43–97.

KASAI, MINORU. 1980. *Gandhi and the Contemporary World*. Poona: Centre for Communication Studies.

KATO, SHUICHI. 1981 (1971). *Form, Style, Tradition: Reflections on Japanese Art and Society* (tr. John Bester). Tokyo: Kodansha International.

LELYVELD, DAVID. 1978. *Aligarh's First Generation: Muslim Solidarity in British India*. Princeton, NJ: Princeton University Press.

MADAN, T.N. 1983a. *Culture and Development*. New Delhi: Oxford University Press.

———. 1983b. 'Cultural Identity and Modernization in Asian Countries: Some Indian Questions Soliciting Japanese Answers'. In *Cultural Identity and Modernization in Asian Countries*. Tokyo: Institute for Japanese Culture and Classics, Kokugakuin University, pp. 130–37.

MARX, KARL. 1853. 'The British Rule in India'. 'The Future Results of the British Rule in India'. In K. Marx and F. Engels, *The First Indian War of Independence 1857–59*. Moscow: Progress Publishers, 1959.

MILLER, ROY ANDREW. 1982. *Japan's Modern Myth: The Language and Beyond*. New York and Tokyo: Weatherhill.

MOOKERJEE, GIRIJA K. 1967. *The Indian Image of Nineteenth Century Europe*. Bombay: Asia Publishing House.

MORISHIMA, MICHIO. 1982. *Why has Japan 'Succeeded'?* Cambridge: Cambridge University Press.

NAKAMURA, HAJIME. 1960. *The Ways of Thinking of Eastern Peoples*. Tokyo: Japanese National Commission for UNESCO.

NAKANE, CHIE. 1970. *Japanese Society*. Berkeley: University of California Press.

NEHRU, JAWAHARLAL. 1941 (1936). *Toward Freedom: An Autobiography*. New York: Doubleday.

NEHRU, JAWAHARLAL. 1961 (1956). *The Discovery of India*. Bombay: Asia Publishing House.

NITOBE, INAZO. 1979 (1905). *Bushido: The Soul of Japan*. Tokyo: Charles E. Tuttle Company.

OKAKURA, KAKUZO. 1964 (1906). *The Book of Tea*. New York: Dover Publications.

SAID, EDWARD. 1979 (1978). *Orientalism*. New York: Vintage Books.

SANSOM, G.B. 1950. *The Western World and Japan*. New York: Alfred Knopf.

SPARLING, KATHRYN (Tr.). 1978. *Yukio Mishima on Hagakure: The Samurai Ethic and Modern Japan*. Tokyo: Charles E. Tuttle Company.

SRINIVAS, M.N. 1962. 'A Note on Sanskritization and Westernization'. In *Caste in Modern India and Other Essays*. Bombay: Asia Publishing House. (Originally published in *The Far Eastern Quarterly*, 15, 4, 1956: 481–96).

———. 1966. *Social Change in Modern India*. Bombay: Allied Publishers.

UNU. 1982. *Development Forum*. 10 July, p. 90.

VOGEL, EZRA F. 1979. *Japan as Number One: Lessons for America*. Cambridge, Mass.: Harvard University Press.

WILKINSON, ENDYMION. 1982. *Misunderstanding: Europe versus Japan* (rev. ed.). Tokyo: Chukoron-Sha.

7

CHALLENGES TO THE PROFESSIONALIZATION OF SOCIAL SCIENCES IN ASIA

M. S. GORE

This paper[1] has several diverse and not a wholly coordinated set of objectives. To begin with, it seeks to address itself to the challenges to the professionalization of social sciences in Asia. In the process it considers some of the dilemmas in research policy formulation faced by major funding organizations like social science research councils. Among other things, it raises some questions about the role of social sciences and the contribution they can make to social policy formulation.

The theme of this paper suggests that the challenge before social sciences in the current decade is likely to be different from the

[1.]This paper was prepared originally under the title 'Challenges to the Social Sciences in the 1980s: Professionalization of the Social Sciences in Asia'.for presentation at the conference of the Asian Association of Social Science Research Councils held at Bangkok on 19-24 October 1981. The author could not attend the conference. The paper is presented here with minor changes.

challenge they faced in the previous decades. Is this really so? Is the challenge of the current decade substantially different from that of the preceding one? I believe that the answer is in part 'yes' and in part 'no'.

In one sense the challenge is basically the same as in the preceding decade or in any of the previous decades. This is the challenge of developing a body of knowledge which can contribute to our understanding of the problems that beset our society and help us to design ways and instrumentalities of overcoming them and improving the quality of life. This search for new knowledge is by its very nature endless and therefore the challenge before social sciences interpreted at this level of generality is constant. (Here I am not entering into a discussion of the question as to whether knowledge must always be looked upon as an instrumentality for achieving certain ends or whether it could be an end in itself.)

While this basic challenge remains, some new questions have been raised about the very nature of social science knowledge and about the process of acquiring and disseminating it—questions that have engaged the attention of scholars and have become important preliminary challenges that the practitioners of social science must face. It is difficult to cover all the aspects of this new questioning in a single paper but some of the aspects will be discussed here.

UNIVERSALITY AND VARIATION IN SOCIAL SCIENCE

One may begin with the question: Is there such a thing as a universal or universally valid social science? This question has at least three different nuances. First, whether on the basis of the various sub-disciplines has anything like a social science—a unified body of knowledge about human beings as individuals and in societies—so far emerged? Second, whether the generalizations or quasi-generalizations of even one of the social sciences have universal applicability across cultural variations? Third, following from the second, whether social science knowledge, if it is culture specific, should be considered a science?

At first glance these questions might appear abstract and unimportant for our immediate purpose, but in reality they are not. If we examine some of the current controversies in the application of social science we will see that they flow out of some of these somewhat abstractly framed issues.

How often have we been told—or, have told ourselves—that 'Western' models of analysis as well as of solving problems have no relevance to the Asian context? Yet no one has seriously suggested that 'Western' ways of analysing physical, chemical or biological events have no relevance in Asia. The problem of the transferability of 'Western' social science knowledge may be at two different levels. First, it may be that the prescriptions of Western social scientists for the problems of Asian societies have no relevance because these problems are different. If this is so, then no basic issues arise with regard to the nature of social science knowledge. Second, if it is asserted that the basic patterns of motivation and behaviour of Indian and Asian peoples are different from those of the people of the West, then questions can be asked about the very possibility of anything like a social science coming into existence and, in fact, about any meaningful communication taking place between these peoples, except at a very elementary level.

It should be obvious that the point made above has a direct bearing on the concept of indigenization of social sciences in different countries. What exactly are the limits within which such a concept can operate without raising this issue. If Indian sociology has to be different from American or British or, for that matter, Japanese sociology, what exactly do we have in mind when we use the word 'sociology'? At the level of describing variations in the social structure, certainly there will be differences in content, but is Indian sociology co-terminus with a description of Indian social institutions? I am not averse to the use of the word indigenization but the limits within which this term can be used with reference to any science must be understood.

MODEL OF KNOWLEDGE SEARCH AND UTILIZATION

Another issue that has attracted attention in recent years concerns the validity of our traditional model of knowledge search and knowledge utilization. The traditional model states that when an important problem exists, scientists will seek to study it; once knowledge about the problem and the way in which it can be solved becomes available, that knowledge will be utilized to solve the problem. We now know that this model of knowledge search and knowledge application is unsatisfactory on several counts. First, it does not tell us how a particular social situation gets defined as a problem or from whose point of view the situation is problematic. The solution identified for a given problem will naturally vary with the perspective from which the situation is seen as problematic. If beggary is a problem from the point of view of the nuisance it creates for the rest of the population, then one solution may be to confine all beggars to an institution. If, on the other hand, the fact that a person has to beg to earn his livelihood is seen as a problem, then the search for a solution would have to be in another direction.

Even after knowledge about the problem has become available, whether or not it will be utilized depends upon several factors, in which the value framework of society, the relative position of various groups in society, and the availability or otherwise of the necessary resources, are important parameters. There are likely to be structured sources of opacity both with reference to the perception of a situation as a problem and the perception of the need to do anything about it.

The linear model of problem perception, knowledge search, knowledge attainment, and knowledge utilization is therefore too simplistic to be of any use. The perception of a problem by a social scientist depends upon his scientific equipment, his framework of values which in turn may be affected by his social position, and the ideological influences to which he has been exposed. His ability to find the necessary resources to undertake a study of the problem depends upon whether his perception of the problem and the importance he attaches to it are shared by those who control these resources. The decision to support a research proposal may itself be governed by value considerations, by the situational pressures upon the agency to utilize the resources made available to it, and by the availability or non-availability of a sufficient number of 'good' proposals, etc. The new knowledge obtained from the study may remain within the folds of a typescript for want of publication facilities, or, if published, it may still not be utilized because the prescriptions following from it are found unacceptable on grounds of cost or of the interests that they would affect.

The role that social values and interest groups in society play in determining the channels into which the activity of knowledge search may flow has been underlined by a vast body of literature over the last two decades. Social science councils cannot themselves be entirely free of these influences, but in so far as they are aware of these issues they may need to provide for ways in which structured biases in decision-making can be minimized. They would also need to undertake conscious responsibility for providing channels for dissemination of social science knowledge. They may need to provide forums from which the implications of new knowledge for the existing forms of social organization can be spelt out. Minimally, since neither the search for knowledge nor the interpretation of available knowledge are value free activities, it becomes important for individual social scientists as well as organizations supporting social research to clarify their value positions.

NEED FOR PRIORITIZATION AND LIMITATIONS

A clearer perception of the goals toward which we are working is essential if social science councils are to utilize the available resources to maximum advantage. Unless the funds available to a council are much larger than the demands likely to be made upon it—this may be seen in the context of 'underdevelopment' of social sciences in some countries—or unless a council decides to use its funds for supporting a number of randomly distributed proposals, the council will necessarily have to adopt some method of priority setting, because between various themes, theoretical perspectives, and/or methodologies of research, a certain degree of pri-oritization becomes inevitable. Very often this priority setting is done unconsciously, thereby reflecting the unarticulated biases of the decision makers. An open priority setting has the advantage that it can be discussed and criticized by the scientific community and thus is likely to get modified in response to informed opinion.

Priority setting is difficult yet necessary. This is primarily because in most cases the resources available are not equal to the tasks that need to be performed—apart from the fact that it is difficult to get any group of scholars to agree on one set of priorities. Further, priorities have to be fixed even between the different objectives that social science councils are expected to pursue. The dilemma in priority setting may appear in the form of 'pure' versus 'applied' research or between different substantive areas of research. Sometimes it is argued that research funding agencies should concern themselves exclusively with the quality of research and with the competence of the research scholar rather than with the importance of the particular subject he is researching. This, however, only begs the question. The judgement of quality of research is not always separable from the subject of research and often involves judgement of the relevance and importance of the subject being researched.

Judgements on priorities in research are closely linked with the social context in which research is being undertaken. This became evident in a recent exercise carried out by the International Federation of Social Science Organisations. In response to a questionnaire circulated by the IFSSO the member councils and individual scholars from developed and developing countries mentioned differing sets of priorities from among a list of given themes. While developed countries chose 'Impact of Science and Technology', 'Unemployment', and 'Income and Welfare Distribution' as the first three priorities in that order, developing countries chose 'Income and Welfare Distribution', 'Rural Development', and 'Social Values and Quality of Life' as the three important themes in that order. 'Population and Development' and 'Education and Development' which ranked fourth in the listing of the developing countries found no mention in the first seven topics listed by developed countries.

It is not surprising that there should be a variation in the priorities set by different councils located in different parts of the world. The fact that priorities vary is often overlooked by the national councils within their own region. In a country like India it is important to bear in mind the possibility of such variation between different regions of the country, depending upon the stage of development of each region as also the stage of development of social sciences in that region. This variation, though negligible in relatively smaller countries, may not be totally absent in any of them. The distinction between developed and developing regions within a country is important for policy formulation by social science councils within the country, because developed regions are usually the ones where social science skills have developed in a greater measure. If this distinction is not given due consideration, developed regions tend to absorb a substantial part of the total resources available to the council. Developed regions have a greater capacity for large-scale absorption of research funds. This should not be a problem except to the extent that the greater needs of a developed region might affect the growth of social science in the less developed areas and thus perpetuate the gap.

What is true of developed and developing regions is equally true of developed and developing disciplines, both at the level of distinction between physical and social sciences and at the level of distinction among the different social science disciplines. Since social science councils are interested in promoting the growth of different social sciences, they must also be conscious of the differential capacity of the various social sciences to absorb (monopolize?) the funds available with them. In India, it was found that economics, sociology, political science, psychology and human geography had absorbed the research grants of the social science council to varying degrees in that order.

DEVELOPMENT OF SOCIAL SCIENCE

Since most social science councils invariably accept the development of social science disciplines as one of their objectives, it may be useful to raise the question: What do we have in mind when we speak of the development of a discipline? One meaning of the term development in this context is obviously an increase in the number of scholars as well as studies in a particular discipline. But quantitative growth is not necessarily indicative of qualitative growth, i.e., growth in the analytical power of the concepts developed in a particular discipline. The body of scientific knowledge must grow in terms of the total amount of relevant information available as also its ability to draw appropriate inferences from this information, so that our understanding of social reality is widened and deepened. Yet research councils—since they focus on growth of research as distinct from growth of a discipline—are sometimes indirectly responsible for a quantitative increase which may be repetitive rather than contributive of new concepts or new insights. Social science councils may have to evolve ways, in collaboration with universities, of promoting the growth of disciplines as distinct from mere proliferation of research studies.

Another meaning of the phrase 'development of social science' is the development of a body of social science concepts uniting the theoretical approaches and insights provided by the different disciplines. In the 1960s and 1970s there was a verbal emphasis on what were called inter-disciplinary or multi-disciplinary studies. This goal of a unified discipline is unexceptionable, but we have to admit that we are still far from approaching it. Even in a single discipline there is a lack of consensus on a theoretical framework among different scholars. On the other hand, it has been recognized that all unidisciplinary insights are partial and for purposes of policy formulation a more comprehensive perspective is necessary. For the present this end is likely to be better served by encouraging scholars from different disciplines who have worked in a common subject area to pool their observations and insights.

Finally, the expression 'development of social science' may be used as indicative of its increased capacity to contribute to the process of social development. This interpretation of the term development provides a specific criterion for assessing the development of social science. In that sense, 'development' can be said to provide a value orientation to social science though the specific meaning of the term social development is itself somewhat vague.

SOCIAL SCIENCE AND SOCIAL GOALS

Social scientists have sometimes taken the position that the choice of goals or ends of action is not their responsibility. But if the development of social science is to be judged in terms of the extent to which it contributes to the process of social development, they would need to be involved in identifying the goals toward which the social development process is itself to be oriented. It is possible that a social scientist may take a value neutral position and only indicate which paths are likely to lead to a particular goal, and leave the choice of goals to politicians and philosophers. This position is logically tenable, but scientists in general are beginning to realise the hazards of this position: that the scientist is merely a technician concerned only with advising on the means to be utilized and not with the ends of social action. This self-imposed limitation is at best an attempt to evade responsibility. A social scientist who is not concerned about the end results of the actions which he recommends forfeits the right to be called a person engaged in the pursuit of knowledge, because his attitude raises a basic question: Knowledge for what? If knowledge does not provide the criteria for judging which ends are desirable, that knowledge cannot be very useful in the choice of means either. The choice of means also involves an ability to calculate relative costs—even social costs—of using a particular means. Social scientists will have to assume the responsibility of helping in the identification of goals and will be required to work out the implications of accepting such a responsibility.

When it is asserted that social scientists must participate in the process of selecting goals and the type of society they would like to live in, it does not imply that they must become politicians or that they must prepare blueprints of a distant Utopia. What is implied is that they must participate in the dialogue as informed persons who have a reasoned point of view based on their knowledge of human beings and societies. They must provide meaning and content to ideas that seem to be vaguely present in the minds of many at a given time.

For example, in recent years there has been a considerable debate in the developing countries of Asia and Africa that the path of development of the industrialized West is not the path they should follow, and that they must adopt a different technology which is often referred to as 'intermediate' or 'appropriate'. While a physical technologist may be able to indicate what this intermediate technology is, a social scientist should be able to assess the kind of social life this new technology would lead to, and the type of social infrastructure and modifications in expectations this new technology would occasion. If, however, developing countries embark upon the familiar path of industrialization and urbanization even without this new technology, their experience may not be exactly the same as that of the West. What are likely to be the experiences of the newly industrializing countries for which they should prepare? What are the implications for social life in a situation where the developing countries have borrowed the aspirations and lifestyles of the Western countries without building up the productive base to support them? These and similar other questions provide a large enough agenda for social sciences and social scientists.

The sub-theme of the conference is 'Professionalization of Social Sciences in Asia'. Our discussion of the concept of development of social science gives some directions along which professionalization of social sciences may be promoted. Social sciences must grow in size, and in the variety and type of information and insights they provide into social life. The growth of social sciences must serve social objectives—objectives which social scientists have examined and have helped in formulating. As the world shrinks and becomes smaller, social scientists must be able to comprehend the challenge and the promise of an emerging new world and help in fashioning the social instrumentalities through which different peoples who lived in relative isolation and pursued narrow loyalties may be called upon to take a broader view both of their larger assets and greater responsibilities. Before something like a world society can emerge there will of necessity be a long period of international cooperation and collaboration. What are the new institutional structures that may have to be created to meet this need? What are the new types of emotional moorings and loyalties that these structures will require for their effective functioning? The ability of social scientists to participate in the search for answers to these questions will be a test of their having achieved professional status. Professionalization is often interpreted merely as the emergence of a boundary maintaining organization for a group of professionals. It is important to state what ends the organization is to serve besides giving a sense of identity to its members.

8

UNAVOIDABLE COMPROMISES IN SOCIAL RESEARCH*

J. A. BARNES

INTRODUCTION

Research, the dignified name we give to the activity in which we set out deliberately to increase the corpus of shared knowledge, has been undertaken sporadically for millennia. It is, however, only in the last few centuries, and particularly since the Industrial Revolution, that it has come to be regarded as a necessary and continuous feature of social life. For many researchers, the pursuit of knowledge has been an end in itself, a source of enlightenment; the more the better. Recognition that scientific research often, and may be always, has an ethical dimension has come only quite recently. The precipitating event that triggered this recognition, most commentators are agreed,

* Earlier versions of this essay were published in 1982 as 'Ethische en politieke compromissen in sociaal onderzoek' in Carolien Bouw et al. (Eds.), *Hoe weet ja dat?* Amsterdam: Arbeiderspers en Wetenschappelijke uitgeverij, pp. 27–37 and in 1984 as 'Ethical and Political Compromises in Social Research', *Wisconsin Sociologist*, 21: 100–11.

was the revelation in 1945 of the medical experiments that had been carried out on prisoners in German concentration camps. Two decades later came the disclosure that cancer cells had been injected experimentally into terminally ill patients in an American hospital. Later still, the aborted Project Camelot of the United States Army, aimed ultimately at forestalling attempts at revolution anywhere in the world, showed that social research, like medical experimentation, also might have serious ethical entailments. The codes of professional ethics adopted by many learned societies during the last 50 years arose in response to these and other similar events.

The latest stage in the institutionalization and bureaucratization of the ethical dimension of research has been the establishment of committees charged, in varying degrees, with assessing the ethical implications of research proposals before they are implemented. Best known are the institutional review boards (IRBs) found in American universities, but somewhat similar bodies have been set up in other countries, including Australia. In the United States pressure to establish these boards came from one of the major research sponsors, the Department of Health, Education and Welfare, as it was then known, and the model provided by medical research was used to draft its ethical guidelines. The Department insisted that these guidelines should be followed by universities and research institutes in assessing the ethical status of all research proposals, whether or not they were biomedical inquiries and irrespective of whether they were to be funded by the Department. In Australia, the National Health and Medical Research Council (NH&MRC), either intentionally or by default, has had much the same effect. Some institutions interpreted its rulings to imply that it would support research only if ethics committees were established to scrutinize all research involving human beings, whether or not the research was supported by the NH&MRC. It laid down ethical guidelines which in some institutions were applied to non-medical as well as medical research. Committees inevitably seek to develop uniform thumb rules for assessing diverse research projects, and thus there was, and still is to some extent, a very real likelihood that a biomedical ethical model may emerge as the criterion against which social science research projects will be usually assessed. America provides a precedent for this process though it is a precedent that in the United States has lost some of its force. American social scientists battled for several years to secure recognition from the National Science Foundation and other major research sponsors that the ethical hazards of social science research are substantially different from those usually encountered in medical research, and that therefore social research requires a separate set of ethical guidelines. Unless the Australian research community can learn from the American experience, there is a strong probability that the same battle will have to be fought again by social scientists in Australia. There are probably other countries where similar conditions are prevalent.

Fighting battles of this kind entails a major diversion of effort and time that otherwise would be available for research. The research activities of social scientists not directly involved in the politicking are likely to be seriously hampered until the battle is won. These detrimental effects are hazards facing not only social scientists in Australia but in all countries where growing public awareness of the implications of social inquiry is accompanied by a growing tendency of governments to control and direct all scientific research. What can be done to minimize the amount of effort required to bring about a state of affairs in which social scientists are able to focus on the research they are trained to undertake, while at the same time paying adequate attention to broader ethical and political issues with which the general public and governments are justifiably concerned?

One of the many necessary steps is to ensure that there is a wider appreciation, not only by social scientists themselves but also by other academics and members of the wider public, of two things: first, that there is an ethical dimension to social inquiry, and second, that in ethical terms there are significant differences between most instances of social research and most instances of medical research. The failure, or slowness, of many social scientists to recognize the first fact, alas, complicates the task of securing recognition of the second. One of the reasons for this failure is the complexity of the issues involved. In this paper I deal only briefly with the question of why ethical considerations are relevant to research in social science, and give greater attention to some of the features that characterize these considerations. In particular I aim to show that in most instances of social research ethical compromises are unavoidable.

A MORAL COMMUNITY WITH DIVERSE INTERESTS

In the broadest terms we can say that research has an ethical dimension whenever it impinges on creatures with whom we have moral relations. Many inquiries impinge only indirectly, or not at all, on such creatures. There is, for instance, no society for the prevention of cruelty to atoms, or to stars, nor is there ever likely to be one. Research on atoms begins to take on a moral component only when the research leads to the construction of entities, such as bigger and better bombs, that do impinge directly on human beings and other creatures. For almost all of us recognize our membership of a moral community encompassing at least all other living human beings, our conspecifics, though we are divided about whether, and to what extent, this community also includes human embryos, dead human beings, non-human animals, or even non-animals such as trees. This moral engagement gives an ethical dimension to all research that affects, or is likely to affect, the interests of members of that community.

In practice, the ethical dimension is closely associated with the political dimension of research, even if in analysis a distinction can be drawn between ethical and political considerations. This is because human individuals and groups, apart from constituting a moral community with mutual responsibilities, also have divergent interests and, in many instances, command resources to protect and further their interests. Decisions about the conduct of research typically aim to take into account political as well as moral constraints. In particular, as the general public becomes increasingly aware of the ethical and practical implications of research, it also realizes what safeguards it may reasonably, and sometimes unreasonably, expect to be incorporated in the research design; it is also better placed to back up its demands.

Different categories of persons become involved in diverse ways in the research process. One category comprises the investigators who, either individually or as members of a team, conduct the inquiry. Often the research can be designed without reference to their political and religious views, their age, gender, ethnic affiliation, family commitments and other attributes of their status as citizens. In other cases, for instance, when continued participant observation is called for, one or more of these attributes have to be taken into account. Whatever the topic of the inquiry, even if it has nothing to do directly with human beings, teamwork always entails moral and, in a narrow sense, political obligations between members of the team.

The rights and interests of those human beings who become the focus of an inquiry, the so-called subjects (Ss), have been the centre of most discussions on ethical research design in social science. Some ethical commentators seem to recognize only the rights of subjects, or at least to regard them as always paramount. But we should not forget that to an increasing degree research is undertaken in the expectation that its findings will facilitate the formulation of public policies that will affect the lives of many people who were not directly involved in the research. So long as 'relevance' serves as a war-cry for politicians, this expectation applies to research in all branches of science even when the inquiry is focused on inanimate objects rather than on human beings. In general, the interests of members of the wider public will diverge as well as overlap. In the limiting case, as perhaps in the provision of cleaner public water supply, the changes that flow from research-based policies may be universally beneficial. But more often some persons will be beneficiaries of the changes and others will be losers, even when the game is not zero-sum. If the losers happen to be, say, corrupt officials, drug pushers, avaricious landlords or polluting factory owners, we may tolerate or even welcome their loss; but we should be aware of the moral judgement we have made and be ready to face the political clout these potential losers may wield.

Most research requires specific funding. Paymasters, or sponsors as we politely call them, quite rightly have an interest in the projects they finance and for which they can never be entirely free of responsibility. Sponsorship encompasses more than the provision of funds, for an institution like a university habitually associated with research lends its name and reputation even when it contributes no funds or facilities. Other persons involved in research are the gatekeepers who control access to the individuals, documents or facilities needed for the inquiry. These may be managers of factories, parents of school children or the custodians of archives, all of whom may require assurances about the conduct of the inquiry before they will open the various gates they control. Colleagues of researchers will expect to read the findings of the inquiry and may also expect to be able to carry out further inquiries on the same topic or in the same place or even on the same individuals. These colleagues have an interest in the maintenance of the canons of reliability and openness that are the distinguishing marks of the scientific enterprise. To some extent these expectations are set out in the codes of professional ethics.

In designing an inquiry we have therefore to take account of the rights and interests of the investigators themselves, their scientific colleagues and their sponsors, as well as the individuals who may be the focus of the inquiry, the gatekeepers and the general public. Our design may be constrained by the codes of professional ethics, though until very recently most of these consisted of sociologically naive exhortations to saintly conduct that could be followed only partially (cf. Galliher 1980: 303–4). Some codes or guidelines are now more realistically phrased, but of necessity most of them still lack teeth. More powerful constraints are constituted by the conditions imposed by sponsors and other parties to the inquiry. In practice, however, it is only very rarely that we can design an inquiry so that all the divergent interests of the various groups are protected and all the moral obligations are fully discharged. Some compromises are inevitable.

Exactly what form the compromise will take will vary from instance to instance, depending on such considerations as the magnitude of the risks and inconveniences—physical, material, financial, mental, political or whatever—which the various parties to the research will have to endure, the relations of power and authority that exist between the parties, and the likely benefits and losses that will flow from the research. These parameters differ widely from one mode of research to another, from, say, the relatively innocuous social survey·aimed at discovering consumer preferences among breakfast cereals to relatively hazardous experiments with slow-acting prescribed new drugs or participant observation of recreational drug abuse. These wide variations preclude the use of simple rules of thumb for determining the optimum design for all inquiries; each has to be looked at on its merits. For instance, securing written informed consent from prospective participants may be an appropriate element in some research designs but quite inappropriate and even counterproductive in others. Some research participants may be offered assurances of anonymity; other participants may rightly demand to be openly identified.

Inquiries that entail risk in their execution and/or that are likely to lead to significant changes in the world are hard to design acceptably. For that reason they may be neglected in favour of easier, safer and less controversial topics that leave the status quo unchanged. This consequence is usually referred to as the 'chilling effect'. Yet, it is precisely through pursuing inquiries that are controversial and difficult that researchers can hope to have a substantial and, with luck, generally beneficial effect on the lives of the general public and at the same time satisfy their intellectual curiosity. It is these inquiries that are, as they say, 'relevant' and which can help to sustain public support for the research community. It is, therefore, both intellectually and pragmatically necessary that researchers and sponsors should overcome the chilling effect and continue to tackle controversial and often unpopular topics, despite the enhanced ethical difficulties these inquiries necessarily entail.

ETHICAL CODES AND GUIDELINES

What advice is available to us in dealing with these difficult issues? Social scientists cannot blindly adopt the guidelines developed for biomedical research without suitable modifications. The balance of power between the various parties to the inquiry differs radically in the two branches of science and the hazards differ. Typically, the medical investigator stands in a much more powerful position vis-à-vis the participant than does the social scientist. Typically, too, the medical scientist is able to offer the participant some reasonable possibility of relief from illness or pain as the outcome of the inquiry, or at least can offer that prospect to future sufferers. Yet at the same time the research may expose the participant to greater risk of injury or death if the investigation misfires. Unlike the medical researcher, the social scientist can offer the participant only enlightenment and perhaps modest material benefits, but he does not usually expose the participant to the risk of major losses. Whenever there is a risk of substantial loss, it is likely to be loss of public reputation, financial loss or punishment at the hands of the law, rather than a threat to one's health.

Biomedical research, particularly when psychiatric considerations are not involved, conforms generally to the so-called natural science paradigm, in which there is a clear division between the investigator and the participant, and where the inquiry is conducted so as to reveal, as far as possible, what happens 'normally', when events are not under the scrutiny of an investigator. Most research in social science conducted before 1960 purported to conform to this paradigm. The investigator tried to collect information about the normal pattern, when, for instance, there was no anthropologist disturbing social life by asking unexpected questions and taking photographs, or when there was no survey researcher seeking opinions about topics previously undreamt of. For a variety of reasons, anthropologists, and to a lesser extent sociologists, have now begun to take account of the fact that the process of inquiry itself often disturbs the phenomenon that is being investigated. Simply by his/her presence the investigator affects what other people do and say.

There is another important difference between biomedical and social science research that occurs when the social scientist works among people whose way of life differs substantially from his or her own. In such circumstances there may be little agreement between the participant and the investigator about what kind of good life is the ultimate goal of the inquiry. The doctor and the patient, even when not members of the same cultural community, are likely to agree that health is better than sickness. But the social scientist and the research participant may not necessarily agree about, say, the attractions of polygyny, the necessity for sub-incision, the guilt of witches, the polluting effects of members of low castes and the legitimacy of exploiting bonded labourers. Whether or not there is a major cultural hiatus between the participant and the researcher, there may well be significant differences in beliefs and aspirations between one participant and another which the researcher cannot ignore. Both kinds of differences affect the research design, particularly when the researcher becomes a participant observer, as in many types of qualitative inquiry. The medical investigator or natural scientist can safely ignore both kinds of complications. Finally, there is a much greater range of intellectual and practical aims among social researchers than there appears to be among medical investigators, and the political and cultural beliefs and opinions held by researchers have a far more direct bearing on the choice and conduct of inquiry in social science than in medicine. Cast-iron ethical prescriptions are, therefore, less likely to be appropriate, and much less likely to be accepted, in social science than in medical science.

Over the last 30 or 40 years a corpus of literature, now of quite substantial dimensions, has been built up which offers ethical and practical guidance to practitioners of social research and which, to a much smaller extent, provides a sociological analysis of why and how the need for this guidance has arisen. Guidance is available in several modes: anecdotes recalled by experienced (and sometimes surprisingly inexperienced) researchers; hypothetical situations spelt out for the reader to wrestle with; and formal codes and guidelines adopted by professional associations and backed by their tenuous authority. Moral philosophers include social research among the activities for which they prescribe norms, often conflating it with research in medicine. There are the guidelines imposed by governmental and private sponsors, with effective sanctions to ensure their adoption.

This corpus of advice, analysis and admonition does not speak with one voice. In particular, there is serious discord between the anecdotes and the professional codes. Many of the anecdotes suggest that even the most conscientious and experienced fieldworker may in practice be unable to meet all the ethical demands he or she accepts as valid. The codes and guidelines, though they often stress the importance of negotiation as part of the process of inquiry, generally lead to the impression that a perfect solution exists to every ethical problem. The fieldworker must be honest, must respect the interests of all respondents, must recognize obligations to colleagues, and so on. My thesis is that this impression is misleading; in most instances of empirical inquiry, no perfect solution exists. In social research there is no immaculate praxis. Even informed consent, which some 25 years ago was the badge of the ethically conscientious investigator, is not a universally effective way of matching research objectives to the participants' interests. Murray Wax, an American anthropologist, has argued that for inquiries involving participant observation in foreign communities where the notion of social science is unknown, the requirement that the persons to be studied should give their informed consent before the inquiry can begin is quite inappropriate. It is, he says, comparable to

a couple… being forced to reverse the usual sequence of courtship, and rather than allowing intimacy to emerge over a period of mutual knowledge and friendship, insisting that they must initially agree in writing that they would be intimate with each other, even prior to any real opportunity for acquaintanceship (Wax 1980: 275–76).

CONFLICT OR CONSENSUS

The necessity to compromise arises in different ways at the various stages in the process of research. The first compromise occurs when we make our choice of the field and topic for research. We might describe this as a compromise between conflict and consensus. Every actual social configuration that might conceivably become the object of empirical inquiry is, broadly speaking, characterized by a certain amount of social conflict and a certain amount of social consensus. A social field characterized by ubiquitous consensus might possibly be easy to study, in that here *everyone's* interests might secure protection. In the attainment of such exceptional harmony this social field would be of considerable theoretical interest. But such field situations are rare indeed and, if they do exist, are unlikely to call for practical intervention. 'For heaven's sake don't rock such a beautiful boat'.

At the other extreme are highly polarized social fields in which positions of neutrality, such as those sought by would-be objective investigators, are simply not tolerated. 'He that is not with me is against me'. In as much as these fields do not in practice disintegrate into a Hobbesian battlefield, a war of all against all, they pose in the most acute form the problem of social order, of why human society is possible, which lies at the very centre of sociological inquiry. Fields that approximate to this polarized type are typically perceived as social problems and they therefore call for practical intervention. Here, research may therefore be usefully linked, directly or indirectly, with the formulation of public policy, and it is here that funds for research are most likely to be available. Yet precisely because of the polarization it may be very difficult for the social scientist who seeks to study the field to achieve for himself or herself any role except that of a committed partisan, who is allowed to see the social scene from the viewpoint of only one of a plurality of contending factions. Hence, in practice, we tend to avoid the extremes of conflict just as much as we neglect the extremes of consensus. We look instead for some field situation in which, though there is conflict, there is still room for a social scientist who can be tolerated as a person not wholly identified with any one faction and who, in some sense, is allowed to remain somewhat removed from the struggle.

In the middle of the conflict–consensus continuum lies an uneasy compromise. Our wish, or our sponsor's wish, to study situations that need intervention, where our research might be perceived from some point of view as 'relevant' and therefore worthy of support from public funds, pushes us toward the conflict end of the scale. However, our analytic expertise is often stronger when we are scrutinizing social fields that are characterized by consensus, for it is these fields that approximate more closely to the structuralist and functionalist paradigms that obstinately continue to pervade mainstream social science. Hence, we are faced with the paradox that the more we are able to speak with professional competence or confidence, the less practical importance there is in anyone listening to what we have to say.

COMMITMENT OR IMPARTIALITY

The compromise between conflict and consensus impinges more directly on the political dimension of research than on the ethical dimension, though investigators may have to make difficult moral choices between their intellectual curiosity and their desire to change the world, as well as facing up to factional pressures to conform. This pressure is highlighted when we consider a second type of compromise, that between commitment and impartiality. This is a compromise between the enthusiasm necessary for practical action and the scepticism that is rightly demanded by science. On the one hand there may be an interventionist or conservationist wish to change the world, or to preserve the existing arrangements that are threatened, and/or an insistence by the subjects we study, or their gatekeepers, that the price of their collaboration is our commitment to their goals. On the other hand is our professional dedication to impartiality, or even to objectivity, to the search for greater understanding via that unquenchable scepticism that professionally differentiates the scientist from the rest of humanity. Our precise position on this continuum is likely to be obscured if, as often happens, we overemphasize our helplessness as a form of protection against importunate appeals that we should intervene, even when in fact we have both the power and the wish to do so. For example, Cleopâtre Montandon (1983: 227–28; 1984: 122–24), a Swiss sociologist, in her study of prisoners housed in a jail where there was considerable tension, continually stressed her powerlessness and inability to help them even though sometimes she would have liked to do so. She had to tell one prisoner that she did not want to hear anything about plans for escape. Had she been told, she would have had to choose between betraying the confidence of the prisoners and acquiescing in their attempts to break out of the prison, a moral choice she wished to avoid.

Though each of the poles, commitment and impartiality, has its attractions, neither is easily tenable. In the field we cannot always avoid taking sides, whether or not we want to do so, and yet we can never endorse any one side as wholeheartedly or uncritically as the actors would like us to do. We cannot easily discard our ingrained scepticism, even temporarily, however much we may try to conceal it, whether for reasons of politeness or prudence. Evans-Pritchard, the pioneer in the study of African witchcraft, stressed that in the field it becomes necessary for the anthropologist to act as if the beliefs of the community were true. He said, 'You cannot have a remunerative, even intelligent, conversation with the people about something they take as self-evident if you give them the impression that you regard their belief as an illusion or a delusion'. He further noted that 'If one must act as though one believed, one ends in believing, or half-believing, as one acts' (Evans-

Pritchard 1973:4). Yet his classic account of Zande witchcraft (Evans-Pritchard 1937) is an attempt to discover why people believe in an illusion. Was he behaving unethically when he gave people the impression that he believed in witchcraft? Was his action any different from that taken by Festinger and his colleagues in the United States, as reported in their book *When Prophesy Fails* (1956), when they joined a small apocalyptic cult group in order to study it? As scientists we cannot become naive converts, however worthy the cause may be. We recognize professionally the importance of myths both in maintaining the social order and in mobilizing pressure to change it, and yet we cannot afford to forget that such myths are only myths and not propositions that have withstood Popper's tests for falsifiability. Thus we cannot expect to become more than half-hearted, and therefore unreliable, partisans. In this sense the social investigator is necessarily a disappointment to the people he or she studies.

SCIENCE OR CITIZENSHIP

The third compromise is perhaps the same as the second, seen in a wider perspective, and is connected with the first. This is the compromise between our roles as scientists and as citizens. Our intellectual concerns are likely to be influenced not only by the insatiable curiosity that marks us as scientists but also by our wish to preserve the world as it is or to change it, by our stance as citizens. If the research we wish to undertake cannot conceivably have any effect on the flow of events we have to put our interests as citizens into cold storage, at least for the time being. Alternatively, if we carry out some routine inquiry not for its intellectual interest but because we expect it to lead to some practical outcome we think desirable, we are then subordinating our scientific interest in favour of our aims as citizens. There is a third possibility, which occurs only too frequently. We make an inquiry neither for its intellectual challenge nor for its expected practical outcome but simply because we are hired to do so, so that we can keep body and soul together. In practice, we often seek to combine all three sets of interests, as scientists, as concerned citizens and as individuals striving to survive. We have to balance one set of interests against the others. The choice we make will influence the type of sponsorship we are willing to accept, the extent to which we are willing to allow the citizens we study to determine how the inquiry is structured, and how we handle the findings of the inquiry.

Once in the field, particularly if the inquiry takes the form of participant observation, we are likely to be continually forced to compromise. Our values as citizens may be in conflict with the values of some or all of the people with whom we are engaged. It is usually foolish either to become insincere copies of the people we study or to cling rigidly to modes of conduct that antagonize them. The first policy undermines our self-esteem as citizens, even if we play our parts successfully, which may be difficult. As Burgess, a British sociologist, notes, remembering a field study in which he tried to conform to the values and lifestyles of teachers in a secondary school, the feelings of guilt that this feigned identification generate may perhaps never be adequately resolved (Burgess 1984; cf. Davis 1961). Some of us may consider the *Weltanschauung* of the British secondary school teacher not too far removed from our own, but Burgess found that his sympathies often lay more with the pupils than with their teachers.

The second policy, of clinging to our own convictions without making concessions to local opinion, may perhaps work in communities where there is a high tolerance of diversity and dissent but in general some concessions are necessary if the inquiry is to proceed. For example, Peter Kloos, a Dutch sociologist who studied a community in Sri Lanka, reports how he reached a compromise with his servant over whether to treat members of a beggar caste as equals or beyond the pale; they were given tea to drink neither in cups with saucers nor in a coconut shell but in cups without saucers (Kloos 1983–84: 128). This may seem trivial but definitely has symbolic importance. A more serious compromise may be forced on social scientists who find paternalism distasteful and yet have to be temporarily paternalistic, to presume to know better than the citizens what their long-term interests are, because there seems to be no other way of providing protection for peoples who are largely ignorant of the wider social arena in which their fate is being decided for them.

FRANKNESS OR CONCEALMENT

There is also a compromise between frankness and concealment. In general the more the social scientist can gain the informed cooperation of the citizens he or she is studying, the higher the likelihood that the inquiry will have a satisfactory outcome. But this is not always the case. The scientist may, for instance, be seeking information that can be obtained only obliquely, whether this be responses to projective psychological tests or other data that can emerge only spontaneously. In collecting these data the investigator seeks a consent from the person being studied that is certainly not informed in any sense defined by the professional ethical codes. The emphasis, in most codes, on obtaining informed consent, contrasts oddly with our practice in our everyday lives, where we continually note, and may indeed be particularly on the lookout for, unguarded remarks, comments made to us on the assumption that we already know more than in fact we do, or that we hold opinions that in fact we do not hold. We usually make use of this spontaneously generated information without betraying the trust of our friends and acquaintances. Often all we can do with such information is to remain silent or to feign ignorance. Likewise in the context of research we should generally be able to utilize similar data without jeopardizing the trust of the citizens we study. At other times we may have to hold our peace and say rather less than we might wish.

Some commentators on professional ethics appear to make a distinction between concealment and deception. It is permissible, they assert, for a social investigator to be less than totally frank about the objectives of the investigation but not deliberately to mislead the persons being studied about what these objectives are. This distinction seems to me to be unsatisfactory, for whatever an investigator may say or fail to say his or her actions are in the field subject to continuous evaluation and speculation by the citizens. Complete frankness is likely to be met with disbelief; it does not occur often in ordinary social interaction. Yet concealment, just as much as deception, may generate wild speculation about what the investigator's real intentions are. A more satisfactory solution, in my view, is to claim an inherent inability ever to be completely frank. Here, for once the biomedical model may have some utility for social research. Physicians, we all accept, can never be trusted to be totally frank with their patients. They never say in advance what they are hoping to find as they examine their patients. After they have made their diagnosis patients do not expect them to reveal all they know, whether or not they would like to be told. These characteristics make physicians slightly uncomfortable companions but we tolerate their lack of frankness because we believe that on balance they do us good. As social scientists we have much less to offer the persons we study but nevertheless we should, I believe, strive for public recognition for our inherent inability

192 ■ J. A. BARNES

to be frank. This recognition may be easier to obtain and maintain if social scientists would also adopt another attribute of the ideal-typical physician, the practice of not disseminating personal information obtained or imparted in confidence. As I have said elsewhere, 'Social scientists should aim at securing public recognition for combining the journalist's sceptical curiosity and the novelist's empathic perspicacity with the physician's professional reticence and fidelity to the data' (Barnes 1980: 77).

Just as the scientist approaches the citizen with caution and restraint, so must the scientist expect less than universal unbridled enthusiasm from the subjects of the inquiry. Many citizens may have good reasons for wishing to conceal what they are doing and thinking. Their actions may be classified as illegal by some powerful authority, or as unfair by some group they are exploiting. They may be in legitimate competition with their rivals and therefore reluctant to reveal their plans. In daily life we constantly restrict, alter and colour the flow of information between ourselves and our fellows; we assume that they do the same. Even those of us who are not ethnomethodologists accept this process as inevitable. Yet curiously many social scientists seem to expect that in the field a radically different mode of discourse can and should be established, in which absolute truth reigns and all colours are black or white. Certainly, in analysis the requirements of statistical techniques and the limited comprehension of computers may force us to group our data into Procrustean categories, even into the extreme categories of true and false. But with most modes of data collection it is definitely advantageous to recognize as sensitively as we can the intrinsically problematic character of all human communication, even if subsequently in analysis much of this quality has to be overlooked.

If everything that the citizens say and do during an inquiry has to be interpreted with a stiff dose of informed salt, what about the statements made by the investigator? Even if complete frankness is impossible, must he or she always be completely honest? In my view, the special circumstances of fieldwork, just as much as the ordinary circumstances of everyday life, may lead the social scientist to lie, particularly when he or she is habitually lied to. Field investigators, like most people, would in general endorse what Sissela Bok calls the principle of veracity, that 'truthful statements are preferable to lies in the absence of special considerations' (1978:30). But what are acceptable special considerations? I think that Peter Kloos oversimplifies the issues when he says, 'I have no qualms in deceiving the authorities of [this] kind, who use their power at the expense of the poor and powerless' (Kloos 1983–84:129). Lying to a citizen, whether or not any practical benefits or dangers are entailed, rules out the possibility of strengthening or enriching the scientist's relation to that citizen in most cases. He or she then becomes an exogenous entity, impinging on that part of the social field which the scientist seeks to interpret and explain, but not encompassed by the explanation. In order to gain a position from which to understand, and possibly also to help, the actors in one part of the field it may sometimes be necessary for the social scientist to deceive other actors, particularly in social situations marked by greater conflict than consensus. Nevertheless we should always regret having to deceive, not only because deception is regrettable in itself but also because of the limits which the deception places on the possible scope of our inquiry. Every inquiry has to have limits. With necessarily limited resources, no social scientist can hope to inquire into everything he or she might like to tackle. Hence, the additional limitation imposed by deceit may well not be inconvenient in the short run. For instance, Pierre van den Berghe, an American sociologist, found that in order to study a small town in South Africa, he had to deceive the local White officials. He succeeded in obtaining the data he sought, although he never received more than reluctant cooperation from the White public servants. Given the inter-racial tension that permeated social life in South Africa, I doubt if he could have gained the confidence of these officials without losing that of other segments of the population. The report of the study, which was openly hostile to the system of apartheid, was said by reviewers in the United States to be 'objective' and 'meeting the highest standards of scholarship', while in South Africa it was described as 'confused', 'sensational' and 'containing several contradictions' (van den Berghe 1964; 1967: 185, 193). In situations such as these the social scientist cannot avoid facing up to Howard Becker's (1967) question, 'Whose side are we on?' but he/she also has to realize that his or her understanding of why and how the other side behaves as it does must necessarily be incomplete.

In the limiting case of social conflict the investigator may have either to conceal his or her identity or else to confine his or her activities to inquiries that can harm no one and change nothing. Many, but not all, social scientists would prefer to avoid the completely covert pole of this continuum, and some would spurn it completely (cf. Dingwall 1980; O'Connor and Barnes 1983), but the other pole, that of bland endorsement of indigenous values and myths, is also difficult to defend. We tend therefore to seek some intermediate position, where we are careful not to tread on too many toes too soon, even if later on because of our inquiries some reputations suffer and some shifts in power are facilitated.

A SOCIAL ETHICAL MODEL FOR SOCIAL RESEARCH

There are other polarities between which the social scientist willy-nilly has to compromise. The compromise between deception and honesty that has to be faced during the phase of data collection is matched by the compromise between openness and secrecy that arises at the stage of publication. There is the conflict between safeguarding privacy and the right to freedom of information (cf. Øyen 1982; Beckford 1982). In broader terms there is a need to compromise between the dissemination of knowledge and the maintenance of necessary ignorance. To discuss these topics, to embark on an examination of the relation of knowledge to power, would take us far beyond the limited purview of this paper (Barnes 1980).

But I hope that I have said enough to make my case. Biomedical research raises serious ethical issues, affecting life and death, and it is quite proper that medical ethics should be the subject of continual public and professional debate. But the comparative maturity of medical ethics, as compared with the ethics of social research, coupled with the comparatively powerful position of the medical profession, is not an adequate reason for seeking to ensure that social research conforms to a biomedical ethical code. Many of the hazards of medical inquiry are not encountered in social research, while on the other hand the social researcher faces a complex set of ethical decisions, most of which do not arise in medical research. Social researchers urgently need guidance in tackling their ethical choices, but the biomedical model does not offer them the guidance they require. A good deal of guidance is already available in the literature on the ethics of social research (e.g., Appell 1978; Cassell and Jacobs 1987; Jowell 1981; Homan 1991; Sieber 1982; Social Research Association 1984) which takes into account the diversity of modes of inquiry, the likely outcomes of inquiries, and the social attributes of those making the inquiries. This guidance is guidance, and not prescription, for it acknowledges that in social research there are no perfect ethical solutions but only uneasy compromises. The hortative but impractical professional codes are being replaced by educationally-oriented ethical guidelines, designed to alert researchers to the complexity of the issues they must take into account and about which they must make their own imperfect decisions. It is this recognition of the unavoidability of compromise that should form the basis for efforts to enhance awareness among social scientists of the ethical dimension of their research activities.

REFERENCES

APPELL, GEORGE NATHAN. 1978. *Ethical Dilemmas in Anthropological Inquiry: A Case Book*. Waltham, Mass: Crossroads Press.

BARNES, JOHN ARUNDEL. 1980. *Who Should Know What?* Cambridge: Cambridge University Press.

BECKER, HOWARD SAUL. 1967. 'Whose Side are We on?', *Social Problems*, 14: 239–47.

BECKFORD, JAMES ARTHUR. 1982. 'The Ideologies of Privacy', *Current Sociology*, 30: 43–69, 71–82.

BOK, SISSELA. 1978. *Lying: Moral Choice in Public and Private Life*. New York: Pantheon.

BURGESS, ROBERT G. 1984. 'The Whole Truth? Some Ethical Problems of Research in a Comprehensive School'. In R.G. Burgess (Ed.), *The Research Process in Educational Settings: Ten Case Studies*. London: Falmer Press.

CASSELL, JOAN and JACOBS, SUE-ELLEN (Eds.). 1987. *Handbook on Ethical Issues in Anthropology*. Washington, D.C.: American Anthropological Association. *Special Publication 23*.

DAVIS, FRED. 1961. 'Comment on Initial Interaction of Newcomers in Alcoholics Anonymous', *Social Problems*, 8: 364–65.

DINGWALL, ROBERT. 1980. 'Ethics and Ethnography', *Sociological Review*, ns, 28: 871–91.

EVANS-PRITCHARD, EDWARD EVAN. 1937. *Witchcraft, Oracles and Magic among the Azande*. Oxford: Clarendon Press.

———. 1973. 'Some Reminiscences and Reflections on Fieldwork', *Journal of the Anthropological Society of Oxford*, 4: 1–12.

FESTINGER, LEON, RIECKEN, HENRY WILLIAM and SCHACHTER, STANLEY. 1956. *When Prophesy Fails*. Minneapolis: University of Minnesota Press.

GALLIHER, JOHN F. 1980. 'Social Scientists' Ethical Responsibilities to Superordinates: Looking Upward Meekly', *Social Problems*, 27: 298–308.

HOMAN, ROGER E. 1991. *The Ethics of Social Research*. London: Longman.

JOWELL, ROGER. 1981. A Professional Code for Statisticians? Some Ethical and Technical Conflicts. *Bulletin of the International Statistical Institute* (Proceedings of the 43rd Session), 49: 165–209.

KLOOS, PETER. 1983–84. 'Nothing but the Truth, a Question of Power', *Journal of Northern Luzon*, 14: 121–37.

MONTANDON, CLÉOPÂTRE. 1983. 'Problems ethique de la recherche en sciences sociales: le cas d'une étude en milieu carcéral', *Schweizerische Zeitschrift für Soziologie*, 9: 215–33.
—— 1984. 'Deception of Host and Self in Field Work: A Case Study', *Wisconsin Sociologist*, 21: 118–27.
O'CONNOR, MICHAEL E. and BARNES, J. A. 1983. 'Bulmer on Pseudo-Patients: A Critique', *Sociological Review*, ns, 31: 753–58.
SIEBER, JOAN E. (Ed.). 1982. *The Ethics of Social Research*, 2 Vols. New York: Springer-Verlag.
SOCIAL RESEARCH ASSOCIATION. 1984. *Ethical Guidelines*.
VAN DEN BERGHE, PIERRE L. 1964. *Caneville: The Social Structure of a South African Town*. Middletown, Conn.: Wesleyan University Press.
—— 1967. 'Research in South Africa: The Story of My Experience with Tyranny'. In Gideon Sjoberg (Ed.), *Ethics, Politics and Social Research*. Cambridge, Mass.: Schenkman, pp. 183–97.
WAX, MURRAY L. 1980. 'Paradoxes of "Consent" to the Practice of Fieldwork', *Social Problems*, 27: 272–83.
ØYEN, ELSE. 1982. 'The Social Function of Confidentiality', *Current Sociology*, 30: 1–42, 71–82.

9

M. N. SRINIVAS:
THE MAN AND HIS
WORK

A. M. SHAH

I first met Professor M. N. Srinivas on 15 July 1951, when he was
35 and I was 20 years of age. He had just joined the Maharaja
Sayajirao University of Baroda as its first Professor and Head of the
Department of Sociology, and I had enrolled as a student in the first
year of the BA programme. The gap between us was wide; however,
with the passage of time it became narrow. The association between
us has been long, intimate and many-sided. I mention these facts at
the outset because although I am writing a biographical account of
Srinivas and not my autobiography, the reader should not expect a
perfectly objective biography. I am, however, helped in reducing my
biases by the several autobiographical accounts provided by Srinivas,
particularly 'Itineraries of an Indian Social Anthropologist' (1973),
'My Baroda Days' (1981) and 'Sociology in Delhi' (1993). I have
paraphrased portions from these accounts.[1]

---

[1] I have also used Parthasarathy's (1991) article on Srinivas. I am grateful to him for
giving me a copy of the typescript.

Srinivas was born on 16 November 1916 in a traditional brahmin family in the city of Mysore, then capital of the princely state of Mysore. His father Narasimhachar was a minor official in the government. The initials M and N in Srinivas' name stand for Mysore and Narasimhachar respectively.

Narasimhachar's native place was Arakere, a village about 20 miles by road from Mysore and about 3 miles from Rampura (real name Kodagahalli) which shot into prominence following Srinivas' anthropological writings. Srinivas named his house 'Arakere' which he constructed in Bangalore city in the 1970s.

Srinivas' family environment was conducive to education. His father had moved from Arakere to Mysore mainly with the intention of providing education to his children. Members of his mother's family had made a name for themselves in the educational field. His maternal aunt was one of the two earliest women graduates in the old princely Mysore state. The other woman was also related to Srinivas. Srinivas was the youngest of Narasimhachar's four sons. His eldest brother had completed his education by the time Srinivas was in school. He had a postgraduate degree in English literature and was teaching in the Maharaja's High School in Mysore. (He was later appointed Assistant Professor in English in the University of Mysore.) When Srinivas' father passed away at an early age—Srinivas was 17 at that time—his eldest brother became the head of the family and took decisions about his younger brothers' and sisters' education.

Srinivas' natal family owned a house on College Road (at it was then called) in Mysore. He lived there till he was in his teens. All the houses on this road were occupied by brahmins hailing from different parts of South India. Most of the people concentrated in the streets behind these houses were Kurubas (shepherds/weavers by caste) and they had migrated perhaps in the early years of this century from their natal villages a few miles to the south of the city. They were villagers who had been urbanized, and a good number of them in the city retained contacts with the village.

The area inhabited by these villagers was known as Bandikeri (literally, bullock cart street) and its culture was different from that of College Road in several respects. Whereas the inhabitants of Bandikeri were non-vegetarian those of College Road were vegetarian. Those living in Bandikeri performed manual work while the residents of College Road did no manual work as they owned land and were literate. The people in Bandikeri celebrated their own festivals, and even when the 'same' festivals were celebrated, there were differences.

Srinivas has narrated in detail how he was fascinated by the life in Bandikeri and how he received many of his first culture shocks there. He writes,

> ... as an overprotected Brahmin boy growing up on College Road, I experienced my first culture shocks not more than fifty yards from the back wall of our house.... The entire culture of Bandikeri was visibly and olfactorily different from that of College Road. Bandikeri was my Trobriand Islands, my Nuerland, my Navaho country and what have you. In retrospect, it is not surprising that I became an anthropologist, an anthropologist all of whose fieldwork was in his own country (Srinivas 1992: 141).

The brahmins living on College Road spoke different languages, and belonged to different sects. College Road spanned nearly 700 yards; Srinivas lived in a section which was about 120 feet in length and housed five families of Sri Vaishnava brahmins, popularly referred to as Iyengars, and followers of Ramanuja, the medieval reformer of Hinduism and propounder of the theological doctrine of qualified monism (*vishishtadvaita*) in contradistinction to Shankara's advocacy of pure monism (*advaita*). But even amongst them there were differences of language, affiliation to a monastery or guru, Westernization, and education.

Srinivas was scrawny and grossly underweight and his relatives and friends thought that he was too delicate to pursue a serious course of study such as medicine or engineering. He did reasonably well at the Secondary School Leaving Certificate Examination (1931) conducted by the University of Mysore, and he could have opted for a two-year Intermediate course in Science in a college in Bangalore like many others who had secured good marks. However, his eldest brother vetoed the idea and advised him to enrol in a course in modern history, logic and mathematics at Maharaja's College in Mysore.

Srinivas passed the Intermediate examination in a third division, securing very low marks particularly in mathematics. In view of his poor performance, considered decision had to be taken about the course he should pursue for the Bachelor's degree. At this juncture, as he has stated,

> Fate intervened in the person of Acharya, a friend of EB's (Eldest Brother's), a Marxist and a rebel. EB asked Acharya what course I should take. He flipped the pages of the university handbook and

gave his verdict: the honours course in social philosophy was a 'broad' humanising one and good for me. I sent in my application for it and was admitted without difficulty (Srinivas 1973).

The course in social philosophy was an ambitious one, it included papers in sociology, ethics, political thought, history of ethics, comparative religion, Indian social institutions, Indian ethics, and political theory. The 'minor' subjects included social anthropology, social psychology, comparative politics, and Indian economics. The curriculum had been designed by A.R. Wadia, the Head of the Department of Philosophy from 1917 to 1942, who was more interested in ethics, sociology, political thought and social work than in metaphysics. The inclusion of sociology, social anthropology, social psychology and politics in a philosophy course was an innovative step if not a courageous one, for the climate in the country at that time was suspicious of sociology as a discipline. Since there were only four other students besides Srinivas in his class, the student–teacher relationship was close.

Srinivas passed the BA (Honours) examination in the summer of 1936, missing a first class by a narrow margin. He has reflected on this performance:

I was an extremely unintelligent examinee and did not know the first thing about preparing for an exam. I thought I had to read conscientiously everything that had been prescribed. All first-class students in arts subjects concentrated on certain topics, if not questions, but gambling was not in my nature. But I became aware of my shortcomings as an examinee only long after I had ceased to take exams (Srinivas 1973).

Srinivas grew up in an environment where he was encouraged to write in English. As mentioned earlier, his eldest brother was a teacher in English, and through him Srinivas came into contact with others in the field of English literature. The most important of them was R.K. Narayan, the celebrated novelist. In an interesting article on Narayan, Srinivas (1994) informs that he had also started writing and used to show his writings to Narayan. Srinivas, of course, did not pursue a literary career in English but he wrote lucid English prose and some of his anthropological works, particularly *The Remembered Village* (1976), are of high literary quality.

BOMBAY PHASE

Having passed the BA examination, Srinivas and his family members toyed with the idea of his appearing for the Mysore Civil Service examination, preparatory to taking up a government job. However, this idea was given up and Srinivas decided instead to go to Bombay to enrol in the Master's course in sociology and to work for a law degree in the evenings. The Department of Sociology at the Bombay University was the first postgraduate department of sociology to be set up in the country and had earned a high reputation within a short period of time due to the distinction of its founder, Patrick Geddes and his successor as head of the department, G.S. Ghurye. Srinivas went to Bombay armed with recommendation letters addressed to Ghurye from Wadia and from his teacher in social anthropology, M.H. Krishna. Ghurye himself had set and evaluated Srinivas' BA paper on sociology and had given him 66 per cent marks.

In those days a student could do his Master's either by taking an examination at the end of two years' attendance at lectures or by writing a dissertation. In view of Srinivas' Honours degree in sociology Ghurye asked him to submit a dissertation. Srinivas believed that this would give him a better chance to prove his abilities than an examination: 'There was no sharp deadline for a dissertation, and I did not have to compete with thirty other students as I would have to if I had to "take papers"' (Srinivas 1973). He completed his dissertation on 'Marriage and Family among the Kannada Castes in Mysore State', drawing upon the available ethnographic literature, folklore, fiction, questionnaire, and a short period of fieldwork. The fieldwork was undertaken mainly to seek information on customs and rituals from informants. The dissertation was completed in 1938, and published in 1942 under the title, *Marriage and Family in Mysore*. It received favourable reviews in professional journals, including an enthusiastic one in *Nature*. (Ghurye has quoted a part of the review in his autobiography [1973: 108–9]).[2]

The Department of Sociology awarded a research fellowship to Srinivas in June 1940 to carry out a field study of the Coorgs of South India for his doctoral degree. Srinivas had for some time toyed with

---

[2] Srinivas studied for LlB at the Government Law College alongside studying sociology at the Department of Sociology. Dr. B.R. Ambedkar was one of his teachers there.

the idea of doing his doctorate on a 'theoretical' subject such as the relation between the individual and society in Indian thought. But Ghurye rejected the idea, saying that no fellowship would be available if he chose a theme which did not involve fieldwork.

Srinivas submitted his thesis, entitled 'The Coorgs: A Socio-Ethnic Study', in December 1944. He is very modest about his fieldwork in Coorg, 'My field study of the Coorgs could not be as deep or thorough as I wanted it to be.... I was forced (due to a stomach ailment) to collect my data in short hit-and-run trips' (Srinivas 1973). But obviously he collected a large amount of data, which enabled him to write an unusually long thesis—two volumes numbering nearly 900 pages. The quality of his work was laudable as testified by the external referee, Raymond Firth, the eminent anthropologist at the London School of Economics, and Ghurye the internal one, in their report on the thesis. Ghurye says that Firth wrote the report and he only added 'I agree':

The referees have read this thesis on the Coorgs or Kodagus with great interest, and regard it as suitable for the award of the Ph.D. degree. In putting forward this opinion the referees have been impressed by several aspects of the thesis, in particular, the very able manner in which the citation and analysis of documentary material have been combined with the results of the candidate's own field research; the quantity and quality of original material collected in the comparatively short period of about five months in the field; and the presentation of the data in a way which draws significant sociological and ethnological inferences from the detailed mass of ethnographic facts set down. Moreover, though the thesis is primarily a study of traditional Coorg institutions, a considerable amount of material is given to show how these institutions are changing and becoming adapted to modern conditions. The treatment of the thesis material is scientific in character and modest in tone. The work is claimed as only a preliminary survey to form a basis for more intensive studies, and the referees hope therefore that Mr. Srinivas will be able in due course to pursue these further investigations, especially on the economic side, and so add to the distinct contribution he has already made to Indian sociology...(Ghurye 1973: 114–15).

Besides the favourable comments of the referees, the quality of ethnographic material was exceptionally high, such that Srinivas later used the same material to write another doctoral thesis using a different theoretical approach.

When Srinivas' research fellowship expired in June 1942 he was appointed as a research assistant in the same department, a post he held till June 1944. The work required him to assist Ghurye in his research, including undertaking field trips to collect data. A part of the data he collected was related to folklore in Tamil Nadu and Andhra, and he published two papers (1943; 1944) using this data.

Srinivas' relations with Ghurye were complicated. He has mentioned that they began to sour in 1943 (see 1973 and 1983). There was one immediate cause:

> Two lectureships were advertised in the department, and Ghurye asked me to apply for one of them. He more than hinted that in view of my publication and extensive field work experience, I stood a very good chance. He said even more. But at the actual selection two others were chosen. Both Wadia and Radhakrishnan were members of the Selection Committee, and they were unhappy with the way things had gone (1983).

Srinivas has also mentioned an intellectual cause for the souring of his relations with Ghurye.

> ...more than eight years of apprenticeship under Ghurye had left me with a feeling of deep dissatisfaction. I had started out wanting to be a theorist of society but had ended up by becoming a conjectural historian and a collector of ethnographical facts without being able to integrate them into a meaningful framework. My interest in ideas had been starved (1973).

Srinivas, however, continued to be decent and at times even cordial with Ghurye.

OXFORD PHASE

After completing his doctorate, Srinivas considered the idea of pursuing higher studies abroad. He was admitted to the B.Litt. course in social anthropology at Oxford, with provision for its later conversion to DPhil with retrospective effect. For his dissertation he submitted a proposal on 'Culture Patterns among Three South Indian Ethnic Groups—Coorgs, Todas and Chenchus'. With financial support from his family, he went to Oxford in May 1945. Later he received a Carnegie research grant for two years.

Srinivas' initial encounters with his teacher A.R. Radcliffe-Brown at Oxford were not happy. The main reason for this was that Radcliffe-Brown did not appreciate Srinivas' idea of studying 'patterns of culture' derived from Ruth Benedict. Instead Radcliffe-Brown advised him to examine—rather re-examine—the relation between religion and society among the Coorgs on the basis of the material he had collected earlier. Srinivas readily accepted the suggestion.

Ghurye has reported in his autobiography (1973: 115–16) that Srinivas was 'very communicative' and wrote to him nearly two dozen letters during his stay at Oxford, some of which Ghurye had preserved. Ghurye has quoted from two letters describing the initial period of his stay at Oxford. In one of the letters Srinivas wrote:

I am quite certain I can never forget what I owe to you intellectually. It is mainly due to this training which I received under you that today I am not swept away by Radcliffe-Brown. He must have found me a 'tough nut to crack' as I rejected his anti-historicism and regarded his functionalism as only supplementary to the so-called historical approach. My fundamental point remains the same—it is because I know it to be correct. I also know that I have derived it from 'you'... I am reading John Embree's 'Suye Mura'[3] which is in our Library. It is supposed to be one of the developments of new anthropology. It is nothing very different from Bhagat's and M.N. Desai's work.[4] I am quite glad I am getting disillusioned.

Nearly a month or so later Srinivas wrote:

R-B seems to have 'warmed up' a bit. He read the Coorgs [the thesis on Coorgs which had earned Srinivas the degree of Ph.D. of the Bombay University] during the 'long vac'. It is this which seems to have changed his attitude. May I thank you as, but for your goading, I wouldn't have taken up that subject, and worked it with sustained enthusiasm.

Although Srinivas (1973 and 1983) has stated that his relations with Ghurye had begun to sour in 1943, these letters do not reveal any tension between the two.

[3] Embree (1946).
[4] M.G. Bhagat's doctoral thesis (1941) was entitled 'The Farmer, His Welfare and Wealth', and M. N. Desai's thesis (1942) was on 'Life and Living in Rural Karnataka'.

The first two years at Oxford were a period of intense intellectual activity for Srinivas, in the course of which, as he says (1973),

I became an enthusiastic convert to functionalism *a la* Radcliffe-Brown. I had the feeling that I had at last found a theoretical framework which was satisfactory but like all new converts I was fanatic. I suppressed my natural scepticism, one of my few real assets, to accept such dogmas as the irrelevance of history for sociological explanation, the unimportance of culture and the existence of universal laws.

Srinivas had completed the major part of his dissertation by the middle of 1946 when Radcliffe-Brown retired. Srinivas then worked for a while under E.E. Evans-Pritchard. He was awarded the DPhil degree in July 1947. Evans-Pritchard's influence had the effect of steering Srinivas away from Radcliffe-Brownian functionalism and towards a more balanced view of social anthropology.

A few days before Srinivas left Oxford in July 1947, Evans-Pritchard informed him of the possibility of a new post of Lecturer in Indian Sociology being created at Oxford, and whether he wanted to be considered for it. This unexpected offer came when 'I was homesick, and eagerly looking forward to going home, and the prospect of returning to England in the immediate future went against my plans'. However, at that moment 'I was overwhelmed to find that I was thought good enough to teach at Oxford... it was no doubt a dream come true...' (1976: 3).

Following the completion of his DPhil thesis, Srinivas planned to do research on an Indian village. He was aware that the village was at the centre of the constructive programme in independent India, that economists, particularly those in Bombay, were studying villages, and Ghurye had also initiated studies on rural communities. It has been mentioned earlier that in a letter to Ghurye (1946) Srinivas compared John Embree's work on a Japanese village under Radcliffe-Brown's supervision with Bhagat's and M.N. Desai's work on rural society in India under Ghurye's supervision. What was required, however, was a village study in India using the new theoretical ideas and methods developed in social anthropology in Britain. Such a study had emerged clearly as the most exciting and fruitful one to undertake Indian sociology and social anthropology at the time. When, therefore, following his appointment as lecturer at Oxford in November 1947,

Srinivas was permitted to devote the first year to fieldwork, he spent almost the whole of 1948 in doing fieldwork in a village in his native Mysore state.

Before leaving Oxford Srinivas had applied for a post in the Anthropological Survey of India. He was interviewed for the post in New Delhi in November 1947, where he had a difficult time with B.S. Guha, the Director. Soon afterwards he received the letter of appointment at Oxford (see Srinivas 1976: 4).

During his second spell, spanning two and a half years, at Oxford, Srinivas of course performed his teaching duties and prepared his thesis for publication. But more important, he was involved in intensive intellectual and social interaction with a large number of scholars, students and others at the time when social anthropology at Oxford was at the pinnacle of its glory. He formed lasting friendships with many eminent persons.

Srinivas' second spell at Oxford was also marked by the dilemma as to whether he should return to India or continue to stay in England. He says,

... underneath my seeming contentment I was homesick for the sun and warmth of India. And I also realized that if I did not make an effort and pull myself out of Oxford before it was too late, I would probably not return home. Throughout the year 1950 I was bothered by the nagging desire to return home (1973).

We learn from Ghurye's autobiography (1973: 127–30) that Srinivas had applied for the post of Reader in the University of Bombay, where a serious dispute arose between the Vice-Chancellor Justice N.H. Bhagawati who favoured Srinivas while the experts on the selection committee, namely, Ghurye, D.P. Mukerji and B.S. Guha, favoured K.M. Kapadia. The dispute was referred to the Chancellor, i.e., the Governor of Bombay, who ruled that the opinion of the experts be accepted. This dispute was perhaps the beginning of the rupture in Srinivas' relationship with Ghurye.

BARODA DAYS

Srinivas has narrated in some detail how he came to occupy the Chair of Sociology in Baroda University. Having failed to secure a job in the Anthropological Survey of India and the University of Bombay,

Srinivas turned his attention to new universities that were being established following the independence of India. Baroda was one such university. His old teacher Wadia was Pro-Vice-Chancellor there.

Wadia played a crucial role in bringing Srinivas to Baroda. Following his advice, Srinivas sent in his application. At Wadia's suggestion, Dr. S. Radhakrishnan also wrote to the Vice-Chancellor Hansa Mehta. (Apart from the fact that Radhakrishnan was an eminent figure in the academic world, he was also the chairman of the committee set up by the Maharaja of Baroda to work out the blueprint of Baroda University.) With such powerful support Srinivas' selection was smooth, though it is worth noting that two very senior sociologists of the time, Radhakamal Mukerjee of Lucknow and Kewal Motwani of Annamalai had also applied.

Wadia visited England in May 1951 and had discussions with Srinivas about Baroda and the work he was expected to do. Srinivas left London on 12 June and arrived at Baroda via Bombay on 15 June and joined Baroda University the same day, the first day of the new academic year.

Baroda University is one of the few universities in India with what is called a unitary structure. That is to say, unlike most other universities it does not have affiliated colleges for undergraduate teaching. Each of its departments offers teaching programmes from the undergraduate level upward to the doctoral level, and the departments are grouped into faculties. A few pre-existing colleges in Baroda city affiliated to Bombay University were merged into the new university and reorganized into departments and faculties. Several new departments were created, sociology being one such department.

Since Sociology Department had been recently set up, Srinivas was faced with the task of organizing the teaching of a new subject at all levels. However, he had an opportunity to make his own appointments, unlike in the other departments which inherited the teaching staff from the pre-existing colleges, and he was at liberty to introduce his own teaching programme.

In the initial years, Srinivas also faced a technical problem in organizing the teaching. Baroda University had decided to continue with the syllabi of Bombay University as long as its own syllabi were not prepared. Since Srinivas was the only teacher in sociology in June 1951 he decided to introduce the teaching of only one programme and that too a minor one, namely, the subsidiary subject of Cultural Anthropology which the BA (Honours) students in other subjects could combine with the main subject. It had two papers, one on 'Social Anthropology' and the other on 'Material Culture'. There were only two students in the first batch, Indubhai Shelat and myself. Srinivas taught Social Anthropology. He discarded all the textbooks prescribed by Bombay University, which in effect meant discarding the textbooks chosen by his teacher, G.S. Ghurye. These were Ruth Benedict's *Patterns of Culture* (1949), Goldenweiser's *Anthropology* (1937), and R.H. Lowie's *Primitive Religion* (1952). Instead, he recommended Evans-Pritchard's *Social Anthropology* (1952), Firth's *Human Types* (1950), and Radcliffe-Brown's unpublished manuscript, 'Method in Social Anthropology' (of which he had a personal copy, which he edited and published in 1959). He also asked us to review two other books: Evans-Pritchard's *Divine Kingship among the Shilluk* (1948), and Verrier Elwin's *Indian Aboriginals* (1949). His prescription of these readings was informal. When Indubhai Shelat and I once asked him about the formal syllabus for examination, he firmly said that we need not worry about the Bombay University syllabus and that we would be examined on what we were taught. Such firmness was obviously rooted in the support he enjoyed from Wadia and Hansa Mehta.

Srinivas' method of teaching was markedly different from that of other teachers who gave formal lectures to classes of 100 or more students. Srinivas adopted the method of dialogue and discussion. Since Indubhai Shelat was less regular in attending classes, often I was the only student whom Srinivas taught. Sometimes the class was held at his house.

A new syllabus for BA Honours was prepared during 1951–52 and became operative from June 1952 onwards. Two more teachers were also appointed by this time, Y.V.S. Nath, an MSc in Anthropology from Delhi University, as Research Assistant, and I.P. Desai as Reader. The syllabus represented perhaps the first attempt at integration of sociology and social anthropology under the rubric of sociology at the undergraduate level in India. A similar new syllabus for the postgraduate level followed in 1955–56.

During the first academic year Srinivas also encouraged students to register for the PhD programme. In all four students registered: three teachers from the Faculty of Social Work—P.T. Thomas, Sugata Dasgupta and C. Gopalan—and one from the Department of Archaeology—H.R. Trivedi. Simultaneously, Srinivas introduced the idea of research seminars. 'They were perhaps the first seminars to be held in the University and well before an expensive "seminar culture" took hold of the country' (Srinivas 1981).

Srinivas had definite views about teaching in general and about teaching Sociology in particular. He believed that a university teacher should not be overloaded with teaching and should have enough time to do research—the two should go hand in hand. He implemented this view in Baroda and later in Delhi. He has narrated (1981) how he struggled to implement it in Baroda.

When Mr. Ramanlal Vasantlal Desai, a member of a committee visiting the Faculty of Arts, 'asked me how many periods I was teaching per week, I told him six (or five). He replied that I ought to be teaching 26 periods a week. I took him on that and told him that since I was expected to do research as part of my duties, any such teaching load was antagonistic to research. I added that I was determined to go on with my research'.

Srinivas had definite ideas about the kind of sociology he wanted to teach in Baroda.

When I joined Baroda, it was usual for universities in western India to copy blindly the Sociology syllabus of Bombay University. I did not want to do that: for one thing, that syllabus had not been revised for some years, and secondly, I had my own conception of Sociology which I wanted reflected in my syllabus. I wanted students to have a firm knowledge of Indian Social Institutions and in a comparative context. Secondly, I found American textbooks of sociology really ethnocentric, uncomparative, and failing to distinguish between sociology and social work. Also, I found the separation of social anthropology and sociology untenable, particularly in the Indian context. Finally, I wanted students to study intensively, at least at the Master's level, a few classics in the subject. And all this had to be while paying attention to the background of the students (Srinivas 1981).

Srinivas had decided to give emphasis to fieldwork in the research at the Department in Baroda. He went on a field trip to Rampura, a village in Mysore, in the summer of 1952 (in continuation of the fieldwork he did there in 1948) and took me along with him to initiate me into fieldwork. Within two years or so of his joining Baroda University, almost everyone in the Department was doing fieldwork. Srinivas secured a grant from the university to purchase two sets of field equipment, such as a camera, pots and pans, plates and a trunk, and pressurized the university bureaucracy to simplify rules for accounting of field expenses.

When Srinivas joined Baroda University, his book *Religion and Society among the Coorgs of South India* was in the press. It was published in 1952 and on all accounts was a landmark in the development of modern sociology and social anthropology in India.

Soon after Srinivas came to Baroda, the results of his fieldwork in Rampura began to appear. He published an article 'The Social Structure of a Mysore Village' in the *Economic Weekly* (1951). He also persuaded other sociologists and anthropologists engaged in village studies in India at that time to publish articles on their work in the same journal. These articles were published in a book entitled *India's Villages* (1955) which was an instant success. He also published several papers on the different aspects of society in Rampura and on the significance of village studies (1952; 1954; 1955a; 1955b; 1959a; 1959b; 1959c). This established Srinivas as a pioneer of village studies in India.

Srinivas was under the influence of structural–functional anthropology during his initial years in Baroda. However, his focus shifted to social change. This shift was clearly discernible in the seminar discussions as well as in the topics he asked his research students to study. For example, he asked N.R. Sheth to study a modern industrial factory and asked me to study historical documents. Among Srinivas' writings the first two major papers on social change were 'A Note on Sanskritization and Westernization' (1956) and 'Caste in Modern India' (1957). The latter was included in a book with the same title (1962).

Srinivas was the most eligible bachelor on the campus of Baroda University and rumours were rife about his relations with eligible women, particularly a few South Indian women. Every one was pleasantly surprised when he decided to marry Rukmini from Tanjore, the centre of Tamil Brahmin tradition. The wedding took place in the South and the newly married couple was given a warm welcome by friends, colleagues and students in Baroda. Rukmini (Rukka to family members and friends) and Srinivas were blessed with their first daughter, Lakshmi, when Srinivas was still in Baroda. I vividly remember how Ramesh Shroff and I bade farewell to Srinivas, Rukka and baby Lakshmi at the Baroda railway station when they left for Delhi in December 1958 to join the University of Delhi. Their second daughter Tulsi was born in Delhi.

As Srinivas has stated,

I had built the Department at Baroda from scratch, and it had been recognized as a good and upcoming one by those who mattered. The University Grants Commission (UGC) had sanctioned in 1958 funds for the expansion and development of the Department, which included a new building, a grant for the library, a few new teaching positions, and a few scholarships for Sociology students.

Nevertheless, 'I did not see myself staying for a long time in Baroda' (1981: 145). 'I wanted to move to a metropolitan city' (1993: 2).

DELHI PHASE

Dr. V.K.R.V. Rao, the Vice-Chancellor of the University of Delhi, had been trying to persuade Srinivas to join the university for some time but Srinivas was reluctant. However, a decisive moment came in 1958. In June when Srinivas was travelling from Mysore to Baroda, Dr. Rao went to the Guntakal railway station to meet Srinivas to invite him to join the university as the first Professor and Head of a new Department of Sociology. The University of Delhi was in the process of becoming a national centre of distinguished scholars in the sciences, humanities, and social sciences. It offered a wonderful opportunity to develop a new department of Sociology.

While Delhi offered new opportunities, Baroda had begun to show signs of decline, at least according to Srinivas. A.R. Wadia, Srinivas' mentor, had left Baroda; a person less distinguished than Hansa Mehta had succeeded her as Vice-Chancellor in 1957; the city politicians had begun to play an undesirable role in the decision-making bodies of the university; and despite the fact that Srinivas and I.P. Desai were very good personal friends, there were visible strains between them in managing the affairs of the department. The growing lack of a broader vision among teachers in social science departments became apparent while considering a proposal to set up a national institute of social sciences in Baroda. While Srinivas and a few of his close friends were in favour of this idea, others opposed it on petty grounds.

Srinivas joined the University of Delhi in February 1959 and the new Department began to function soon thereafter. The first major task in setting up the Department was to prepare a syllabus for the Master's programme. He gave it more or less the same general thrust that he had given to the syllabi in Baroda: a broad comparative perspective entailing integration of sociology and social anthropology. The themes of research for PhD students had a similar thrust: a broad spectrum varying from the traditional themes of social anthropology such as caste, kinship and religion to the traditional themes of sociology such as urban community and industrial and other complex organizations. In dealing with these varied themes, Srinivas' emphasis was on the method of intensive fieldwork or participant observation. As a result there was a tilt towards anthropology in the Department. He justified this tilt in his writings and lectures around the world by firmly asserting that it was the best strategy for developing a sound study of Indian society and culture for many years to come.

Srinivas gave close attention to the organization of the postgraduate teaching programme. First, to keep the teacher–student ratio low, so essential for good teaching, he enrolled a small number of students. Second, he emphasized a vigorous tutorial and seminar programme besides lectures. This was possible due to the small number of students. Third, he ensured that all teachers, irrespective of their rank, shared the teaching work, including tutorial work, equally.

When Srinivas took over as the founder Head of the Department there were only a few posts, one of Professor and three of Lecturers. At the end of his tenure as the Head in January 1970 there were four posts of Professors, five of Readers, and four of Lecturers. The number of Research Fellowships for doctoral students had also increased from 2 to 11, and the technical and office staff from 3 to 9. In addition, the Department had its own building and other infrastructural facilities.

Srinivas made ceaseless efforts to build up the Department. Apart from monitoring the teaching and other activities within the Department, he also cultivated relationships with people outside the Department and influenced and lobbied them in the interest of the Department. He frequently agreed to be a member of a committee or to attend a seminar not necessarily because of its intrinsic worth but because it gave him an opportunity to promote the interests of the Department. Unlike other heads of academic institutions who refused to meet 'clerks', even 'glorified clerks', and hence jeopardized the interests of their institutions, Srinivas always agreed to meet low ranking bureaucrats. Of course, a lot of his scholarly work was sacrificed in the process. Many of his detractors often said that Srinivas had become an administrator!

During his 12-year tenure as Head of the department, there was always some exciting new development or activity taking place in the department. The high point, however, was the academic year 1967–68 during which several important developments took place one after another. First, the UGC set up a Special Cell for the Development of Sociological Study of the North-Eastern Hill Areas and the Pakistan Area Studies Programme (in collaboration with the Department of Economics) in the department. Second, the department undertook the teaching of BA (Honours) programme in sociology. And third and most important, the UGC recognized the department as a Centre of Advanced Study.

A.R. Wadia played an important role in the decision regarding the Centre of Advanced Study. He was at that time a member of the UGC. He was appointed chairman of the UGC's Visiting Committee to assess the department's request for status as a Centre of Advanced Study. The other members of the Committee were Srinivas' friends, M.S. Gore and R.N. Saksena. The Committee as well as other friends in the UGC helped the department in securing both high status and funds for further development.

Having successfully established the department, Srinivas turned his attention to devoting himself entirely to scholarly work.

For many years, I had been dreaming of getting away from my teaching and other professional activities to write an authoritative book on the social structure of Rampura. I had done fieldwork in Rampura in 1948 and in the summer of 1952, and I had tried hard to organize my field notes in the intervals of teaching and administrative duties (1993).

But the final planning, thinking and writing remained to be done. A one year fellowship at the Center for Advanced Study in the Behavioral Sciences at Stanford in 1970 gave him an opportunity to do just that. 'I was itching to go to Stanford', Srinivas said (1993).

Srinivas' stay at Stanford, however, proved to be disastrous. On 25 April 1970, all the copies of his processed notes on Rampura were burnt in the fire started by anti-Viet Nam War arsonists at the Center. However, at Professor Sol Tax's suggestion Srinivas wrote the book *The Remembered Village* (1976) based almost entirely on his memory of field experiences in Rampura.

The new building for the Sociology Department was nearing completion when Srinivas returned to Delhi from Stanford in July 1971. It was inaugurated on 27 September 1971 by Dr. V.K.R.V. Rao. The new building was symbolic of Srinivas' efforts to create an excellent department with an identity of its own.

AT ISEC, BANGALORE

The day the Department's new building was inaugurated, Dr. V.K.R.V. Rao informed Srinivas that he was setting up a new institute—the Institute for Social and Economic Change (ISEC) in Bangalore and he wanted Srinivas to join it as Joint Director. Srinivas accepted the offer. When this plan was announced, it was by all accounts considered to be a momentous event in social sciences in India. Its importance lay not so much in Rao founding yet another institute—he had founded the Delhi School of Economics and the Institute of Economic Growth in Delhi—but in his success in persuading Srinivas to migrate from Delhi to Bangalore. A number of people considered it to be a kind of scoop and Rao proudly stated that he had highjacked a scholar of Srinivas' stature from Delhi to Bangalore. (By this time Rao had acquired the image of being a politician.) He went so far as to say that while in the naming of the earlier two institutes he had given primacy to the economic factor, he had given primacy to the social factor in the naming of the new institute, because he believed the social factor to be more important than the economic factor in changes taking place in India. He was also implying that Srinivas would play a vital role in the new institute.

On his part, Srinivas usually gave two reasons for moving to Bangalore. First, he had been planning to settle down in Bangalore after his retirement from Delhi, and this offer only hastened his departure. Second, he believed that sociology was not well developed in South India—there was a lot of truth in this belief—and that his moving to Bangalore would have an impact on the development of the discipline in the south. While both these reasons were convincing, there were all kinds of rumours about Srinivas' real intentions. Far more important, however, was the widely held belief that Rao was such a difficult person that Srinivas would not be able to get along with him. This was precisely the argument that Dr. Sarup Singh, Vice-Chancellor of the University of Delhi, offered—rather bluntly—to Srinivas (in my presence) in his efforts to persuade him not to leave Delhi.

Srinivas joined the ISEC in May 1972. Initially things proceeded smoothly. But soon Srinivas began to complain about the load of administrative work and its adverse effect on his academic work. He gave up the Joint Directorship; and relations between him and V.K.R.V. Rao began to sour after a few years. What followed was bitterness and confrontation. Never before had anyone seen Srinivas in such a mood. Only formal resignation and consequently retirement as a faculty member in January 1979 put an end to this.

CONTRIBUTION TO PROFESSIONAL ORGANIZATIONS

One of Srinivas' lasting contributions to the profession of sociology in India has been the unification of two professional organizations, the Indian Sociological Society and the All-India Sociological Conference in 1967. The Indian Sociological Society, founded by Ghurye in 1952, published a journal, *Sociological Bulletin*. The Society was a legally registered body and conducted its financial and other affairs in a systematic manner. However, for various reasons it began to languish around 1965. Moreover, it was perceived to be dominated by Ghurye and his pupils, mainly in western India. On the other hand, the only activity of the All-India Sociological Conference was to organize conferences. It was neither a legally registered body nor were its affairs conducted in an organized manner. For example, its accounts were in shambles. More important, it was perceived to be a north Indian organization.

With Srinivas' migration from Baroda to Delhi, he emerged as a sociologist who could unite sociologists in all the various parts of the country. It is this perception which led to the unification of the two bodies. The All-India Sociological Conference was merged into the Indian Sociological Society under Srinivas' leadership. He became the first President under the new arrangement. The office of the Society was also shifted to the Department of Sociology at the University of Delhi. Since then sociology is perhaps the only social science which has only one representative professional association in the country. Other social sciences have each two or more rival associations.

Srinivas has a high reputation as a committee man. He has been not only a member but also chairman of many committees. He has won admiration for his being fair but firm, open to differing views but able to cut through them and arrive at a meaningful conclusion, always making witty remarks to make the proceedings smooth and lively but taking firm and unpleasant stands when necessary.

Srinivas has received widespread recognition for his contributions to sociology and social anthropology and to academic life in general.

He has been conferred with honorary degrees and visiting professorships and fellowships of many universities, research institutions and foundations; medals, prizes and awards; honorary memberships and fellowships of learned societies and associations; invitations to deliver lectures; etc. The list is too long to be given here. Srinivas, however, wears his successes very lightly.

A SYNOPTIC VIEW OF SCHOLARLY WORK[5]

Srinivas' fieldwork experience has been long, varied and widespread. Beginning with the work for his Master's degree on marriage and family in Mysore, he collected Tamil and Telugu folk songs as Ghurye's Research Assistant. His marathon two-volume thesis on the Coorgs for his doctoral degree is a testimony to the richness of data he had collected. Using the same data, he wrote another thesis, with a different theoretical orientation at Oxford. His fieldwork reached high standards when he worked in Rampura. In addition to the theoretical sophistication he had cultivated at Oxford by this time, he had also acquired intimate knowledge and understanding of the fieldwork done by such luminaries as Evans-Pritchard, Firth, Fortes and Gluckman as well as of the failures of a number of lesser known anthropologists. He put this knowledge and understanding to good use in his own work in Rampura. I had the privilege of observing him when he did his fieldwork in Rampura in the summer of 1952. He worked very hard from early morning till late in the night and made detailed notes, frequently interspersed with theoretical comments. Not even a tenth of these notes have been used in his publications.

Though Srinivas has written on many aspects of Indian society and culture he is best known for his work on religion, village community, caste, social change, and methodology. While most of his writings are based on intensive fieldwork in South India in general and Coorg and Rampura in particular, his writings on Indian society at large provide a synthesis of his personal observation and knowledge and the existing literature on different regions of the country. His concepts of 'Sanskritization' and 'dominant caste' have been used by a wide range of scholars to understand Indian society and culture, past and present, and have become part of the public discourse in India. The distinction

[5] This section is based on my article on Srinivas (Shah 1991). An elaborate evaluation of Srinivas' scholarly work is the focus of the rest of this volume.

he made between the 'book view' and the 'field view' in the study of civilizations has tremendous significance.

Srinivas does not describe himself as belonging to any 'school' or 'ism' except empiricism. His writings are free from jargon and from references to grand sociological theories. His empiricism is related to his belief that for many years to come field studies, particularly intensive studies, will provide deeper insights into Indian society and culture, although he is not averse to using data from macro surveys and developing overall perspectives of social processes.

While Srinivas tends to disagree with some of his critics that he is a structural–functionalist, he has frequently mentioned that the ideas of social structure and function have had a profound influence on his work. He has also maintained that the full potential and implications of the idea of social structure have not yet been worked out. Though Srinivas has not propounded any general anthropological theory, his discussions of the contributions of Radcliffe-Brown and Evans-Pritchard, including his editorial introduction to Radcliffe-Brown's posthumous work, *Method in Social Anthropology*, have provided illuminating commentaries on theoretical developments in anthropology. As far as fieldwork is concerned he has demanded from his students not only methodological competence but also the sensitivity of a novelist.

To disseminate the knowledge and insights of anthropology among the common people, Srinivas has contributed to numerous newspapers and magazines and has frequently delivered lectures in public forums.

Srinivas has remained active even after his formal retirement from the ISEC. He has taught at several universities, colleges and institutes both in India and abroad as a visiting professor. He has also been involved in writing and publishing, delivering lectures, sitting on important committees, and performing many other public functions. By a happy turn of events, his differences with Dr. V.K.R.V. Rao were resolved, so much so that at Rao's initiative Srinivas was elected chairman of the Board of Governors of ISEC in 1990. Srinivas has not really retired. He is in good health and is active and agile. May God bless him with many more years of active life.

REFERENCES

BENEDICT, RUTH. 1949. *Patterns of Culture*. London: Routledge & Kegan Paul.
ELWIN, VERRIER. 1949. *Indian Aboriginals*. Bombay: Oxford University Press.

EMBREE, JOHN F. 1946. *A Japanese Village: Suye Mura.* London: Kegal Paul, Trench, Trubner.

EVANS-PRITCHARD, E.E. 1948. *Divine Kingship of the Shilluk of the Nilotic Sudan.* Cambridge: Cambridge University Press.

——. 1951. *Social Anthropology.* London: Cohen and West.

FIRTH, RAYMOND. 1950. *Human Types.* London: Thomas Nelson.

GHURYE, G.S. 1973. *I and Other Explorations.* Bombay: Popular Prakashan.

GOLDENWEISER, ALEXANDER A. 1937. *Anthropology: An Introduction to Primitive Culture.* New York: Crofts.

LOWIE, R.H. 1952. *Primitive Religion.* New York: Grosset & Dunlap.

PARTHASARATHY, V.S. 1991. Mysore Narasimhachar Srinivas. Supplementary Dictionary of National Biography. Calcutta: Institute of Historical Studies. Typescript.

RADCLIFFE-BROWN, A.R. 1959. *Method in Social Anthropology* (Ed. M.N. Srinivas). Chicago: The University of Chicago Press.

SHAH, A.M. 1991. 'M.N. Srinivas'. In *International Dictionary of Anthropologists.* New York: Garden.

SRINIVAS, M.N. 1942. *Marriage and Family in Mysore.* Bombay: New Book Company.

——. 1943. 'Some Tamil Folk-Songs. Parts I and II', *Journal of the University of Bombay*, XII, Parts I and IV, July 1943 and January 1944: 48–80; 55–86.

——. 1944. 'Some Telugu Folk-Songs. Parts I and II', *Journal of the University of Bombay*, XIII, Parts I and IV, July 1944 and January 1945: 65–86; 15–30.

——. 1952. 'A Joint Family Dispute in a Mysore Village', *Journal of the Maharaja Sayajirao University of Baroda*, 1, 1: 7–31.

——. 1954. 'A Caste Dispute among the Washermen of Mysore', *Eastern Anthropologist*, VII, 3 and 4: 148–68.

——. 1955a. 'The Social System of a Mysore Village'. In Mckim Marriott (Ed.), *Village India.* Chicago: The University of Chicago Press.

——. 1955b. 'Village Studies and Their Significance', *Eastern Anthropologist*, VIII, 3 and 4: 215–28.

——. 1956. 'The Social Structure of a Mysore Village', *Economic Weekly*, 30 October: 1051–56.

——. 1956. 'A Note on Sanskritization and Westernization', *Far Eastern Quarterly*, XV, 4: 481–96.

——. 1957. 'Caste in Modern India', *Journal of Asian Studies*, XVI, 4: 529–48.

——. 1959a. 'The Study of Disputes in an Indian Village'. *Regional Seminar on Techniques of Social Research.* Calcutta: UNESCO Research Centre.

——. 1959b. 'The Case of the Potter and the Priest', *Man in India*, 39, 3: 190–209.

——. 1959c. 'The Dominant Caste in Rampura', *American Anthropologist*, 61, 1: 1–16.

——. 1973. 'Itineraries of an Indian Social Anthropologist', *International Social Science Journal*, XXV, 1–2: 129–48.

——. 1976. *The Remembered Village.* Delhi: Oxford University Press.

——. 1981. 'My Baroda Days', *Journal of the Maharaja Sayajirao University of Baroda*, XXX, 2: 171–82.

——. 1983. 'All Is Not Lost If Your Plans Go Awry', *Deccan Herald*, 25 December.

——. 1992. *On Living in a Revolution and Other Essays.* Delhi: Oxford University Press.

——. 1993. Sociology in Delhi. Typescript.

——. 1994. 'The Creator of Malgudi', *The Times of India*, 5 June.

BIBLIOGRAPHY OF
M. N. SRINIVAS

BOOKS

1942.   *Marriage and Family in Mysore*. Bombay: New Book Co.

1952.   *Religion and Society among the Coorgs of South India*. Oxford: Clarendon Press. (Bombay: Asia Publishing House, 1965. Bombay: Media Promoters and Publishers, 1978).

1959.   With Y. B. Damle, S. Shahani and A. Beteille. *Caste: A Trend Report and Bibliography. Current Sociology*, Special Number, VIII, 3.

1962.   *Caste in Modern India and Other Essays*. Bombay: Asia Publishing House. (In Gujarati, 1968).

1966.   *Social Change in Modern India*. Berkeley: University of California Press. (Delhi: Allied Publishers, 1967. Delhi: Orient Longman, 1972. In Gujarati and Hindi, 1968).

1976a.   *The Remembered Village*. Delhi: Oxford University Press. (Berkeley: University of California Press. In Russian, 1988. In Hindi, 1995).

1976b.   *Nation-Building in Independent India.* Delhi: Oxford University Press.

1977.   With E.A. Ramaswamy. *Culture and Human Fertility in India*. Delhi: Oxford University Press.

1978.   *The Changing Position of Indian Women*. Delhi: Oxford University Press.

1980.   *India: Social Structure*. Delhi: Hindustan Publishing Corporation.

1983.   With T.S. Epstein, M.N. Panini and V.S. Parthasarathy. *Basic Needs Viewed from Above and from Below—The Case of Karnataka State, India.* Paris: OECD.

1984.   *Some Reflections on Dowry.* Delhi: Oxford University Press.

1987.   *The Dominant Caste and Other Essays.* Delhi: Oxford University Press.

1989.   *The Cohesive Role of Sanskritization and Other Essays.* Delhi: Oxford University Press.

1992.   *On Living in a Revolution and Other Essays.* Delhi: Oxford University Press.

EDITED BOOKS

1955.   *India's Villages.* Calcutta: Government Press. (Bombay: Asia Publishing House, 1960. In Gujarati, 1968).

1959.   *Method in Social Anthropology*, by A.R. Radcliffe-Brown. Chicago: University of Chicago Press. (Bombay: Asia Publishing House, 1961. Delhi: Hindustan Publishing Corporation, 1983).

1977   With S. Seshaiah and V.S. Parthasarathy. *Dimensions of Social Change in India.* Delhi: Allied Publishers.

1979   With A.M. Shah and E.A. Ramaswamy. *The Fieldworker and the Field.* Delhi: Oxford University Press.

PAPERS, ESSAYS AND NOTES

1942.   'The Family versus the State', *Aryan Path*, 13: 68–70.

1943.   'Some Tamil Folk-Songs. Parts I and II', *Journal of the University of Bombay*, XII, Part I, July 1943: 48–80. Part IV, January 1944: 55–86.

1944.   'Some Telugu Folk-Songs. Parts I and II', *Journal of the University of Bombay*, XIII, Part I, July 1944: 65–86. Part IV, January 1945: 15–30.

1946.   'The Social Organisation of the Coorgs of South India', *Man*, 46, 86: 98–99.

1947.   'A Note on Sociology and Social Work in England Today'. *Silver Jubilee Volume of the School of Economics and Sociology*, Bombay: University of Bombay, pp. 83–98.

1951.   'The Social Structure of a Mysore Village', *Economic Weekly*, 30 October: 1051–56.

1952a.   'A Joint Family Dispute in a Mysore Village', *Journal of the Maharaja Sayajirao University of Baroda*, I, 1: 7–31.

1952b.   'Social Anthropology and Sociology', *Sociological Bulletin*, 1, 1: 28–37.

1953.   'Prospects of Sociological Research in Gujarat', *Journal of the Maharaja Sayajirao University of Baroda*, 2, 1: 21–35.

1954a.   'A Brief Note on Ayyappa, the South Indian Deity'. In K.M. Kapadia (Ed.), *Professor Ghurye Felicitation Volume.* Bombay: Popular Book Depot, pp. 238–43.

1954b. 'Varna and Caste'. In S. Radhakrishnan et al. (Eds.), A.R. Wadia—Essays in Philosophy Presented in His Honour. Bangalore, pp. 357–64.

1954c. 'A Caste Dispute among the Washermen of Mysore', Eastern Anthropologist, VII, 3 and 4: 148–68.

1955a. 'The Social System of a Mysore Village'. In McKim Marriott (Ed.), Village India. Chicago: University of Chicago Press. (Bombay: Asia Publishing House, 1961).

1955b. 'Village Studies and Their Significance', Eastern Anthropologist, VIII, 3 and 4: 215–28.

1955c. 'Castes: Can They Exist in India of Tomorrow?', Economic Weekly, 15 October: 1230–32.

1956a. 'A Note on Sanskritization and Westernization', Far Eastern Quarterly, XV, 4: 481–96.

1956b. 'The Industrialisation and Urbanisation of Rural Areas', Sociological Bulletin, V, 2: 79–86.

1956c. 'Mysore Gilleya Ondu Halli', Kannada Gudi, 8, 2: 4–13 (in Kannada).

1956d. 'Radcliffe-Brown: The Man and His Work'. In L.K. Balaratnam and A. Aiyappan (Eds.), Society in India. Madras: Social Science Association, pp. 49–53.

1956e. 'Sanskritization and Westernization'. In L.K. Balaratnam and A. Aiyappan (Eds.), Society in India. Madras: Social Science Association, pp. 73–115.

1956f. 'Regional Differences in Customs and Village Institutions', Economic Weekly, 18 February: 215–20.

1956g. 'Indian Marriages', Transport, Special Issue of the TAAT Fifth Convention, Bombay: 25–33.

1957. 'Caste in Modern India', Journal of Asian Studies, XVI, 4: 529–48.

1958a. 'Hinduism'. Encyclopaedia Britannica, pp. 574–577.

1958b. 'The Nature of the Problem of Indian Unity'. Report of the Seminar on National Integration. New Delhi: University Grants Commission, pp. 20–31.

1958c. 'Caste and Its Future', Akashavani, 19 October: 10–11.

1958d. 'Foreword'. In F.G. Bailey, Caste and the Economic Frontier. Manchester: Manchester University Press.

1958e. 'Foreword'. In A.M. Shah and R.G. Shroff, 'The Vahivancha Barots of Gujarat: A Caste of Genealogists and Mythographers'. In Milton Singer (Ed.), Traditional India: Structure and Change. Philadelphia: American Folklore Society. Also in Journal of American Folklore, 71, 281: 246–48.

1958f. 'A Note on Mr. John Goheen's Note on Professor Milton Singer's "Cultural Values in India's Economic Development"', Economic Development and Cultural Change, VII, 1: 3–6.

1959a. 'The Study of Disputes in an Indian Village'. Regional Seminar on Techniques of Social Research. Calcutta: UNESCO Research Centre, pp. 144–51.

1959b. 'The Case of the Potter and the Priest', Man in India, 39, 3: 190–209.

1959c. 'The Dominant Caste in Rampura', American Anthropologist, 61, 1: 1–16.

1959d. 'Social Anthropology and the Study of Rural and Urban Societies', *Economic Weekly*, Annual Number, XI, 4, 5 and 6: 133–40.

1959e. 'The Changing Social Pattern in India', *Illustrated Weekly of India*, 25 January: 20–21.

1959f. 'Bhavi Bharat Me Jatipratha', *Samaj Vikas*, 12, 5–6: 91–95 (in Hindi).

1960a. 'The Indian Road to Equality', *Economic Weekly*, Special Number, June: 867–72.

1960b. With A.M. Shah. 'The Myth of Self-Sufficiency of the Indian Village', *Economic Weekly*, 10 September: 1375–78.

1960c. 'Ustroj Kastowy i Jego Przyszlosc', *Spotechzno Ekonomiczne Problemy Indii, Warszawa* (in Polish).

1961a. 'Changing Attitudes in India Today', *Yojana*, Special Number, 1 October: 25–28.

1961b. 'The Changing Face of the Villages', *Illustrated Weekly of India*, 22 January.

1961c. 'There is a Vested Interest in Backwardness', *The Statesman* (New Delhi), 9 October.

1961d. 'Sociological Aspects of Indian Diet', *Agricultural Situation in India*, XVI, 3: 246–48. Ministry of Food and Agriculture, Government of India, New Delhi.

1962a. 'Pursuit of Equality', *The Times Survey of India* (London), 26 January.

1962b. 'AIR Discussion of "Ensuring Social Justice in Economic Development"', *Yojana*, 16 September: 5–7.

1962c. 'Changing Institutions and Values in Modern India', *Economic Weekly*, Annual Number, February: 131–37. Reprinted in *The King's Rally*, XXXIX, 11, Jan-Feb 1963: 259–72. Also in T.K.N. Unnithan *et al.* (Eds.), *Towards a Sociology of Culture in India: Essays in Honour of Professor D.P. Mukherji*. New Delhi: Prentice-Hall of India, 1965, pp. 428–38.

1963. 'National Integration: Can We Take it for Granted?', *Yojana*, Republic Day Special Number: 24–38.

1964a. 'The Changing Indian Village', *Indian and Foreign Review*, 1, 7, 15 January: 11–12.

1964b. 'Social Structure', *Sociological Bulletin*, XIII, 1, March: 12–21.

1964c. With Andre Beteille. 'Networks in Indian Social Structure', *Man*, 64, November-December: 165–68.

1965a. With Andre Beteille. 'The "Untouchables" of India', *Scientific American*, 213, 6, December: 13–17.

1965b. 'Social Structure'. *The Gazetteer of India*, Vol. 1. New Delhi: Publication Division, Government of India, pp. 501–77.

1965c. 'Reducing Inequalities', *The Times Supplement on India*, 14 August: ix.

1965d. 'Sociological Studies in India', *Economic and Political Weekly*, 1, 3, 3 September: 119–20.

1966. With M.S.A. Rao and others. 'A Sociological Study of Okhla Industrial Estate, Delhi'. In *Small Industries and Social Change*. Delhi: UNESCO Research Centre, pp. 33–89.

1967a.   'Cohesive Role of Sanskritization'. In Philip Mason (Ed.), *Unity and Diversity: India and Ceylon*. London: Oxford University Press.

1967b.   'Is the Sun Setting?', *Seminar*, 90, February: 12–16.

1967c.   'The Future of Fission', *The Times of India*, 16 November.

1968a.   'Changing Food Habits', *The Times of India*, 3 February.

1968b.   With A.M. Shah. 'Hinduism'. In *International Encyclopedia of the Social Sciences*, Vol. 6. New York: Macmillan, pp. 358–66.

1968c.   'Mobility in the Caste System'. In Milton Singer and Bernard Cohn (Eds.), *Structure and Change in Indian Society*. Chicago: University of Chicago Press.

1968d.   'Politics of Scarcity', *The Times of India*, 12 and 13 July.

1968e.   'Education, Social Change and Social Mobility in India'. In T. Mathias (Ed.), *Education and Social Concern*. Delhi: Jesuit Educational Association of India.

1969.   'Towards Smaller States', *The Times of India*, 14 August.

1970a.   'Sociology and Sociologists in India Today', *Sociological Bulletin*, XIX, 1, March: 1–10.

1970b.   'The Problem. Modernization', *Seminar*, 128: 10–14.

1972a.   With R.D. Sanwal. 'Some Aspects of Political Development in North Eastern Hill Areas in India'. *North Eastern Research Bulletin*, I. Also in K. Suresh Singh (Ed.), *Tribal Situation in India*. Simla: Indian Institute of Advanced Study, pp. 117–24.

1972b.   'Foreword'. In Milton Singer, *When a Great Tradition Modernizes*. New York: Praegar, pp. 7–10.

1973a.   'Itineraries of an Indian Social Anthropologist', *International Social Science Journal*, XXV, 1/2: 129–48.

1973b.   'Foreword'. In A.M. Shah, *The Household Dimension of the Family in India*. New Delhi: Orient Longman.

1973c.   'Comments on Hanna Papanek's "Pakistan's New Industrialists and Businessmen" and Richard Fox's "Pariah Capitalism and Traditional Indian Merchants, Past and Present"'. In Milton Singer (Ed.), *Entrepreneurship and Modernization of Occupational Cultures in South Asia*. Monograph No. 12. Durham, North Carolina: Duke University.

1973d.   'Whither Our Union', *Seminar*, 164, April.

1973e.   With M.N. Panini. 'The Development of Sociology and Social Anthropology in India', *Sociological Bulletin*, 22, 2, September: 179–215.

1974a.   'The Dynamics of Indian Culture Today', *Indian and Foreign Review*, II, 10, 1 March: 12–13.

1974b.   'Village Living: A Source of Insights for the Social Scientist', *Research Methodology*, A/D/C/ Teaching Forum, 35, January.

1974c.   'Review Article on *South India: Yesterday, Today and Tomorrow* by Scarlett Epstein', *South Asian Review*, 7, 3, April: 85.

1974d.   'Why I am a Hindu', *The Illustrated Weekly of India*, 17 November.

1975a.   'Social Environment and Management's Responsibilities', *Economic and Political Weekly*, X, 11, 15 March: 487–91.

1975b.   'Status of Women in India', *The Times of India*, 18 and 19 April.

1975c.   'Indian Village: Myth and Reality'. In J.H.M. Beattie and G. Lienhardt (Eds.), *Studies in Social Anthropology: Essays in Memory of Sir E.E. Evans-Pritchard*. Oxford: Oxford University Press.

1975d.   'Village Studies, Participant Observation and Social Science Research in India', *Economic and Political Weekly*, Special Number X, 33, 34 and 35, August: 1387–94.

1976a.   'Foreword'. In Kalpana Das Gupta (Ed.), *Women on the Indian Scene: An Annotated Bibliography*. Delhi: Abhinav.

1976b.   'Foreword'. In R.D. Sanwal, *Social Stratification in Rural Kumaon*. Delhi: Oxford University Press.

1976c.   'Rural India through a Microscope: Interview with H. Kusumakar', *The Times of India*.

1976d.   'Tradition and Modernization'. Valedictory Address. In S.K. Srivastava (Ed.), *Tradition and Modernization*. Allahabad: India International Publications, pp. 206–11.

1977a.   'Changing Position of Indian Women'. T.H. Huxley Memorial Lecture. *Man*, 12, 2: 221–38.

1977b.   'Science, Technology and Rural Development in India'. R.R. Kale Memorial Lecture. Pune: Gokhale Institute of Politics and Economics.

1977c.   'The Dual Cultures of Independent India'. Gandhi Memorial Lecture. Bangalore: Raman Research Institute.

1977d.   'Village Studies, Participant Observation and Social Science Research in India'. In Biplab Dasgupta (Ed.), *Village Studies in the Third World*. Delhi: Hindustan Publishing Corporation.

1977e.   'Caste Today. Special Report on India', *The Guardian*, 7 November.

1978.   'Reply to Critics on *The Remembered Village*', *Contributions to Indian Sociology*, 12, 1: 127–52.

1979.   'The Dual Cultures of Independent India'. In G.P. Misra and B.C. Das (Eds.), *Gandhi in Today's India*. Delhi: Ashish Publishing House, pp. 93–109.

1981a.   'India—Society—Social Structure'. In *Collier's Encyclopaedia*, Vol. 12, pp. 577–84.

1981b.   'The Role of Caste in India: Present and Future'. Review of Pauline Kolenda's *Caste in Contemporary India: Beyond Organic Solidarity*. *Reviews in Anthropology*, 7, 4, 412–30.

1983a.   'The Observer and the Observed in the Anthropological Understanding of Cultures'. Singapore: Faculty of Arts and Social Sciences, National University of Singapore.

1983b.   'All is not Lost if Your Plans Go Awry', *Deccan Herald*, 25 December.

1983c.   'Karnataka Elections: Emerging Indian Radicalism', *Indian Express*, 10 March.

1984a.   With M.N. Panini. 'Politics and Society in Karnataka', *Economic and Political Weekly*, XIX, 2, 14 January: 69–75.

1984b. 'The Insider versus Outsider in the Understanding of Cultures'. In Chie Nakane (Ed.), *Social Sciences and Asia*. Tokyo: Institute of Oriental Culture, University of Tokyo.

1984c. 'Some Reflections on the Nature of Caste Hierarchy', *Contributions to Indian Sociology*, n.s., 18, 2: 151–67.

1984d. 'Some Thoughts on the Sociological Aspects of Food in India'. In Mahipal Bhuriya and S.N. Michael (Eds.), *Anthropology as a Historical Science: Essays in Honour of Stephen Fuchs*. Indore: Sat Prakashan.

1986a. 'On Living in a Revolution'. In James E. Roach (Ed.), *India 2000: The Next Fifteen Years*. Maryland: The Riverdale Company. (New Delhi: Allied Publishers), pp. 3–24.

1986b. 'Religions in a Sociological Perspective', *Social Compass*, 30, 2–3.

1987a. 'Caste System and Its Future'. In Paul Hockings (Ed.), *Dimensions of Social Life: Essays in Honour of Professor David Mandelbaum*. Berlin: Mouton.

1987b. 'Development of Sociology in India: An Overview', *Economic and Political Weekly*, XXII, 4, 24 December: 135–36.

1988a. 'Social Changes in South India', *The Economic Times* (Bangalore), 1 October.

1988b. 'Le System Social D'Un Village Du Mysore', *Miroir De L'Inde* (Paris), 49–89.

1988c. With E.A. Ramaswamy. 'Culture et Fecundite', *Miroir De L'Inde* (Paris), 312–49.

1988d. 'Religionens Sociala Betydelse', *Mot Indien, Kulturhuset*, 29 August 1987–14 February 1988, 99–116.

1989. 'Using the Village Teashop as an Information Centre', *The Times of India*, 16 May.

1990a. 'Society and Culture'. In Manjulika Dubey and Bikram Grewal (Eds.), *South India*. Bangalore: Apa Publications.

1990b. 'The Mandal Formula', *The Times of India*, 17 September.

1991a. 'Encounters with Graham Greene', *The Times of India*, 21 April.

1991b. 'Dateless Diary from Berkeley', *The Times of India*, 13 October.

1991c. 'India's Cultural Ethos: Centrality in Development Process', *The Times of India*, 9 December.

1992. 'Employment Quotas in India', *Anthropology Today*, 8, 2: 19–20.

1993a. 'India—People—Society'. In *Collier's Encyclopaedia*, Vol. 12, pp. 562–67, 577–84.

1993b. 'Changing Values in India Today', *Economic and Political Weekly*, XXIII, 19, 8 May: 933–38.

1993c. 'Towards a New Philosophy: Renewing Faith in God as Saviour', *The Times of India*, 9 July.

1993d. 'The Cultural Revolution Moves North', *Indian Express*, 12 December.

1994a. 'Tamilnadu—Past and Present', *The Times of India*, 19 March.

1994b. 'The Creator of Malgudi', *The Times of India*, 5 June.

1994c. 'Sociology in India and Its Future', *Sociological Bulletin*, 43, March: 9–19.

1995a.   'Sociology in Delhi'. In Dharma Kumar and Dilip Mookherjee (Eds.), *D. School*. Delhi: Oxford University Press.

1995b.   'Reminiscences of a Bangalorean'. In *Bangalore: Scenes from an Indian City*. Bangalore: Gangaram and Sons.

1995c.   'Gandhi's Religion', *Economic and Political Weekly*, 24 June.

NOTES ON CONTRIBUTORS

JOHN A. BARNES was former Professor of Sociology at the University of Cambridge, England, and now works at the Australian National University, Canberra. He is the author of *Three Styles in the Study of Kinship* (London, 1971); *Ethics of Inquiry in Social Science* (Delhi, 1977); and *Models and Interpretations: Selected Essays* (Cambridge, 1990).

I. P. DESAI was Professor and Head, Department of Sociology, Maharaja Sayajirao University of Baroda, and Founder-Director, Centre for Social Studies, Surat. His publications include *High School Students in Poona* (1953); *Some Aspects of Family in Mahuva* (Bombay, 1964); and *Craft of Sociology* (Delhi, 1981).

J. V. FERREIRA was previously Professor of Anthropology and Head, Department of Sociology, University of Bombay. He is the author of *Totemism in India* (London, 1965); and is the co-editor of *Outlook Tower: Essays on Urbanization in Memory of Patrick Geddes* (Bombay, 1976).

M. S. GORE was Principal, Delhi School of Social Work; Director, Tata Institute of Social Sciences, Bombay; and Vice-Chancellor, University of Bombay. Professor Gore has written extensively and has several books to his credit including *Urbanization and Family Change* (Bombay, 1968); *Immigrants and Neighbourhoods: Two Aspects of Life in a Metropolitan City* (Bombay, 1970); *Non-Brahman Movement in Maharashtra* (Delhi, 1989); and *Indian Education: Structure and Process* (Jaipur, 1994).

P. C. JOSHI was earlier Professor of Sociology, and Director, Institute of Economic Growth, Delhi. Professor Joshi is the author of *Land Reform and Agrarian Change in India and Pakistan since 1947* (Delhi, 1970); *Institutional Aspects of Agricultural Development: India from Asian Perspectives* (Ahmedabad, 1987); and *Culture, Communication and Social Change* (Delhi, 1989).

R. S. KHARE is Professor of Anthropology, University of Virginia, Charlottesville. He is the author of *Changing Brahmans* (Chicago, 1970); *Hindu Hearth and Home* (Delhi, 1976); and *Untouchable as Himself* (Cambridge, 1984).

T. N. MADAN, Professor of Sociology, was previously Director, Institute of Economic Growth, Delhi. Professor Madan has written extensively and is the author of *Family and Kinship: A Study of the Pandits of Rural Kashmir* (Bombay, 1965); *Doctors and Society: Three Asian Case Studies* (Delhi, 1980); *Non-renunciation: Themes and Interpretations of Hindu Culture* (Delhi, 1987); and has edited *Religion in India* (Delhi, 1991).

A. M. SHAH, Professor of Sociology, University of Delhi, is the author of *The Household Dimension of the Family in India* (Delhi, 1973), and the co-author of *Division and Hierarchy: An Overview of Caste in Gujarat* (Delhi, 1988).

MILTON SINGER was Professor of Social Sciences in the College and in the Department of Anthropology, University of Chicago. He published extensively and his books include *Traditional India: Structure and Change* (editor, Philadelphia, 1959); *Structure and Change in Indian Society* (co-editor, Chicago, 1968); *When a Great Tradition Modernizes: An Anthropological Approach to Indian Civilization* (New York, 1972); *Man's Glassy Essence: Explorations in Semiotic Anthropology* (Bloomington, 1984); and *Semiotics of Cities, Selves and Cultures: Explorations in Semiotic Anthropology* (Berlin, 1991).

INDEX